Cattle, Concrete & Guided Missiles

Stephen Lock

Edward Gaskell
Publishers
DEVON

First published 2023
Edward Gaskell Publishers
Mulberry Lodge
Oldways End
Devon
EX16 9JQ

isbn (13) 978-1-906769-88-8

Cattle, Concrete & Guided Missiles
Stephen Lock

Please note: The author and the publishers have made every effort to credit all photos
used where applicable and if any are missed we would extend our apologies. If such
omissions are forwarded to us we will do our utmost to rectify this in any future edition.

Typeset, printed and bound by
Lazarus Press
Mulberry Lodge
Oldways End
Devon
EX16 9JQ

To my wife Christine who has
put up with me for 50 years.
It is with her encouragement
that I wrote this book

Contents

Foreword

I wrote this book to show what life was like driving lorries in the 1970s, 80s and 90s. Roads were different then and lots of towns were not yet by-passed. Many motorways didn't exist and those that did had a lot less traffic on them and there were not endless roadworks.

There were no mobile phones for communication.

No trackers in vehicles.

There were transport cafés that did excellent food at reasonable prices and gave free parking for road transport. Lorry drivers were known as 'Knights of the Road' and they helped anyone who needed help.

They were allowed to give lifts to people. They could take their children, the transport drivers of the future, for a ride with mum or dad. Towns had lorry parks, transport was welcome for lorry drivers had money in their pockets and they were looking to spend it.

The job of the lorry driver, was and still is, to collect and deliver goods, on time and in good order. Drivers take pride in achieving this and will do their utmost to make it happen. Remember, nearly every thing you see around you has, at some time, been on the back of a lorry.

I believe this book is different to many others on the same subject. It is about one man's journey on the road, local and long distance driving. The highs and lows of the job and the camaraderie of the industry.

Laughter, tears, rebellion and jubilation are in this book and it is written with the love and memories of those great men and women who were on the road every day of the year, to keep this country going.

These are my memories and may not be exactly historically correct and some names may have been changed to save people from embarrassment and from me getting sued.

Stephen Lock
2023

Thanks to:

Jeffrey Binding
Nigel Blunt
Geoff Colwill
Brian Coppledick
Roxann E Cuthbertson
Dover Transport Museum
Jack Heywood
Geoff Horrell
Andrew Jury
Marcus Lester
Jude Moore
NA3T
Frank Pidler
Pat and Colin Richards
Graham Roberts Autos
Caroline Russell
Adrian Richards
Tiverton Museum of Mid-Devon Life
Susan Uttley
Mervyn Way
Nick Way
Stephen Wilks

Glossary - General

AA: Automobile association

ABC: A chipboard company owned by Aaronson Brothers

Artic: Articulated vehicle. A vehicle where a semi-trailer is coupled to the tractor via a 5th wheel coupling

Artic unit: Vehicle for pulling a semi trailer.

Block & Quayle: Original name for B&Q Do it Yourself stores

BMC: British Motor Corporation

Bob tail: Driving the tractor unit with no trailer attached.

Butt, Bucket: The body of a tipper.

Diff' Lock: Device for locking the differential of a back axle of a vehicle

ERF: Edwin Richard Foden, A lorry manufacturer 1933-2000

Headboard: The upright part fitted to the front of a flat bed vehicle.

HGV: Heavy Goods Vehicle.

Janner: A regional nick name given to a native of Plymouth.

MAN: MaschinenFabrik Augsburg-Nurnberg AG.

MPH: Miles per Hour

R.A.F.A: Royal Air Force Association

Rave: The metal side of a flat trailer.

Road form: A length of steel channel designed to lock together, 100mm or 150mm in depth held in place by steel pins. Used in concreting roads and drives

RHA: Road Haulage Association

R.S.P.C.A: Royal Society for the Prevention of Cruelty to Animals

Semi trailer: A trailer without a front axle and designed to be coupled to a fifth wheel of a tractor unit.

Shunter: Cab unit of an Artic used for loading and unloading trailers on a companies yard.

Shunter: A driver that loads and unloads trailers on the premises or at local companies.

Sheets: Tarpaulins, covers for loads. Usually made of thick plastic or waterproofed linen.

Tractor unit: A motorised vehicle for pulling semi-trailers. The trailers are directly coupled to the tractor unit via a pin and fifth wheel unit.

WRAF: Woman's Royal Air force

Wrecker: A breakdown lorry. Recovery vehicle.

Glossary CB (Citizen Band) Radio

CB Radio Transceivers broadcast over a 15 mile (approx) distance and in the days when there were no mobile phones Lorry drivers found they were an ideal aid to their job. Most CBs were the same size as a normal car radio and easily fitted in the cab of a lorry. By using CB radios drivers could talk to other drivers and receive up-to-date road and weather reports and talk to anyone else who had a CB radio. When a driver got near to his delivery address he might try to speak to someone who could direct him to his destination. My CB radio had 40 channels. Channel 9 was kept for emergencies. Channel 19 was the one usually used by lorry drivers. If one was going to have a long conversation it was polite to move away from channel 19 so one didn't 'bleed over'. CB radio had its own language and here is a list of some of the more common phrases:

Advertising: An emergency vehicle with its blue lights on

Back door: Rear vehicle in a convoy

Bears (Smokey Bears): Police

Big 10-4: Yes! (with feeling)

Bleeding over : Adjacent channel signal heard on tuned channel

Bone Box: Ambulance

Blow the doors off: To quickly pass or overtake

Bodacious (totally bodacious): Good signal, clear transmission

Back down: Reduce speed

Back out: Stop transmitting

Basement: Channel one

Base station: Non mobile transmitter. One in a home or office.

Break or Breaker: Word used to join a conversation

Chicken coop: Truck weigh station or toll booth

Clean and green: There are no police or hold ups ahead

Copy: Received transmission

Ears on: Listening for a transmission

Eighteen wheeler: Articulated tractor and trailer

Feed the bears: Pay a fine

Flip flop: Return trip

Front door: First vehicle in a convoy

Good buddy: Friend

Handle: CB nickname

Hammer: Accelerator

Modulation: Talk, conversation

Motion lotion: Diesel fuel

Over your shoulder: Opposite of the direction you are travelling

Pregnant roller skate: A Volkswagen Beetle

Rocking chair: All positions between the lead and rear vehicle in a convoy

Seat Covers: Girls in a car

Ten four: Yes, I acknowledge

Ten Ten: Goodbye

Wall to wall: Everywhere, loud and clear

1

In the beginning

I suppose where I got my love for lorries was from my family. Two of my older brothers, Jimmy and Maurice, and Uncle Percy and his son Brian, all drove lorries for the local cattle haulage firm of F.C.E. Moore in South Molton

Jimmy eventually moved to Bickington and worked for National Benzole and then British Petroleum (BP) driving fuel tankers, based in Fremington, North Devon.

Holidays and some weekends I would ride with Jimmy in his tanker. He would park it at the end of our road and come into to see mother and have a cup of tea. Then he would take me with him to various petrol stations around North Devon and North Somerset. He was not supposed to take passengers with him but it got me away from mother for a few hours. I was the youngest of ten children and with me out the way mother could put her feet up for a couple of hours.

I could not stay in the lorry while fuel was being unloaded so I had to sit in the office or shop which usually meant squash, tea and biscuits or chocolate. I was returned home a very happy little boy. I suppose I was about eight years old when I first went with him.

Maurice used take me in the cattle lorry which was probably more dangerous than petrol tankers. Some animals do not like being loaded, especially bullocks, as they are used to roaming free in fields. Very often when half way into the lorry they would turn and charge out again. Some Aberdeen Angus bullocks did this once when Maurice's son, Russell, was with us. Maurice moved to one side and Russell and I ran to a nearby fallen tree trunk, dived over it and hid behind it while the bullocks went over the top of us. It was like a Wild West film. It shook us all up a bit but the bullocks had to be loaded so we tried again and finally did got them loaded.

The body, or float, of a cattle lorry was a complicated piece of equipment. At the front there was an area the width of the body that overhung the cab of the lorry. This was called the box and usually hay and straw was stored here. At the front on each side of the box was a door three to four feet high, often calves were unloaded through these doors. At the rear of the lorry was a ramp that was fastened, in the up position. with two large nuts with a handle welded on to them. The nuts were fitted each side along with a hydraulic ram to assist in raising the ramp. In the middle of the ramp was a rope used to pull the ramp down. On later lorries the ramp was operated by compressed air.

Behind the ramp and fitted to the lorry body were two interlocking gates that went the full height of the body, the gates were often used to push reluctant livestock inside.

Inside the box there were more gates about three feet high. They could be used to partition off parts of the body. Also the were metal bars that could be fitted across the body and fold away floors could be let down to make the vehicle into two stories for carrying small animals. This description is of cattle lorry bodies manufactured in the nineteen sixties. Many of the bodies were produced by Tiverton coachbuilders. Most bodies were removable and were usually held on by four big bolts. With the body removed the lorry was used as a standard flatbed vehicle.

Myself and a few of my friends would wander down to the cattle market on a Thursday. There were plenty of lorries there, mainly belonging to F.C.E.Moore and another company call Watts who also had their South Molton Yard in Cook's Cross, next to Moore's yard. Many drivers were happy to take a lad with them for the day, it was another pair of hands to help load, especially with sheep who needed to be pushed in and partitioned off. The danger here was that a sheep would decide not to go where it was told and would turn ready to head butt the small lad behind him. A tap on the nose soon sent the sheep in the right direction.

There were also farm and field gates to open and close, this was the boy's job.

I got on very well with a driver called Albert Alderman who drove a Dodge lorry. The Dodge had a bonnet shaped like a parrots beak. These lorries were known as parrot nose, or Kew Dodges after the part of

London where they were built. Because the engine was in front of the cab there was plenty of room inside the cab, which was fitted with three seats. This was my favourite lorry to ride in.

At the end of the day the lorries returned to the yard. The first job was to fill them up with diesel, another job for the lad. The diesel pump was sited at the end of a big shed and if a lorry was fuelling up it blocked the entrance to the rest of the yard. On busy days there would be a queue of lorries waiting to get in.

The pump it self was known as a lift pump, it was fitted with a handle which was turned three times in one direction, then three times in the opposite direction to put the fuel into the tank of the lorry.

I estimate that each cycle put in one gallon, therefore to put in forty gallons, the average capacity for a lorry diesel tank in those days, would take one hundred and twenty turns of the handle in both directions. This was not a quick job but most drivers gave a small cash reward for doing it.

The next job was clean the back of the lorry. Remove the straw bedding and the muck and then wash every part of the inside with a power hose. Only then was the lorry parked up ready for the next morning.

For kids it was a great day out and maybe a bit of pocket money at the end. More so if there was more than one lorry to fuel up and clean.

While the lorries were being fuelled and cleaned the driver would be in the office, talking with Derrick Moore, the manager. Fred Moore was the owner of the company and Derrick was his brother. Many years later my brother Maurice owned the company.

Another great day was Sheep Fair, there were three or four during the summer holidays, with South Molton being one of the biggest in the area. The day started around six in the morning with picking up sheep at local farms until the lorry was full. Sheep from different farms were kept separate in the back of the lorry. The entrance to the sheep fair field was through the housing estate of Kingsway and by ten o'clock there was a long queue of lorries through the estate waiting to unload.

Once unloaded it was off to get another load. After the second was delivered it was time for lunch while the sheep were sold.

In the top corner of the field there were all sorts of stalls, including swing boats. My mother was usually there, along with many other people, for Sheep Fair was a great social occasion.

Drivers used lunch-time to have a nap or to talk to farmers and maybe get a free tea from one that had achieved a successful sale. Then it was time to take the sold sheep to their new homes, often a field quite a way from the farm. It was no problem to an experienced driver who seemed to know every farmer and his fields. The day ended sometimes at eight or nine o'clock in the evening, a long day for every one.

Another thing that drew me to lorries was the army recruiting party that would arrive in South Molton with shiny four-wheel drive Bedford lorries and a big gold griffin painted on the mudguard. Who wouldn't want to drive one of those?

When I was about fourteen my brother-in-law, Ray Weeks, took me on a trip to London and Surrey. The lorry belonged to Shapland and Petter, Barnstaple, who made wooden doors, windows and wooden packing cases

One place in London did not allow passengers in the lorry, so I was left in a café while the delivery was done. Later we were travelling through the East End between two high walls. Ray heard the sound of bells (used on emergency vehicles before the two tone horn) so he slowed down and moved a bit closer to the kerb. An ambulance came from the opposite direction so Ray accelerated and moved out a bit and just missed another ambulance going the same way as us.

Always check your mirrors.

We were away for two nights and we slept in the back of the lorry which had a box van type body. It was a real adventure for a fourteen year old.

2

North Devon Farmers

After leaving school and doing various jobs, at the age of twenty I was employed as a storeman/driver by North Devon Farmers, Station Road, South Molton. This company sold agricultural machinery and repaired the same. It made and sold animal feed, most of which was milled at their own large mill at Braunton Road, Barnstaple.

In the mill yard were the main company offices. The company had depots in Bideford, Barnstaple, Dulverton in Somerset and South Molton.

My job was to assist the feed storeman and also deliver materials using the fifteen hundredweight Bedford pick-up truck. The feed storeman, Tony Mitchell, was a hard working man but easy to get on with and I enjoyed working with him. I knew him and his brother, Walter, before I joined the firm. The large feed store (now part of Wickes) had two entrances at the front of the building, each fitted with double doors. At night and weekends two lorries were parked inside the store. On the left side was a Commer lorry driven by Charlie Kingdom and on the right was a Bedford KM driven by Maurice Bendle.

Saturday mornings the store was open and the Bedford had to be moved out to allow customer access and put back inside when the store closed. Tony was happy for me to do this.

The pick-up was used three or four days of the week, delivering animal food to farms and stables, and even private houses, around Exmoor and North East Devon. Sometimes it was used to do part deliveries of bigger orders when no lorries were available. This happened one winter when Exmoor was covered in about four feet of snow.

I was told to take some feed to a farm near the village of Withypool. Just before I got to the open moorland I met Tony Mitchell's brother, Walter, coming in the opposite direction. Walter was driving a tipper lorry belonging to E J Kingdom, a local building firm. The snow had been cleared by a snow plough but was only wide enough for one vehicle so it meant that I had to reverse back. There was a road junction about three hundred yards behind me and I started to reverse; I hadn't gone too far when the cab tilted, I had put the nearside front wheel into a ditch. I got out of the vehicle and Walter stopped his lorry and walked over to have a look.

'What be goin' to do now?' says he.

I thought for a minute. Only the one front wheel was in the ditch the rest of the wheels were ok although the offside rear wheel was off the ground.

'If the load is moved and stacked above the wheel that is off the ground it may level the truck up' I said.

In a couple of minutes the bags of feed were moved and indeed it did look like my idea had worked. So I get into the cab and gently eased backwards, with all the weight on the back axle the Bedford came out of the ditch. I reversed back to the road junction so that Walter could pass.

'You should get to Withypool alright if you can keep out of the ditches,' he shouted as he passed.

Sometimes I would be required to go with one of the lorries if they had a large load for one farm. I did not mind doing this as some of the drivers knew that I wanted to be a lorry driver and they would let me drive theirs. Usually when we got to a farm, one driver, Charlie Kingdom, would say to me, 'You can turn the lorry around as you need the practice - anyone can drive them forward.' His Commer was a short wheel-base type and was pretty easy to manoeuvre.

The other lorry that I drove a lot was Maurice Bendle's Bedford KM. This was a long wheel-base, maximum length, four-wheeled lorry and was more difficult to turn and drive around in farmyards although it did turn a lot sharper than the Commer.

This was in the days before the big sheds and concrete yards when farmyards were small and every thing was stacked in small sheds and barns. The benefit was that we usually unloaded near the farm house and were often rewarded for our labours with cups of tea and occasionally scones, or bread and cream.

The Commers were designed for small farm yards and the Bedford KM was designed for long-distance work and originally belonged to Mitchell's Transport of Bideford before being transferred to North Devon Farmers. Mitchell's transport did the long-distance work, going to feed mills outside of Devon, to collect animal feed and other necessities

The fleet was mainly Commers, with a couple of Bedfords and Mitchell's had an eight-wheeled Atkinson. There were two Bedford CA pick-ups, one based in Bideford and one based in South Molton. These had a column gear change, sliding side windows and a drop side body.

On February 2nd, 1970 the government introduced the Heavy Goods Vehicle driving licence. One had to be twenty-one years old to drive a heavy goods vehicle over three tons unladen weight and also pass an appropriate driving test for the same. The problem with this was I wasn't twenty-one until January 1972.

Early in 1972, I was at the Bideford branch, where vehicle repairs were done. My Bedford CA needed some welding done on it. While I was there I went to see Mr Percy Mitchell, the transport manager for Mitchell's Transport and North Devon Farmers. I told him that I wanted to be a lorry driver and asked would there be any chance that I could learn to drive with North Devon Farmers. He asked me a few other questions and then he said that I could learn to drive as long as my branch manager, Mr Jutsam, allowed me the time off.

One of the conditions of the Heavy Goods Vehicle licence was that you needed an appropriate Medical Certificate and a few days later I passed a medical examination and received my certificate.

After the examination I asked the doctor how much will it cost and he said, 'The invoice is normally sent to the employer.'

'Fine,' I replied. 'But if they do not pay then I will.'

The following week I was called to the office to see Mr Jutsam.

'I have received a bill from the medical people,' he said.

'That's right the doctor told me he was going to send it to you,' I replied.

'What is going on?' he asked

I told him of my discussion with Mr Percy Mitchell the previous week. It appears that Mr Mitchell had forgot to tell Mr Jutsam, who was now not a happy man.

Although work was quiet for the next few months Mr Jutsam always said the branch was too busy to let me have some time driving the lorries. I think he did not want to lose me and have to employ another storeman.

Then, one day, the inevitable happened a man came to the store driving a very clean cattle lorry and we got talking. He was Mr Shapcott and he owned a firm in the nearby village of Bishop's Nympton. He said that he was looking for a lorry driver, he interviewed me on the spot and after he left I went and gave in my notice to Mr Jutsam.

3

Shapcott and Son

Henry Shapcott and Son where agricultural feed merchants. They had a yard, just south of the church, in the Devon village of Bishop's Nympton. As you entered the yard on the left was the Shapcott house and office. Straight ahead was the feed mill operated by the son Nick Shapcott. On the south side was the village bakery owned by the Chanter family; the baker was Tony Littson from South Molton. The delivery driver was 'Dince' Kingdom.

There were hot pasties for lunch from the bakery, made by Tony Litson, and if you met 'Dince' in a country lane there was always a cake - I couldn't let them go stale.

The company had a coal yard and storage facilities at the nearby Molland station.

They did cattle haulage using the vehicle that I was to drive.

There were three lorries altogether, Two seven ton Commers and one ten ton Ford D1000. Seven and ten tons being the maximum weight they carried.

Les Chilcott drove the Ford, Tony Bradford drove one of the Commers and I drove the other.

The cattle lorry was garaged in a Dutch barn at the South end of the village. When not in use the cattle body was lifted from the lorry using chains hanging from the roof beams of the barn, the lorry was moved away, and the body was dropped onto empty forty gallon steel drums.

Les went to Avonmouth most days to collect animal feed, some times doing farm deliveries on the way back.

Tony delivered animal feed to local farms and I did the same when there was no livestock work.

Everybody helped with coal deliveries which was done using one of the Commer lorries.

Mr Shapcott, we did not call him Henry, was my co-pilot for a few weeks as I was a learner driver.

Most days were spent delivering animal feed and Shapcott and Son were unusual in the fact that the feed was put into the different bins: cattle cake in the cow shed, pig food in the pig shed etc. and the empty paper bags taken away. At least by the time I'd passed my test I knew where most of these bins were to be found.

I quickly settled in and driving the Commer proved to be quite easy: most of the roads we travelled were B and C roads around the edge of Exmoor. The Commer was fitted with a five speed gear box and could achieve seventy mph although most of the time it was more like twenty five.

Tony Bradford was following me one day and could not keep up even though he was driving an identical lorry. The next quiet day Les, Tony and myself had a look at Tony's lorry to see if we could find any cause for the poor performance. We discovered there was a lot of play on the throttle linkage and the accelerator pedal moved half way before any change in the engine speed was noted. A quick bit of spanner work took up the slack and Tony did a test drive, he came back and said it felt like he was driving a new lorry.

Life grew into a steady routine, animal feed deliveries, with one or two days delivering coal to the local villages and pubs and every pub we went to would offer us a drink. Two of the pubs stick in my mind, one was the Jubilee Inn on the South Molton to Bampton road and the other was the London Inn at Molland. The Jubilee Inn was a bit posh and glasses, bottles and a bottle opener were left outside near the coal bunker. We left the delivery note under one of the bottles and always had, 'thank you, for the beer,' hand-written on the bottom. The cheque, for the coal, would be sent in the post. At the London Inn the coal was delivered and then we would go into the bar where the landlady, Mrs Buckingham, had already pulled us each a pint of beer. After consuming our drinks and indulging in a little small talk she paid us for the coal.

Mrs Buckingham was well into her eighties and, with the help of her son Donald, still ran the pub. They were happy, pleasant, wonderful people: typical Exmoor folk.

Thursday was usually spent taking cattle to South Molton Market and often the Farmer would ride in with us. One farmer's wife in particular, would give us tea and bread with clotted cream while she went and changed out of her working clothes. The Commer had three seats so there was plenty of room for her. I do not know how she got home, she never went back with us.

At the market we would unload the livestock and I would wash the lorry and the cattle box, inside and out. Mr Shapcott would go to the George Hotel were he met with farmers who hopefully then paid last week's invoice. This was a long-standing tradition that went on for many years.

While Mr Shapcott was at the hotel I had time to wander around the market and also have my lunch. At the appointed time, usually two o'clock Mr Shapcott would return and if there were no animals to take back we would return to Bishop's Nympton and put the lorry in the barn. Then I would take the boss's car, a Humber Hawk, to Molland station to bag-up coal for Friday's Bishop's Nympton coal round. If we had to take livestock to a farm on the way back then Mr Shapcott went home and changed and both of us went to Molland station. There was usually between five and six tons of coal to get bagged by Friday morning. By Thursday there would already be some coal bagged as we would often bag coal during the week when we had some spare time.

I used to love driving that big executive Humber, remembering to remove my overalls and put them in the boot, take out the paper sack and put it in the driver's footwell. At Molland, remembering to park well away from the coal bagging.

It was nice and peaceful at the station, the railway line having closed down in 1996. I enjoyed listening to the sounds of nature as I worked. When the requisite amount was bagged I then returned to Bishop's Nympton. If it was after five o'clock and as I had a lot of free time during the day I didn't get paid any overtime. I thought this was fair and I usually got back by five, the official time to leave work.

The Friday coal-round was interesting with a bit of competition to get to a certain house first. The young lady that lived there would get out of bed late and always answered the door in her see-through baby doll nightie. After the coal had been delivered she still had not dressed and one would have to wait while she looked for her purse to pay for the coal. I am sure she took great delight teasing us young men and to be honest we thoroughly enjoyed it.

For the coal-round we had leather waistcoats and leather shoulder bags for the money collected.

One Friday Mr Shapcott, Tony Bradford and myself were delivering the coal and when finished we all returned to the office where the money collected was handed over and counted. The amount of bags of coal left on the lorry were counted and the value was deducted from the original load. Then the value of the amount sold was calculated and should tally with the amount of cash in front of Mr Shapcott. However this day there was a pound missing, the exact price of a bag of house coal.

Mr Shapcott asked if either of us had mistakenly put a pound some where else instead of the purse. All three of us checked our pockets and then the cab of the lorry was checked, no pound note, even the area around the lorry was searched, nothing. Returning to the office Mr Shapcott gave a little lecture on the importance of taking care of other people's money. In fairness, in those days, a pound amounted to a third of a day's wages.

During this lecture a lady appeared at the door and said 'I'm sorry to interrupt you, Mister Shapcott but after you delivered my coal this morning I went outside the back door and found this pound note on the floor. You must have dropped it on your way out.'

Mr Shapcott went a bit red in the face, thanked the lady and told us to carry on with our work. Tony and I got outside and burst into laughter.

A few of trips with the cattle lorry come to mind. The first was to Farmer Wally Snell's farm, called East Avercombe, about a mile to the East of Bishop's Nympton. The wide entrance to the farm is halfway up a steep hill. This particular day we went into the farm to collect a heifer for transportation to Lloyd Maunder's slaughter-house.

We already had several bullocks on board and this was the last pick up. Mr and Mrs Snell and their daughter Janet, were waiting for us, but this was not the easy job that we hoped it would be.

We pulled down the ramp and opened the gates but as soon as the heifer saw the bullocks she would not move. We took the bullocks off the lorry and loaded the heifer, then as we put the bullocks back in the heifer came charging out. This was a challenge. One should never hit animals with anything especially if they are going to slaughter as the bruises will show and devalue the carcase, we had to think of some way to get this reluctant lady into the lorry.

We got the heifer to the bottom of ramp using gates then Farmer Snell got hold of one of her legs, Mr Shapcott another, I had the third leg and Janet, who stood about five foot tall, took the fourth. Mrs Snell opened the lorry gates a little way and we walked the reluctant heifer into the back of the lorry. Mrs Snell shut the gates and then let us out one at a time. The ramp was shut and then it was deciding which way to exit the farm yard. Previous experience told me that going out through the gate way and turning up hill with a full load would result in the lorry leaning at an alarming angle and the front wheel coming off the ground. This was something that the boss did not relish and would take hold of the grab handle fitted inside the cab.

Plan B was put into operation I drove through the gate at an angle facing down hill. If the lorry did turn over at least it would fall against the hedge. Slowly I drove it out of the yard keeping the back wheel on the hedge and as soon as I was through the gateway I turned sharp left toward the hedge. At that stage the lorry was leaning alarmingly and the boss had his hand around the grab handle and was pushing onto it trying to keep upright. I was watching the rear wheel on my side because if that came of the ground we would be in trouble. Very slowly the lorry straightened and the cows in the back spread out a bit, which brought the lorry back up right. We drove to a farm at the bottom of the hill, turned the lorry around on some flat ground and drove back up the hill. With a wave to the Snell family we went on our way to Lloyd Maunder's slaughter house at Willand. With a full load of cattle we were on our maximum load weight and because these animals can move about, caution was taken when cornering and braking. It is easy to drive safely with a moving load (cattle, liquids etc.) just imagine that you are driving on ice.

A similar situation arose moving bullocks for another customer. The previous autumn we had taken four or five loads of bullocks from Molland Common, part of Exmoor, to Starcross, South of Exeter. Starcross is near the sea and in winter is a lot warmer than the deep snow of Exmoor. In the spring we brought the bullocks back to Molland Common where they had acres of moorland to graze on during the summer. I drove onto the common and parked with the rear of the lorry pointing towards the moor. The ramp was lowered onto the moor so that the hooves of the cattle could get a good grip.

One gate was opened as far as it would go and then the second was opened with me jumping sideways off the ramp at the same time. The bullocks came charging out, running, jumping and kicking their heels as they raced across the moor. It was an amazing site to see and it always makes me laugh. These bullocks were here for their summer holidays and they loved it. I also loved doing this job as it meant a round trip of ninety to hundred miles twice a day.

There were two routes we could take. The first was through Tiverton to Exeter and then on to Starcross. It was fairly flat but had several narrow bridges and villages to negotiate. The second would be through South Molton, pick up the A377 and follow it to Exeter and then to Starcross.

Being an 'A' road this was a better road to travel and that was the way I drove with the first load. I had forgotten that Crediton High Street is on a slope. As we drove along it the lorry was leaning pretty well with Mr Shapcott holding on to the grab handle.

'I don't think this is the best road to take and perhaps we should go through Tiverton,' said the boss man.

We agreed that for the rest of the loads we would go down through Tiverton loaded and come back through Crediton when empty, a nice round trip.

A few days later I had to take my driving test in Exeter. The lorry was washed inside and out, the lights and the number plates were polished. On the way I stopped and took a stick out of the hedge; I put it directly in line with the rear of the lorry and then, on the mirror, I drew a line exactly where the stick was.

'Why did you do that,' asked Mr Shapcott?'

I replied, 'On the test you have to reverse and stop with the rear of the vehicle in line with a thick line painted on the floor. All I have to do is get the mark on the mirror in line with the one on the ground.'

We arrived at Exeter on time and met the examiner. We all walked around the lorry to make sure all the lights were working correctly and every thing was legal. We found that one of the rear light lenses was missing along with chrome ring that held it in place. The examiner said the lorry was not road legal and we could not go on the road, so the test would have to be cancelled. He said that if the boss could get back with a new light lens before we finished the manoeuvres in the yard then we would do the road work. This is not the way to do a test, wondering if you are, or are not, going to be able to finish it. All the manoeuvres were completed with no problem. I'd had plenty of practice reversing through narrow gateways and around small farm yards. The trick with the stick worked perfectly. Thankfully Mr Shapcott returned in time and the rest of the test went ahead. We had left the cattle box off so I didn't have to worry about low trees, shop signs and lamp standards. I thought it went pretty well, remembering that I'd never had any lessons with an official driving instructor. The lorry was eight years old but in a very clean condition and that always makes the examiner happy. I have to say I am a good driver, I am now over seventy years of age and can still put my van through a gap if it is two inches wider than the van.

The last part of the test was knowledge of the highway code and the mechanics of the lorry. I had studied this for several days before hand. Christine, my girlfriend at the time, and now my wife, used to test me, before I was allowed to go down the pub and play pool.

I was over the moon that I passed and the man testing me said that I did very well considering the mental stress that I had been put under because of the missing light lens. Mr Shapcott was delighted as now he could look forward to staying in the office on cold rainy days.

We used to do a regular job for Lloyd Maunder's at Willand. Once a month we would visit a few farms around Bishop's Nympton and collect various animals and then take them to the slaughter house. While I washed out the box, after unloading the animals, Mr Shapcott would go to the Butcher's shop at the front of the slaughter house and stock up with meat for a few days. If I was lucky he would bring back a couple of pasties for our lunch. After passing my test I used to do this run on my own. From the shop, I had to collect the meat that Mr Shapcott had already ordered and buy my own pasty.

At first it was a bit scary going out on my own, Twenty-one years old and in charge of a lorry. I soon settled down, the main difference was that Les Chilcott took the place of Mr Shapcott, doing Friday's coal-round. The Commer engine was fitted horizontally and therefore inside the cab the floor between the seats was not very high and that allowed three seats to be fitted. On longer journeys I used to sit at a slight angle, sit back and put my left leg on the engine cover and not bother to use the clutch to change gear. This is very easy after a little practice and something that I continued to do throughout my driving career. Just a couple of years ago (2017) after the clutch disintegrated in Bideford, I drove my Citroen van the twenty miles back home

One Friday afternoon I was told to fit the cattle box to the lorry and make sure that it was spotlessly clean. Saturday morning Mr Shapcott told me that we were off to the other side of Taunton to move a family, who were living on a farm, back to Bishop's Nympton.

It was quite normal in the seventies to use cattle lorries as removal vehicles. This was a nice change from carrying cattle and a round trip of a hundred miles; also lots of overtime pay.

Every thing went according to plan. The furniture was loaded in the back along with Mr Curtis, the customer, and his four children. Mrs Curtis was sat in the cab with me and Mr Shapcott.

On the return journey the sun was out and it was starting to get a bit warm in the lorry. We traversed the narrow road bridge at Waterrow and climbed the hill out of the village.

After a few minutes Mr Shapcott said, 'If there was a pub near here I would buy everybody a drink.'

He must have been thinking of a nice cool light ale after seeing the pub at Waterrow. I drove on for a few minutes before I said, 'What did you say just now I was concentrating on the road?'

He repeated what he said as I started to go around a long bend. A couple of hundred yards further on the right was the Barleycorn Pub. I pulled up on the left-hand side and looked at him. Like most people of his era he was careful with his money but he would buy the odd drink when the weather was hot. At least today he was making a bit of extra money so I don't think he minded fronting a round.

We three exited the cab and the rest of the family were let out of the back and we crossed the road to the 'Barleycorn.' Like the kids my pint was Coca Cola with lots of ice - beer is not the stuff if you've got a load of furniture to unload. The rest of the trip was uneventful and the Curtis family were back in the village of Bishop's Nympton where they had lived before their move to Taunton.

I was sent to a farm in the hamlet of Ashmill, to move some sheep. The farm was on a narrow 'C' road. The farmhouse was beside the road with the yard entrance on the west end of the house. The farmer said, 'Point the rear of the lorry toward the yard entrance and we can put some gates across the gap.' Now sheep do have a habit of escaping through such barriers so I was not too keen to do this.

I said 'Why don't I back into the yard entrance?'

'Nobody has ever backed in there before,' replied the farmer. With the help of the farmer, I reversed in at the first try.

There were just a few inches either side of the lorry. 'That will be easier to load them now,' I said getting out of the lorry.

The farmer looked at me and said 'That is the first time anyone has done that since I've lived here.' To me that said a lot about some so-called drivers; as previously stated the lorry was eight years old and I definitely was not the first driver.

In Bishop's Nympton there were two shops in 1971, a general store next to the north side of the yard and the bakers to the south side. I used to park outside the general store as the road was quite wide there. Sometimes I would forget that there was a metal sign sticking out from the wall. Strangely, I always remembered it when I came *out* of the shop. The procedure was always the same: I would have to then drive the lorry into the middle of the road, climb up the box (this was quite easy because of the ventilation slats) lean across and pull the sign out square with the wall. Now the world would know that the shop sold Bristol cigarettes.

The same manoeuvre was used to access a tall holly tree at the side of the road to get Christmas holly.

Occasionally straw would be carried on the flat bed of the lorry and a valuable lesson was learnt at farmer Verney's farm. The straw was loaded from a barn straight on to the lorry but I forgot that the lorry was on a slope. I built the load parallel with the straw in the barn and then I moved the lorry forward on to a flatter area. The load was about fifteen foot high and definitely on a lean. The good thing was that I only had a few miles to travel but it was challenging trying to avoid hitting the tops of our tall Devon hedges while driving along the narrow roads.

After about twelve months I was getting a bit disappointed with the pay. The promised amount of overtime did not happen which left the take-home around fourteen pounds. It was time to spread my wings again.

4

Tone Vale Transport

Tone Vale Transport, Wiveliscombe, Somerset were advertising for Heavy Goods Vehicle drivers, so I decided to attend an interview. The interview was done by the transport manager, known as Prickle, and the boss, Ken Thorne.

It went a bit like this:

'Hello Stephen, can I see your Heavy goods Vehicle licence' he looks at the licence. 'I see that you only have a four wheeler licence.'

'Yes'

Ken Thorne, 'We only have one four wheeler and we already have a driver for that.'

Me, grumpily, 'If you already have a driver why did you ask me to come here today?'

Prickle, 'If we take you on then we will put you through a Class one (articulated vehicle) driving course.'

I had never thought about driving a lorry that bent in the middle, that would be totally different to driving a rigid vehicle.

There were a few more questions about my limited driving experience. Having driven livestock was a bonus as it proved that I could drive carefully and in a safe manner.

They offered me the job and I was told that the wages were twenty three pounds a week for forty hours, over time rates were time and half and double time Sundays. Monday to Friday was normally paid ten hours per day, if the legal limit of eleven hours was worked then the extra hour would be paid.

This was an awful lot to take in, there was plenty of work and it all sounded like an opportunity to print money. With a bit of thought I calculated that I could double my take home pay even with travelling to and from Wiveliscombe a couple of times a week I was still going to be a lot better off financially.

I agreed to take their offer and told them that I could start Monday week (third July nineteen seventy two). I was told to ring the Saturday before and I would be told what I was to do on the Monday.

Before I even started on Tone Vale Transport I received notification of my Artic driving test (13th July 1972).

I started work at eight o'clock, Monday morning and was introduced to the shop steward who showed me around. As well as the office there was a workshop on site and a large lorry park, much of it on a slope. There was also a rest room and on the wall were wooden 'pigeon holes' each one with a driver's name on it. In your personal hole would be put your instructions for the following day.

I was also taken to Norton Fitzwarren were Tone Vale Transport had various storage sheds on the old Army camp. The stores foreman used a Land Rover, painted in the company colour of yellow, with Tone Vale Transport written on the door. This vehicle was used a general run about.

The sheds were huge and most of the doors were ten feet wide. The company used several sheds which were used to store cardboard boxes, ICI fertiliser, eggs and much more. There was an old Guy lorry used for moving trailers around the site. This type of operation is called shunting and the vehicle (in this case the Guy) and driver moving the trailers is called a shunter.

As well as the stores at Norton Fitzwarren there were depots in London and Southampton.

The Wiveliscombe fleet consisted of one four-wheel Ford, six ancient six-wheeled Albion Reivers, one twenty-ton Leyland Badger tractor unit, three ERF LVs, Two Mercedes, one Leyland and two brand new Leyland Buffaloes, all four-wheeled, thirty-two ton tractor units (lorries are classed by the amount of wheels you can see, although most lorries have duel rear wheels, for classification they are classed as a single wheel). There were probably many more lorries owned by Tone Vale Transport but the above were the ones that I mainly came into contact with.

Four of the Albion Reivers were flat bed lorries, one was fitted with an insulated box van and one had a standard box van.

There were twenty-foot box trailers fitted with a single axle, twin axle thirty-three foot box trailers, thirty-six and forty-foot flat trailers.

Taunton Meat Haulage and Eurofrigio Ltd of Ireland were incorporated into Tone Vale Transport. Although Taunton Meat Haulage had their own yard in Taunton, they shared the London office.

During the first three days of my employment I helped out where ever I was needed. Some times driving the Ford, as Bo, the normal driver, had the week off.

Tone Vale stored new flattened cardboard boxes and one job I did was to deliver a load of these boxes to Heathcote's factory in Tiverton.

Why I remember this trip is that the goods-in part of the factory had two people working there. One was a middle-aged man and the other a young lad who was Down's Syndrome. The young lad seemed to do everything. Showing me where to park, helping unload - he was one of the hardest working youngsters that I ever came across and a credit to the company. Heathcote's was a weekly delivery and enjoyed by every one. I used their phone to ring Tone Vale for the next job. There were no mobile phones in those days and after loading or unloading one had to ring-in to tell the company of your particular status using the phone belonging to the company where you were, or else find a telephone box. The beauty of using one of Heathcote's phones was that I used to flirt with their secretary while she connected me to an outside line.

On the fourth day I started my Articulated Lorry training at the Road Transport Industry Training Board, Bridgwater.

My instructor was named Alan. There should have been another learner-driver from Showerings at Shepton Mallet but he never turned up so I had double the amount of training time. The morning was spent in the class room learning about the stresses that play on a driver. I learnt through experience the worst is tiredness, this can be offset by just stopping and walking around the lorry a couple of times. I tried to not drive for more than three hours without stopping even if it was only for a few minutes.

Back to the schooling. Alan used model lorries to show what happens if you brake at the wrong time. Basically when you slow down while pulling a trailer the weight of the trailer and load will be pushing the tractor unit. On a thirty-two ton articulated vehicle the weight of the trailer and load is four fifths of the total weight. At all times the trailer will want to go straight so when you drive around a corner one should slow down a little before the bend and then gently accelerate through the bend therefore pulling the trailer and not letting it push you. If you break going into the bend then you risk jack-knifing the whole thing. Jack knifing is where the trailer goes straight on and causes the tractor unit to slide sideways and then go backwards in the same direction as the trailer. This situation can cause serious damage to the tractor unit and possibly seriously injury to the driver.

I was given the Police Driving Manual to read as well as the highway code. By lunch time the class room training was finished. Alan drove us to a café for lunch. From the café Alan drove the lorry to Weston Zoyland airfield.

In one corner of the airfield a test course was laid out and Alan showed me the manoeuvres needed to pass a test. I was told to practice them and then drive around the perimeter road, turning right at each junction and that would bring me back to where we were. There was no hurry as there was another training vehicle doing the same thing. Alan then walked over to a little hut where the other instructor was standing drinking tea

So off I went, forward, zigzagging through some traffic cones before coming to a stop in a straight line. Reversing back through the cones and stopping in a parking bay with the rear of the trailer in line with a white band painted on the ground.

It was the same procedures as I did in my Class three test the year before. Then it was drive straight down the road in front of me. As the other lorry was approaching the reversing area I had plenty of time for the drive around. It was the first time that I had driven this lorry so I decided to practice a few gear changes and get used to where the controls were. The lorry was a G-cabbed Leyland with a five speed gearbox and a two speed axle, the trailer was a flat one around thirty-six feet long with the axles right at the end. This type of trailer cut corners quite a lot.

The two speed axle was popular in the seventies, allowing half a gear change instead of a full gear. If the lorry was struggling to climb a hill one could change down half a gear and that would give you a better power to weight ratio. The lorry would then 'pull' a bit better. The axle control was fitted on the gear lever. You hooked two fingers under the knob on top of the axle control and pulled it up to engage the higher ratio and pushed the knob down for the low ratio. There was no neutral on it. The axle automatically changed speed when the clutch was depressed.

During the course I had to change all the gears in order, from first gear to top gear and back down to first. Ten gears without exceeding thirty mile per hour. It could have been worse, for example a Volvo had sixteen gears.

After about an hour I was getting thirsty so I parked the lorry to one side and joined the two instructors to have cup of tea. While I was enjoying my tea the other instructor asked how long had I been driving articulated vehicles. I told him that I had driven the shunter around the army camp the day before.

'You don't seem to have any trouble reversing the trailer,' he said.

'I've been driving agricultural tractors and trailers for about seven years - artics have a longer trailer but the principle is the same.'

On the Friday I continued my learner-driving with Alan by driving various roads around Bridgwater including going to a farm to get some potatoes and eggs for his weekend. The concentration when learning is intense so we stopped around every two hours, rested with a cup of tea and discussed my progress. Remember this was when there was a café every ten miles or so.

We were driving along the A361, through the Somerset levels, when Alan said, 'Stop swinging on the steering wheel. You are over correcting and wiggling down the road like a snake.' His criticism was right and the rest of the day was ok.

I had the weekend off and Monday we started driving around and through Taunton. Tuesday was the same, two hours driving and then half an hour rest.

Wednesday Alan said 'You have a choice today. Drive on the motorway or go to the seaside.'

I picked the seaside and, with Alan navigating, I drove toward Exeter. We encountered heavy holiday traffic and chaos around the Exeter ring road but finally arrived at Dawlish Warren, a town designed around the horse and cart. We found a place to park and enjoyed tea and an ice cream. All to soon it was time to return Bridgwater.

Thursday 13th July was the day of the test. I arrived at Bridgwater and was met by Alan and his boss. The boss was to accompany me to the test station at Norton Fitzwarren. Alan shook my hand and wished me luck. I had an hour driving around Taunton before we made our way to the test centre.

We got to the centre and Alan's boss asked me if I was happy with the training. I replied 'Yes. How did I do this morning, driving in?'

He said 'You gave those cyclists plenty of room as we came into Taunton but you didn't notice that you were doing thirty two miles an hour instead of thirty. You have to watch that. Keep as close to thirty all times but do not go over it.'

When the examiner came Alan's boss said that he was the worst of the examiners. First I did the manoeuvring around the bollards and into the parking bay, then off we went into Taunton. I drove to a straight bit of road and did the gear changing exercise. All good so far. Then we went around some country roads with hills and narrow sections. Then the gremlins arrived. Going up a hill the lorry started to struggle so I selected low on the two speed axle but it did not engage. We were freewheeling up hill and slowing quite quickly. Without taking my eyes of the road (that would have been an instant fail) I pulled the axle button up and changed down two gears with the gear lever. Thankfully the gears engaged. I accelerated and then changed up a gear and put the axle into low. It did not engage again so I put it into high axle and changed down a gear. I then accelerated and changed up to the next highest gear. The instructor said, 'You seem to be having trouble with the two speed axle.'

I replied, 'Yes, we oiled the switch earlier so I think the problem must be at the axle end.'

'You have done the gear changing exercise therefore there is no reason to use it again' said the examiner.

A little happier we went through Taunton. We came to a straight two lane road with both lanes marked Bristol. I took the right hand one and then realised there was a sharp right turn at the end. I suddenly realised that I wouldn't be able to turn right without the trailer crossing the pavement. That would be a certain fail. I checked the left hand mirror, clear road, so I indicated left and pulled into the middle of the road. No worries about the trailer now but would this manoeuvrer get me a pass? The examiner was watching carefully as we went around the bend.

'Take the road to the town centre,' he said.

As we approached some traffic lights I slowed right down for a cyclist on the left and the lights were on red. I gave the cyclist the regulation six feet. I had almost got level with him when he got off his bike and walked in front of the lorry.

'Oh my God!' exclaimed the examiner.

A picture of a newspaper headline saying, 'Cyclist killed in Taunton by heavy goods vehicle driver,' flashed through my mind. Not good for the industry. I stood on the brake and the lorry came to an instant stop, helped by the fact that I was slowing for the lights. The cyclist ambled across the front of the lorry unaware of how close he had come to being seriously hurt or killed.

The lights went to green and the examiner told me to make our way back to Norton Fitzwarren, not even telling me which road to take.

He actually looked quite shook up, realising how close we had come to a serious accident.

It was only a short drive back and the speedometer was on thirty most of the way. I just kept thinking three strikes and your out. I believed I had acted correctly at all times but did the examiner think the same? Three separate problems: had I handled them well enough to pass?

There were no more incidents on the way back to the test centre. I was asked questions on the highway code and was confident that my answers were correct. Then the examiner showed me a picture.

'What is that?' he asked

I replied 'It is a railway crossing but I cannot remember the correct name for it.'

'It is a continental half barrier crossing,' he said, quite loudly. He closed his big book and looked at me. 'What is the last thing you do before pulling away after you have coupled up a trailer?' I was asked.

Confidently, I said 'Check that the trailer reflectors are clean and the lights are working.'

In an even louder voice the examiner said 'There are three different lights on a trailer.' He looked at me.

Very quickly I said, 'Stop lights, side lights, indicator lights and the front marker lights.' (He had forgotten about the front marker lights, but would I get bonus points for them. I didn't think so).

He said very slowly, 'Young man you have passed, but only just.'

Apparently this was something that he said to everyone. The test had taken two and a half hours.

He gave me my pass slip and turned and walked away. The boss of the training school congratulated me and told me to drive back to Bridgwater. When we got to the village of North Petherton I was told to stop outside the Swan Hotel.

'You know the way back to the yard don't you?' he asked.

'Yes,' I said. 'Well I am going to pop into the Swan for lunch, you can take the lorry back on your own.' And he got out.

Well I didn't expect this. I thought, Mr Lock you are a fully qualified Artic driver - so drive.

I passed my car test, class three and class one Heavy Goods Vehicle first time. My motor-bike test was second time. The first test was stopped because the examiner thought that the bike had too many mechanical faults. I passed a few weeks later with a different bike. The whole test took eight minutes. I do get a bit nervous before hand but as soon as a test starts I just get on with it.

I got back to the yard, parked up and gave Alan the keys of the lorry.

'You obviously passed,' he said, 'or else the boss would be having a late lunch. Where is he, in the Swan?'

'Yes' I said.

Alan asked me how it went. I told him, good and also mentioned that the two speed axle needed checking.

He told me that the examiner was strict but fair. He said I did the right thing when the axle played up. I had kept the lorry under control at all times. If it had rolled to a stop I would not have passed. He said he was sure I *would* pass and if there had been any doubt the test would have been cancelled. I would have faced another week's training.

Goodbyes were said then I drove to North Petherton for lunch at the transport café. Then it was back to Wiveliscombe to give the good news to the transport manager.

A happy 'Prickle' told me that there was a job in my pigeon hole.

There was an envelope with the delivery notes inside and a lorry registration number written on the front. In the yard l found the lorry I was to drive: it was one of the Albion Reivers, fitted with a flat body. I checked the oil, the diesel tank was full, the tyres ok and the lights were clean and in working order. The ropes were tight, so we were ready to go - destination, Burton on Trent, Derbyshire.

Albion Reivers didn't have power steering so it was hard work steering at low speed. The same cab was shared with Leyland and Dodge and was known as an LAD cab, (Leyland, Albion, Dodge). The interior was all metal, no heater, no radio, no bed and a large, curved engine cover taking up a lot of room. There were two seats. The engine cover sloped down to the floor a few inches from the rear of the cab. There was an inspection plate on the side of the engine cover and was originally fitted with a rubber seal, now missing. I covered the plate with my sleeping bag and a couple of blankets. This deadened most of the engine noise and kept out the majority of fumes. The six-speed gear lever came up from the floor between the engine cover and the back of the cab. To select odd numbered gears the lever was pushed forward which caused the lever to go down as well. Caution was used doing this, with the flat of your hand, that stopped you banging your knuckles on the steel engine cover; something a wise person only did once.

There were four small dials on the dashboard and a central speedometer. Logbooks were filled in to record the journey times.

I looked at the maps in my AA book and set off on my first job as a Class One, Long Distance Heavy Goods Vehicle driver. At first it was a bit strange, I had never driven a six wheeler before, longer than a four wheeler but shorter than an Artic.

The M5 was still being constructed and the bridge across the Avon had not been built, so it was straight through Bristol and out the other side. Then to Walsall where the small lorry park was full. I had been up since six, it was now nearly ten at night and I was getting tired. I was stopped and contemplating what to do next, when a man came over and asked if I was looking for somewhere to park. He drove for BRS (British Road Services) and had parked just around the corner on some waste ground, opposite the Police station. I drove around the corner and there was a BRS Artic. So I parked up beside it and turned the engine off. The man had followed me, we talked for a while and I told him it was my first trip as a long distance driver and I had passed my test that day.

'Come on,' he said 'that is some thing to celebrate.' We went to the nearest pub, he brought me a pint of Ansell's bitter, I brought him one back. Then we went to the chippy for a driver's supper which we ate as we walked back to the lorries.

'Where are you going?' he asked. I looked at the delivery notes. They said a Bonded warehouse, Burton on Trent (possibly the one on Derby Road, I can't remember the exact address). He then asked what I was carrying.

I said I had no idea as I hadn't looked.

'Bonded warehouses store goods where tax is paid when the goods are moved on, stuff like alcohol and tobacco,' said my new friend.

What I was carrying was about twelve tons of wine, on a lorry were even the doors didn't lock.

I was too tired to take in what could happen, high-jacks, theft, what ever. I put some ropes in the gap between the engine cover and the back of the cab, climbed into my sleeping bag and slept like a log. The end of my first day as a distance driver. As time went on I discovered that the gear lever, on Albions, were held in with a pin. Remove the pin, move the gear lever and there was more sleeping room.

As a new driver I was given older lorries to drive, mainly the Albion Reivers. These Reivers had double drive, meaning both axles drove the lorry which is probably why they used to be hard to steer. The worst thing was that when it was raining and the white lines of a Zebra Crossing were wet, the front wheels of Albions would not grip causing the lorry to go straight on. This is ok on a straight road, but it seemed to be there were thousands of crossings on a bend especially in London.

I had a load one day for British Aerospace near Manchester. I stopped at one of the services on the M5. I was going to have a cup of tea and then go into the shop and look at one of the maps to see if I could find my delivery address. My AA book wasn't the best thing for this. As I was having my tea two blokes came over and one asked if I was going toward Manchester.

I said 'Yes, why?'

He explained he was a lorry driver and had given the other chap a lift but now he had to turn off. I asked the younger one if he knew where British Aerospace was. He told me that he wanted to get to the same area and I could drop him at the end of the road. So off we went, as good as his word when I dropped him off he pointed to the end of road and said that is where British Aerospace is.

After unloading I was sent to a wire works in Warrington. I slept in their canteen that night and loaded in the morning coils of wire for Poole. That evening I parked in Tone Vale's Southampton Depot. As I didn't have much money I asked if I could have my night-out allowance. Normally wages were paid by cheque and night-out allowance and other expenses were paid in cash, Both at the end of the following week.

He gave me the money and said, 'Ring me in the morning after you have tipped (unloaded)'.

'Why is that?' I asked.

'There is a load of flour to be collected at the docks,' I was told.

That evening I accompanied some of the other company drivers who introduced me to the Juniper Berry pub. In the seventies it was the haunt of Transvestites and other various fun-loving people; well known for a place to have a good night out.

The following day I arrived at Poole and the wire was unloaded. While unloading I folded the tarpaulin, known as the 'sheet'. I asked the forklift driver if he would put the sheet on the back of the lorry. This is normal practice for forklift drivers to do this but strangely he never answered and drove off.

Tone Vale used to carry a lot of waste paper and because of this the sheets were quite wide as well as long. They were made of thick plastic and weighed about a hundredweight and a half, around seventy five kilos in new money.

I was really going to struggle to lift it up on my own, so I unrolled it again. Then I folded it in half and pulled it up to the end of the lorry. I took one end and put it onto the bed of the lorry and then pulled it up to the head board, the vertical part of the body against the cab. Then I bent over the back of the lorry and pulled up the remainder of the sheet and folded it over the sheet on the floor of the lorry. Then I rolled it up, job done.

At the nearest telephone box I rang Wiveliscombe and told them I was empty. I was sent to Express Dairy at Honiton to load butter. Christine's uncle Clifford was the load foreman. Later the butter would be trans-shipped into an insulated box van or one of Taunton Meat Haulage's fridges.

When I returned to the yard I was told off for not going back to Southampton to load the flour. I made out that I had forgotten; flour is loaded from a chute at the end of the lorry. Each sack weighs one hundred weight (three hundred in total) to be loaded and there is a lot of walking up and down the lorry. Who wants to do that on a Friday?

Six-wheeled Albions Reivers seemed to be what I would drive for a while. Thursday afternoon a flat bed Albion would be loaded with new flat packed cardboard boxes. The load was for Toshiba at Southway, Plymouth to be delivered on Friday.

The return load would be from Stonegate Eggs at Loddiswell in the South Hams or Bovey Tracey, both are in Devon. On the way back I had to pick up three or four wooden egg crates from Halberton. I would meet with a farmer and trans-ship the boxes from a Land Rover to the Albion.

Eggs were normally packed in cardboard boxes and would be loaded using metal rollers. The boxes were taken off the rollers and stacked by hand. This was usually done by three or four people. The roots of Tone Vale Transport was in egg transportation and in the seventies they stored and transported eggs across Southern England for Stonegate Eggs.

One Thursday afternoon I was being loaded by Ron, the forklift driver, when he disappeared at high speed out of the door and shot up the road toward the site entrance. This site was the size of a small town with several large warehouses. I decided to make a cup of tea and wait for the forklift to return. After about forty minutes Ron and forklift returned, a bit slower than when he left.

'What's going on?' I asked.

'Well, at lunch time I went down the pub for a pint and got a lift back with Colesy, one of the drivers,' said Ron.

'So why did you suddenly rush off just now, mid-afternoon?'

Ron replied, 'You know the postman leaves his bike in the shed by the gates. Well I sort of borrowed it to ride down to the pub (about four hundred yards away). Then I got a lift back and I forgot about the bike. So I've just been down to recover the bike as I didn't have permission to ride it.'

'Why have you been so long? It is only just down the road' I asked.

'Well you can't go to a pub and not have a quick pint' said Ron.

This was when pubs closed afternoons but Ron always knew a way to get a pint, whatever the time of day.

Another egg story involved me returning home to Wiveliscombe one afternoon and travelling around the notorious Exeter ring road when the traffic came to a stand still. This was not normal during the week so I wondered what the problem was - an accident or a breakdown? No, it was an escaped prisoner from Dartmoor prison at Princetown and the Police were checking every vehicle. When they got to me they asked what I was carrying. I told them eggs.

'Let's have a look please,' said one of our boys in blue. This trip I had a box van, so I opened the back doors and the policemen looked at the stack of boxes. There was a gap of around twelve inches between the top boxes and the roof of the lorry.

'When you crawl along the boxes try to keep your weight on the sides of them and not in the middle,' I said.

They looked at each other. I'd seen slimmer policemen.

'Did you load the lorry?' asked one of them.

'Yes, I did' I replied.

'Have you stopped since you loaded.'

'No, and I haven't been on Dartmoor either,' says I.

'Carry on driver,' said the other.

'If you get to your destination and find you have a stowaway give us a ring. You know the number.'

Aren't our policemen wonderful.

I had been on the firm for about three weeks and I was given a multi-drop load to deliver around Cornwall on a Reiver. I travelled across country to the A30 and headed west. I hadn't gone very far when the clutch stopped working. I found a telephone box and phoned mission control. After being told of the problem, 'Prickle' said, 'Carry on, keep in touch.' This was a three day trip - with no clutch! So carry on I did.

On the second day, a Tuesday, I arrived at a Cash & Carry in Truro. I gave the delivery tickets to the fork lift driver. He looked at them and said, 'You are not booked in until Thursday.'

Now, forklift drivers can make life hard or easy for a lorry driver and this guy had just made it hard for a person that is not too patient. I walked over to the cab of the lorry, got a piece of paper and wrote something on it. I walked back to the fork lift driver and gave it to him. 'What's this?' he asked.

'That's the name, address and phone number of the company. The clutch has gone on the lorry and it is going back to the depot to be repaired. It will be in the garage Thursday so if you want your consignment you can collect it from Wiveliscombe or I will deliver it next week when the lorry is back on the road. Your choice.'

I know that these places only have small storage areas. The idea being that products should be on the shelves to sell and not in store. Under the circumstances and as it was only a couple of pallets the 'forky' decided that he could make room for them in the store this time. After unloading I thanked him for putting himself out and went on my way, picking up a load of eggs for the return load back to Wiveliscombe.

Every Saturday drivers that had only worked five days in a row were expected to work Saturday mornings, I hated doing this as it meant a least an hour's round trip to drive to Wiveliscombe. Then I drove a spare tractor unit (the newer ones had a dedicated driver). The older units, like the six-wheelers, were used twenty-four hours a day when possible with no regular driver.

It usually meant taking an empty trailer over the hills to Watchet docks and returning with a loaded trailer. At Watchet the trailer was dropped wherever there was space, possibly on Dock Road. The trailer park was beside the railway line fence with a low wall along one side and the dock road the other. In this long rectangle were park up to sixteen trailers, four rows of four

Your allocated loaded trailer was then found, there was usually three trailers in front of it. After a bit of shunting the allocated trailer was parked in Dock Road and the others back in the trailer park The loaded one was roped down before it was taken back to Wiveliscombe.

If there were two or three units present the trailers to be collected were found and working together they could probably be shuffled around in the trailer park. There were also other companies collecting trailers and, without care, the area could soon get choked with trailers. It would have been better to knock down the small wall and park the trailers at an angle. Now the docks have closed for commercial traffic and the trailer park is a car park and, yes, the wall has been removed.

All this messing about with trailers took time and did use to annoy me greatly. After a couple of weeks doing it I told 'Prickle' that I wasn't too happy with the situation. He told me that it was company policy the only other options were to stay out Friday nights or work Sunday.

The agency that dealt with Naval maps was situated in Taunton. I collected a load of maps for the aircraft carrier HMS *Ark Royal* which was berthed at Devonport, Plymouth.

I was pretty excited at the thought of getting up close to such a famous ship. There were two ways to get to the Docks. One road took you opposite the entrance to the base and one could drive straight across the road and into the naval base. The other road followed the perimeter wall and when one got to the entrance there was a sharp left turn to enter the base. I took the straight route and stopped at the gate office.

'I have a delivery for *Ark Royal*,' I said and showed the gate man the delivery notes.

'Straight down the end,' he told me. 'It's a big ship with a flat top. Even a chap from Somerset should be able to find it.'

I thought that was quite rude and stored it in the memory bank in my head.

A few weeks later I had an Artic loaded for Devonport. This time I came the other route which meant a sharp left turn into the base. There was a line of bollards down the middle of he road which meant the gate man had to move them all so that I could drive in.

While he was doing this a Naval police woman came over to me.

'You look happy,' she said looking at my smiling face.

'I normally come down the other road but I was here a few weeks ago and that bloke was taking the 'mickey' out of people from Somerset. I thought that if he has all that hot air inside of him I'd help him get rid of some of it by giving him a bit of exercise'.

Then she smiled at me.

'It's worse than that,' I said, 'I was born and still live in North Devon.'

She laughed so loud that the gate man looked across to us.

As I drove off I said to the happy policewoman 'You can tell him what I said - that should make his day.'

On my first trip to London every thing was fine until I got on the M3. The lorry, an Albion Reiver, started making a noise, it sounded like the silencer had fallen off. A quick check and I could not see anything wrong with the exhaust system so I carried on to Worcester Park where I stayed with Doris and Chas, my auntie and uncle.

The next morning I went to Bermondsey and delivered my load of cheese.

I rang the London office and was told to go to the London depot situated between St Pancras and Euston station. Due to my lack of knowledge of London it took nearly 2 hours to find Phoenix Road where the depot was. Eventually I found the road, I drove down it but could see no yard. I drove around the block and stopped halfway along the Phoenix Road. There was a National Car Park all along one side with what looked like industrial units underneath it at street level. I walked up the ramp to the roof top park with the idea of asking the parking attendant if he knew where Tone Vale transport was. When I got to the top of the slope I could see some yellow lorries at the other end of the car park and the attendant confirmed I was at the right place. I went back to the lorry and drove it down to where the others were parked.

A sign on the side of a big wooden shed declared it to be the London office of Taunton Meat Haulage, Eurofrigio (Ireland) and Tone Vale Transport.

Above: The Cook's Cross entrance to Moore's yard.

Below: The Entrance to Moore's yard as seen from the yard. The diesel pump is on the side of the shed. Both images by the author

Above: A close up of the now rare blue and white diesel pump.

Below: The Commer lorry that was driven by the author's brother Jim.

Top image by the author. Bottom Image Tiverton Coach builders.

Brother Jim's Commer lorry on contract to the Fatstock Marketing Corporation. The picture is believed to have been taken at the Devon County Show. People: from left to right. Pat Moore, Arthur Bryant (another of Moore's drivers), Fred Moore, Derek Moore and Jimmy Lock. The boys are left, Alan Seatherton and right Desmond Moore, Derek's son.

Image courtesy Fatstock Marketing Corporation.

The rear of a cattle lorry showing the two rear gates. Inside, above the slats, the upper deck is visible. Two more would be put down for ramps and when loaded the two ramps would be hung on the centre chains hanging from the roof.

Above: A Bedford CA pick-up identical to the two that North Devon Farmers had. The photo was taken by the author at the Dover Transport Museum.

Below: A very new, 1958, seven-ton Commer that has been in an accident with a car. All North Devon Farmer's Commers were fitted with drop sides. The man closest to the cab is Jack Heywood, driver and then Distribution Manager for North Devon farmers.   Image Jack Heywood.

Above: The front end of the accident. It happened early in 1958. The lady driver from Instow was overtaking at the time. Jack Heywood was driving the lorry.   Image Jack Heywood

Below: This 1947 registered lorry was built by North Devon Farmers. Owned by Mitchell's of Bideford it has a Bedford chassis, fitted with a Perkins engine and a five speed gearbox. The cab and body were built by North Devon Farmers in Bideford.   Image Jack Heywood

Above: A Wolseley Titan rotavator, with Briggs and Stratton engine purchased from North Devon Farmers. It was still in use in 2019. Image by author.

Below: North Devon Farmer's company plate on the top of the rotavator.
Image by the author

Above: An Albion Reiver fitted with the LAD cab (Leyland, Albion, Dodge).
Image by the author

Left: A badge from an Albion Reiver. Albions were made in Glasgow. The badge shows the flag and thistle of Scotland. The model of lorry, in this case a Reiver, was written along the bottom of the badge. The Albion motto was 'As Sure as the Sun Rises.'

Image by author.

Above: An ERF (Edwin Richard Foden) LV with single axle box trailer. The author drove a lot of miles in this vehicle.   Image Edward J Beazley @ NA3T.

Below: Watchet harbour.

Above: The old trailer park at Watchet. The wall has been removed and the trailer park is now a public car park.   Image by author

Below: Present day office block at the Watchet docks.   Image by author

Left

RHA Driver's handbook

Below

Three drivers.
With the beard,
Francis Pidler.
Centre, the author.
Right, Jeffrey Binding.

Above: Wandsbrough paper mill, Watchet. Image by Stephen Wilks

Below: Another view of Wandsbrough paper mill, Watchet. Image by Stephen Wilks

There were two managers, one for the two meat haulage companies and one for Tone Vale Transport. The latter stood about five foot eight high and was about five foot six wide, answered to the name of Graham, and he wasn't very happy. He told me I should have been there at least an hour earlier. I told him that it was my first time driving in London and also there seems to be a problem with the lorry.

'So I heard,' said the man-mountain. He picked up the phone, spoke to someone and then told me to take the lorry down to the workshop that was under the car park.

The mechanic told me later that the engine had dropped a piston, which had to be replaced.

I liked parking in Phoenix Road. There was a pub nearby called The Cock, and the barmaid seemed to like the drivers from the West Country, with their strange accent. I used to get served pretty quick. Then I would sit and watch the television in the bar. There was another pub close by called the Coffee Bean. They used to have Karaoke nights but that was not my cup of tea. Also nearby was a nice café run by a Greek family, although the taxi drivers used to kick up if we sat in what they thought was their area.

The next Monday was the start of a regular run for me and I was to start at five o'clock in the morning. The load was eggs for Poole, Southampton and Hastings. I checked the lorry over and left about fifteen minutes after five and got to Poole in a couple of hours. There was no one at the delivery point. I ate a sandwich and unloaded the ten boxes of eggs on to the unloading dock. About a quarter to eight a man arrived, signed my delivery note and I drove to Totton, near Southampton. I had a timed delivery at a Cash and Carry store and half of the load was unloaded very quickly. An hour later I was on my way to Hastings, Sussex.

Somewhere between Southampton and Portsmouth I went through a town that was full of policemen, I found out later that they were from a police training college.

From Lewes to Hastings the road is often very busy with holiday traffic and it takes ages to get to Hastings. Eventually I got to my destination in Hastings - another Cash and Carry belonging to the same company as the one in Southampton. The lorry now empty I telephoned London. Graham told me that the lorry has to be in the yard for six in the morning so the shunter can load it at a fruit market.

I had completed my driving hours so I went to the lorry park on the sea front with the intention of parking up for the night. The lorry park is used by coaches during the day and if there is no free parking spaces then you kept driving around the town until a coach left and freed up a parking space. The problem was that there were always three or four lorries trying to park.

The lorry park was at the east end of the sea front, right on the beach, alongside Rock-A-Nore Road. The other side of the road was a small pub that did wonderful cottage pie which was my first port of call that evening. There were other drivers that parked in Hastings every Monday and I soon got to know them and enjoyed many a good night out there.

A four o'clock start the next morning meant I was in the London yard by six and handed over the lorry to the shunter. I then went for an early breakfast. Graham arrived at the yard about eight.

Once, Graham was having a go at me when Gordon Hartnoll, one of the other drivers came in. He grabbed Graham around the neck and told him to stop bullying me or there would be trouble. After that Graham treated me with a bit more respect and we got on really well.

Graham told me that he was supposed to get another shunter but couldn't get one and asked me to deliver a load for ten pounds cash - half a week's wages. I told him that I would be delighted to help him out.

He gave me some keys and delivery notes and told me to deliver the load to Greenford, Middlesex. He didn't tell me that it was four hundred dusty sacks full of coffee beans to be hand-balled off (un-loaded by hand). The lorry was a Leyland tractor unit and a forty foot trailer, the first Artic that I had driven in London. All went well and as I had started early Graham gave me the afternoon off and I still got ten hours' pay.

This was to be the start of a wonderful working relationship and of course we kept it to ourselves. Graham would tell the Wiveliscombe office that he could not get a load back to the West Country and they would tell him to find something for me to do. There were always loads to sort out for the night trunkers. These were the drivers who did the night deliveries, mainly fruit, that was loaded during the day. Much of this fruit went to Frank Mann at Plymouth and Torquay.

Another benefit of staying in London for a couple of days was driving to different parts of the city and also exploring roads that I had not previously driven. With an empty lorry and diesel for four hundred miles I used to drive many different routes, always remembering where I went. A lot of the loads were from the docks and delivered to various places in the London area.

One evening, myself and another driver came back from the Cock. Graham was in the office which was strange, normally he went home at five pm. He called to us and said as it was cold we could sleep in the office. Even stranger, because no one was ever allowed to sleep there.

Then about one o'clock he woke us up and said he had a job for us. We got into his car and he drove us to an industrial estate in Slough. On a car park, in front of a factory, was a Taunton Meat Haulage fridge trailer on its side and a Mercedes tractor unit beside it. The driver of the Mercedes had dropped his trailer on the car park and drove off to get some fish and chips. While he was gone one of the landing legs at the front of the trailer went through the hard surface of the car park. The trailer was loaded with 20 ton of pig carcases hanging on hooks from the roof of the trailer and the further the trailer sank, the more the weight went to that side of the trailer eventually the weight turning the trailer onto its side.

A little while later a lorry with an empty fridge trailer arrived. The doors on the 'dead' trailer were opened and the empty trailer was reversed up to it. Then our work began, the two drivers unhooking the pigs and passing them up to us and we hooked them up in the empty trailer. The trailer was about three-parts empty when a four-wheel wrecker (recovery truck) arrived. We stopped for a rest while the recovery man had a look at the situation. He owned the company who recovered our stricken lorries and was very good at his job. He told Graham that there wasn't too much damage done to the trailer and it should be lifted upright with a mobile crane. It would probably be ok to use once the broken landing leg was repaired. If he pulled it upright now, with the wrecker, it would cause too much damage and the trailer would probably have to be scrapped. Graham told him to go and get a crane as quick as possible, and off he went.

We finished loading the pigs and waited for the crane to arrive. Then a huge Scammell recovery lorry arrived, it was covered in orange and white lights. I had never seen any thing like it. He backed up to the trailer and started to unload chains and straps. Graham asked what they were doing and he was told that the other chap had sent them to recover the trailer. Graham told them it was going to be lifted with a crane. The two guys said that the first guy had changed his mind and had sent these two to do the job with their bigger lorry. Graham was still discussing it when the first guy arrived back with a small mobile crane.

It appears that in the recovery world once you start a lift then it is your job. The guys in the Scammell had intercepted a radio message from our recovery man and had rushed down to do the job before the crane got there.

Soon cars started to arrive at the factory with workers and the owner wanted to know what on earth was going on. He said that one of his staff had phoned for the police to come and sort out the situation. Then the driver of the crane and the driver of the Scammell stared arguing, with Graham trying to sort it out. It got out of hand and the two recovery men started to fight just as the old Bill arrived with blue lights flashing.

The scene that met the police was one dead trailer, one Artic unit, one unit and trailer, one large wrecker across the road, one small crane in the middle of the road and several cars trying to park. Two people in overalls fighting, four people covered in pig fat trying to stop them, two men in suits arguing and several people watching it all. The police told the driver of the Scammell and his mate to leave and the loaded Artic was moved and parked a little way up the road. The police then left and the trailer was, at last, lifted upright and the Mercedes unit reconnected to it. There were only a few scratches and a bent leg. It was coupled to the tractor unit and driven away to be repaired. The crane left and Graham drove us to a nearby café for breakfast - none of us had eaten for several hours. We got back to the yard nine hours after we left it, the night before. We got paid for ten hours and had the rest of the day off. From the insurance company I got a complete set of new clothes, including shoes. We hadn't taken our overalls because we didn't know where we were going, or why. The driver of the Mercedes got a written warning.

One morning I was given the Leyland Badger to drive, this was to be a trip I would never forget, for all the wrong reasons. It was connected to a box trailer loaded with eggs for delivery to railway arches under Waterloo station.

I decided to go up the A361 to Shepton Mallet and across country to Hungerford and then the M4 into London. At Shepton Mallet, I slowed for some traffic lights but the lorry did not seem to respond to the brakes. I went through the lights at green a bit faster than I intended and had to turn right. As I turned right I had to brake really hard and the tractor unit started to lean a bit. To avoid a jack-knife I straightened up and stood on the brakes, as the lorry slowed, and using a bit of pavement I managed to accelerate and regain control. For the rest of the trip I drove carefully on to London.

The eggs safely unloaded I made my way to the town of Potters Bar, just north of London. Here I loaded foam rubber, each piece being the size of a small van. The total weight was about three tons.

There was no M25 in those days so I made my way to Slough and joined the M4 there and settled back for a nice drive to Bristol. Being around six o'clock the traffic was busy but would thin out as I travelled West.

A little while later I was overtaken by a new AA transit van and what caught my eye was the big orange light in the middle of the roof. I hadn't seen one of them before.

About twenty minutes later, as the light started to fade, further down the motorway I saw a lot of brake lights and in the middle a big orange flashing light.

There was a slight curve in the motorway and the orange flashing light didn't seem to be on the hard shoulder, nor did it seem to be on the other side of the motorway. This made me think it must be in the middle. As I got closer, maybe a half a mile away I could see the orange flashing light was definitely in the middle of the motorway, surrounded by lots of brake lights. There were still cars going past at great speed. I slowed down a bit - there was obviously some thing really serious going on ahead.

There were lots of brake lights but the speeding cars could not see them because of the vehicles in front of them. I was a few hundred yards away and I could just make out the middle and outside lanes were blocked with stationary vehicles. Three lanes of fast moving traffic were trying to get through using one lane, I decided to take to the hard shoulder and slowed to about forty miles per hour and then to thirty, unfortunately there were no hazard warning lights fitted to vehicles in those days.

Cars were now swerving across the motorway and causing other vehicles behind to brake sharply. All of a sudden three cars came onto the hard shoulder in front of me, braked hard and slid to a halt. Even on a good day (the road was dry) a lorry is not going to stop in fifty feet. I had no choice but to take to the grass verge. But between the grass verge and the hard shoulder is a trench full of chippings. Will the lorry sink and tip over if I go across these chippings? I had no time to think, it was an automatic reaction. I swung the steering wheel to the left, changed down a gear and accelerated, probably holding my bum cheeks tight together.

The grass verge was on a slope and the badger shot up that slope like he had seen a long-lost cousin. I travelled a fair distance and seeing I was well away from the hard shoulder I turned parallel to the motorway and drove along the verge hoping that the lorry wouldn't sink and fall on its side. The load was light and a bit of speed would help. I didn't have time think about drains or any thing else that may be hidden in the grass. The cars below me had passed the obstruction were now going back on to the motorway so I drove down the verge and across the chippings and rejoined the motorway myself.

At the next services I stopped, and had a cup of tea, to get my heart rate down to normal speed.

I went across to the garage and put some diesel in the lorry. While the young lady was dealing with that I disconnected the blue air line from the trailer and pushed the brake pedal. No air came out, I turned off the isolation valve for that line and pushed the brake pedal, air came out. I reconnect the air line. I could not believe it, some idiot had fitted the handle of the valve the wrong way around. Worse still was that previous drivers had not told anybody. This was not a new valve.

The lady attendant said if she charges for ten gallons more fuel than has been put in the tank we could have half the cost of extra fuel each. I said what do you want the money for? She said that she was saving up for a car. 'Well Tone Vale aren't paying for it,' I replied rather harshly. I was still wound-up about the brake valve. In twenty years of driving that was the only time I was asked to do some thing illegal like that. Mileage and fuel consumption are always monitored by companies - so why risk your job for a couple of extra pounds.

The rest of the journey went ok and the brakes were great - it would stop on a sixpence as people used to say. When I got back to the yard the next day the fitter changed the valve handle to the correct position.

The London docks were still open in the seventies and Tone Vale Transport did a lot of work from them. Fruit, timber and flour were just a few things that were collected from there. One day I was sent there with the Badger to collect a load of bananas. The dockers helping to load told me that if I can smell banana while loading then I should take the yellow bananas out of the box as they were over-ripe for delivery. Bananas are shipped green and would ripen too quickly if the yellow ones are left in. So I did that and when I took over-ripe ones out I replaced them with green ones. At the end of the load I had eight boxes of over-ripe. Nobody seemed to care so I put them at the back of the load, next to the trailer doors. I returned to the London depot with a load of fruit and the some over ripe the same colour as the bright yellow lorry that drove. When I went into the office Graham said 'get your gear out of that lorry, it's going on night trunk.'

'I want to show you some thing outside' I replied.

'What's up' he said when we got to the lorry.

'Eight boxes of over ripe.'

He went and got his car and put four boxes in the boot and put four in another lorry. This is the lorry I was driving the next day. I really was his mate now. I gave one box to my mum, most of the bananas she gave other mums on the estate where we lived. The other three I sold to the green grocer down the road.

The depot moved to Fyffe Munro's yard, Dock Road, Silvertown, East London. Dock road was just off Silvertown Way. The benefits to the driver was that it was closer to the docks and the industrial East End but further to get to the M3 and M4 and the other routes to the West Country.

There was also a lot of animosity from the Fyffe Munro drivers who had to share their rest room with us western yokels. The yard was also a lot smaller than the large car park that we were used to.

The first time that I had to go back to Somerset from the new yard a Taunton meat driver said, 'Just follow me.' Off he went down the East India Dock Road (the A13) and I followed. He turned left down into Branch Road and that is where I lost him. I turned left and went to the end of the road past the tunnel Approach Road, I knew that was not the way. At the T junction I turned right onto the A1203, called the Highway, and headed for Tower Bridge. The driver in front of me was driving a Mercedes and I had an Albion: a bit like a horse and cart chasing a sports car. I got to end of the Highway and immediately on my left was Tower bridge. There was no sign of my guide so I drove across Tower bridge and then turned right and followed the road along side the river Thames. This was a route that I had used before. While travelling along the Albert Embankment at Vauxhall I looked across the river and there was my guide, level with me, going along Millbank. I got to Vauxhall Bridge and crossed back to the North side of the river but I never saw the Taunton Meat Haulage lorry again. I turned left at the end of the bridge for I knew that this road would eventually take me to the A4 and then the M4.

One dark evening I was heading homeward along the A4 and the traffic was going very slow for a three lane road. After some aggressive driving I got to the front and there were three motorbikes, one in the middle of each lane. They were deliberately riding slowly and ignoring my lorries hooter. I was in the middle lane and I gave the motorbike in front of me a little nudge with my bumper. The rider turned around and read Albion across the front of the lorry and decided to get out of my way. He accelerated away and I also accelerated. As I got level with the bike on the right I started to cross into his lane and he fled off into the night. I then went into the right hand lane and the other rider also accelerated away. I then stayed in the middle lane as it was marked M4, the same as the right hand lane. The left hand was marked A3. Cars started to pass both sides of me, blowing they're hooters and waving. Now they had realised why I had been driving like I was.

The Monday morning egg run was getting quicker, time-wise. I started at five thirty and didn't stop to eat until after I had delivered at Totton. There was a café a few hundred yards from the Cash and Carry where I ate before going on to Hastings. After going under a low bridge in Southampton I realised I was lucky. I had forgotten to use the alternative route. It was the only time on that run I was driving a flatbed lorry, if it had been a box it would have hit the bridge. I was advised at Totton, in the future, to go through the city, as there were no bridges there.

From Lewes to Hastings the road was always very busy and traffic could be slow moving. The man at the Hasting Cash and Carry told me a better route. From Lewes head north towards Royal Tunbridge Wells. As I left Lewes follow the B2192 to Hailsham, then onto Battle. At Battle follow the road marked 'station' and the road to Hastings which would take me right past the Cash and Carry. Going this route saved a lot of time and I was able to drive on to London before my total legal driving hours were exhausted.

The move to Silvertown meant that it took a lot less time to get to the yard from Hastings, using the Blackwall Tunnel. It meant no more good nights in Hastings but I didn't have to get out early in the morning. I had many good nights in Hastings with other regular drivers. After the pubs closed we would go back to the lorry park and do a bit of trading. Cyril, the manager of Stonegate eggs at Bovey Tracy, originally came from Barnstaple in North Devon and had married my cousin Pat. I was an usher at his wedding and we always got very well. When I loaded eggs at Bovey Tracy he always gave me three dozen eggs. As my father kept chickens and I didn't strictly need these eggs I used them for trading on the road. Over time I obtained various goods such as an antler suitcase, a dozen bottles of Co-op jam and a new kitchen table.

Gradually the regular drivers that parked in Hastings were moved to other routes and the last time I parked at Hastings there were no drivers there that I knew.

In the London Inn I got talking to a local who asked me where they had all gone. I told him that deliveries change and routes change. He told me he was a fisherman and invited me into the lounge bar. The lounge bar was used exclusively for fishermen and anybody else was definitely unwelcome. As I was invited I had no problem, in fact they were a great bunch and it was a challenge to pay for a drink. My drink always seemed to be paid for - they really knew how to look after their guests and all because I bought matey a drink in the bar.

Graham told me one morning that he wanted two trailers loaded at Spillers Millennium Mills at Royal Victoria Dock and he would pay me ten pounds for each trailer. Well of course I said yes, that was nearly a week's wages. This meant hand-balling 800 x cwt (fifty kilo) bags of flour. The first trailer was a thirty-six footer which I backed up to a chute as instructed. The chute was fixed to the wall and ended vertically about four feet from the deck of the trailer. The bags would come down one at a time and when that one was removed another would come down.

I put a line of bags vertical across the trailer, leaning against the head board. After about four rows I stacked three rows of bags, laying them flat across the trailer. I carried on like this until there was about six foot of space left at the end of the trailer.

A voice on the tannoy said, 'Tone Vale you have forty bags left to load.' A quick calculation and I came to the conclusion that they wouldn't all fit. I had to stack them higher which meant throwing some bags on to the ones already stacked, then climb up and stack them correctly.

Finally the trailer was loaded, after what seemed to be miles of walking up and down it. The load was roped and sheeted and taken back to the yard. The extra height on the rear didn't look very professional but because the trailer axles were fitted at the end of the trailer there was no worry about the axles being over-weight.

For the next load I picked up a forty-foot trailer and returned to the flour mill.

I had already calculated how many bags fitted on four foot of the last trailer, multiplied by ten meant that four hundred bags would easily fit on a forty foot trailer. The second load had been taken back at the yard and, my money collected, I went into the restroom and had a well-deserved cup of tea, also making one for Graham and his fellow manager and for any other drivers there. This was a way of getting in the good books of the Fyffe Munro drivers.

It started the same as any other Monday but today, for me, was going to be the day that all drivers dread. I arrived at the Wiveliscombe yard at five thirty in the morning to find 'Prickle' was waiting for me.

'I thought that you started at five to do the south coast egg run,' he said.

'No,' I replied. 'I have altered the route and now I can start at five thirty, do the three drops and still get to London in my hours.'

'Anyway things have altered; you are going to Cornwall with that Leyland Beaver Artic.' He pointed to a lorry parked outside the office.

'I've checked it over for you and it's already to go. Ring when you are empty.'

I put my overnight bag in the cab. Read the delivery notes and off I went. The weather was fine and it was great to drive a vehicle with a forty-foot trailer. The Beaver was a more modern cab than the LAD one. It had two seats and a very high engine cover that sloped down to the wind screen. It was like sitting in a box and it was a bit more comfortable than the LAD cab. It was also fitted with a heater and a demister.

I delivered the load and then went to Stonegate eggs at St Columb Major and swapped my empty trailer for loaded one. I decided that I would stop at a café the other side of Bodmin for something to eat.

I drove across Goss Moor to the A38 and set off North-East toward Bodmin. Near the old wireless station at Lanivet the road curves to the right, widens into three lanes and drops down hill to a roundabout.

One lane going down the hill and two coming the other way. One lane used as an overtaking lane. As I drove towards this curve I saw a Bedford Caravanette coming up the hill passing a 'Mother's Pride' Artic. I was almost at the bend, the caravanette had passed the Artic but made no effort to pull in front of it. To my horror the vehicle came straight on across the double white lines making no attempt slow down. I realised it was going to hit me head on. I turned left onto the grass verge and braked but it was too late.

The front offside of the Bedford hit the offside front of the tractor unit. The cab started to squash up and the windscreen shattered. The lorry started to jack knife and I gripped the steering wheel and turned it hard left at the same time throwing my weight against the door.

The next thing that I remember was sitting on the A38 not really knowing how I got there. I must have been thrown out of the cab. Did I go over the roof of the Caravanette or behind it? To this day I do not know.

I did an assessment of my self, my hands hurt and my head a little bit but every thing seemed to be working ok. Then, in front of me, on the road, I saw the cigarette that I was smoking in the cab just a few moments before. At least I assumed it was mine. I picked it up and saw a few inches in front of where the cigarette had been was my metal sandwich box and my wrist watch both of which had once been leaning against the windscreen of the lorry. I picked them both up and then, suddenly, I felt myself slowly rising above the road. Gently I went higher and higher. Is this what it is like to die? No flash-backs from my childhood, just a very confused brain. Just a few seconds ago I was sitting in a nice lorry thinking of lunch and now I am levitating above a Cornish road. I got about four foot above the road and stopped rising. I heard a voice in my ear. The driver of the Mother's Pride lorry had stopped and had come over. Seeing that I was moving around he had picked me up, carried me to the side of the road and set me down on the grass verge.

I remember seeing the squashed cab of the lorry leaning against the hedge, just like it had been reversed into it. A little further away was the Caravanette the front corner of it was under the front corner of the trailer. The front of the trailer on one side was ripped open and sticking out a couple of feet. The back axle of the lorry and part of the chassis was in a big heap under the trailer. The tractor unit was completely broken in half.

The next thing that I remember was being in a hospital minibus, apparently they had run out of ambulances in Cornwall. I asked the driver where we were going and he told me Treliske hospital at Truro.

'Could we not go to Bodmin?' I asked. 'It's a lot closer.'

'Sorry, no, all accidents go to Treliske,' he informed me.

'It wouldn't take long under blue lights,' I replied.

'No blue lights. As long as the patient is conscious and feeling ok. Do you feel ok?' he asked.

'Apart from a few small aches, I feel fine. I guess I will just sit back and enjoy the ride.'

On arrival I was taken to the accident department and handed over to a lovely nurse. Because of the wound on the back of my head I was assessed straight away. The nurse told me that I needed a few stitches to the wound which she did immediately. She then got two red cross nurses to attend to my hands. There was no skin on any of the knuckles on my fingers. I think that when I was thrown out of the lorry my judo training had kicked in. As I hit the ground I put out my hands and used my arms as shock absorbers to take the weight off my body.

Two nurses cleaned and dressed my wounds and asked if there was any thing else that she could do for me. I told them that I had not had anything to eat since the morning and I was getting hungry.

'What would you like?' they asked.

'Sausage, egg and chips would go down well,' I said hopefully.

They went off and some minutes later returned with my request and a cup of tea.

They sat with me while I ate and then showed me to a telephone. I phoned 'Prickle' who asked me how I was and what had happened. The accident had been on the television, some one had died, but they didn't give any details.

I told him that I had some grazes on both hands and a cut on the back of my head. The rest of my body was aching a bit but I could walk ok.

The nurses told me that I was to stay in the hospital that night because of the head injury. They showed me to a small ward with four beds. Two of the beds were occupied and I was told that both patients had just had nasal operations. I told the nurses that I really needed a cigarette and I was told that I could sit beside the window and blow the smoke out of the open window.

I had my cigarette and then decided to go to the toilet. Dressed in only my pyjama trousers I passed the Women's ward twice as it was between the ward I was on and the toilet. I hadn't been in bed for too long when the Matron arrived. She asked me how I felt. I told her that I was fine. She then told me that someone in the women's ward had complained that I was walking around the hospital semi naked. I told her that I only had pyjama trousers.

'If you go to the toilet again wear a T-shirt as well,' she told me and bade me good night.

The next morning after being examined by the doctor I was released from hospital. I made my way to the railway station and bought a ticket to Exeter. While I waited for the train I telephoned 'Prickle' and told him that I was out of hospital.

'Make your way to Lanivet, he said. 'There's a lorry going down there to pick up the crashed unit and he will bring you back to the yard.'

I told him that I had a train ticket for home and would ring him in a couple of days. Then I hung up the phone.

At Exeter I had to change trains for Barnstaple. I asked what time the train for Barnstaple left and I was told not for another hour. I decided to walk outside the station and see if I could get a lift using the log book I still had. Within five minutes a lorry had stopped and offered me a lift. The driver was going to Barnstaple and I asked if he could drop me off at Eggesford station. As I had a big bandage on my head and my hands were both bandaged he asked me what had happened. I told him that I worked for Tone Vale Transport and that I had been in an accident the day before. 'Not the one on the front page of the paper?' he asked.

'Yes,' I answered. (The accident was also in the first issue of a road safety magazine issued by Devon and Cornwall Constabulary. It high-lighted the dangers of driving when tired).

I was dropped off at Eggesford before the train had left Exeter. The plan was to go to the village of Chawleigh, about a mile from the station, to see my girl friend Christine and then get my brother Philip to come and pick me up and take me home

At the station was a man called Roger who, with his father, ran the garage at Chawleigh and also the local taxi firm. Roger was around my age and I knew him quite well.

'Are you going back to Chawleigh?' I asked.

'Yes,' he answered.

'Can I hire you to take me to Chawleigh?'

'I'll give you a lift but there won't be any charge as the person I brought to the station paid for both ways,' said Roger smiling. I got into the car and told him I would buy him a beer the next time I saw him in the Royal Oak.

Fed and Watered by Christine's mum, Betty, and having convinced Christine I was feeling a lot better than I looked I was collected by Philip and taken home.

After a couple of days rest I telephoned 'Prickle' and told him that I would like a few more days off as my hands and head needed to heal completely. He asked me if the accident had put me off driving lorries. If so he would let me have a lorry and I drive it wherever I want. I told him that I believed the accident was not my fault and therefore I was happy to come back to work as soon as I felt fit enough. I also said that when I came in to pick up my car we could fully go through the accident then. Before he hung up he told me that Martin, a driver who started the same day as me, had also had an accident. He had loaded eggs at Loddiswell in the South Hams and a few miles down the road he had collided head on with a council lorry. Martin was in hospital with injuries to both legs. It was not a good week for the company.

In time I attended the inquest about the accident. There were four lads from Scotland in the Caravanette and they had all been killed, just a few miles from their destination. They had driven from Scotland to Cornwall in ten hours and could not have had much rest. Remember that there was very little dual carriageway and motorway at that time.

Only one of them had a driving licence and it was concluded that he had fallen asleep at the wheel. There were two main witnesses, both lorry drivers. One worked for British Road Services and was on holiday from Surrey. He was behind me at the time of the accident and confirmed my speed was less than the maximum forty miles per hour and that I had braked hard before the collision. The other witness was the driver of the 'Mother's Pride' bakery lorry and he came from Plymouth. Both of these drivers stated that in their opinion there was nothing that I could have done to avoid a collision. It was comforting to know that there was no blame put on me for the accident but the sad loss of the young men still stays in the back of my mind.

One morning, in London, Graham said there are two Reivers out in the yard, take them to Thames Nitrogen, just down the road in Essex, and load fifteen ton of fertilizer on each one.

Before I left the yard I put ten good wooden pallets on one of the lorries and went off to the fertilizer plant. At the plant one is supposed to take the bags (thirty - weighing one hundredweight each) of fertilizer from their pallets and load it onto your lorry either on pallets or straight on to the flat bed.

I said to the forklift driver that I have ten good pallets here and you could swap them for the pallets that you have there and that would save a lot of time and effort for both of us. Then you can load those pallets with another fifteen ton for my next load. He thought that would be a good idea so that is what he did.

Loaded and sheeted I drove back to the Silvertown yard and did exactly the same again. Just after twelve o'clock I walked back into the office and told Graham I'd done as he asked. He looked at me and said, 'There are two of them.'

'I know they are both loaded.'

'They can't be, you can't load thirty ton handball that quick,' he argued. 'Let's have a look.' He walked out to the yard with me following. 'You little shit [or words to that effect]. You have put them on pallets!' I pointed to my head and then to my feet and replied 'Up here for thinking and down there for dancing.' Back in the office he gave ten pounds. I only got five pound for a six wheeler but I was happy enough.

At the north end of Silvertown Way, on the East side, just a couple of hundred yards from our depot was Silvertown Transport Motel where the food was acceptable.

Also from our yard it was just a short walk up George Street and then into Shirley Street to the 'Rose of Denmark' pub.

Performing in this pub were dancing topless 'Go Go' girls. They were mainly students and we got to know them well as we visited the pub quite often. Sometimes young male customers would enquire why these lovely girls sat with us and did not want anything to do with them. One of the drivers would say, 'That one over there is my niece and the blond one is her best friend.' I would say 'That other one is my cousin.' After that they used to lose interest and the girls always thought it was amusing having such gallant West Country minders. I can't remember any driver going out with one of them or walking one home. After all they just wanted to do their stint and then sit and have a quiet drink with friends.

There was another pub not far from the new yard. It was near the Tate and Lyle factory on North Woolwich Road. One night I visited this pub in the company of Maurice Williams and Geoff Roberts. Both drivers came from North Devon: Maurice from South Molton (same as me) and Geoff from Bideford. Maurice drove for Tone Vale Transport and Geoff for Taunton Meat Haulage and both were in their thirties.

As we got to the pub Maurice said, 'In this pub men are men and women are women and for half a crown they'll prove it.'

Geoff said, 'Keep yourself to yourself and don't go into the Lounge.'

Geoff went into the pub first, followed by Maurice, and me last. On the left there was a little raised area with a disc jockey and his turn table and when I looked at him he blew me a kiss. Opposite was a fire place with four foreign sailors drinking small glasses of something. When the glasses were empty they threw them into the fire.

We sat at a table and drank a couple of beers and then I went to the Gent's toilet. Of course, on the way back, contrary to Geoff's advice, I went through the lounge were 'Ladies of the Night' plied their trade. One of them looked up at me and said, 'If you want to hang on love, I'll be with you in 'alf a jiffy.' Needless to say I kept on walking.

When I got back to the bar Maurice said 'You've been in the lounge. You're all red in the face.'

Geoff agreed. 'That'll teach you not to do what you're told.'

When I went to the bar to buy a round I pointed to the sailors by the fire. I said to the landlord, 'Why do you allow them to do that?'

He said, 'At £3 a round they can do what they want with the glasses.'

I have to say drinking in the East End of London certainly improved my education in the university of life. I remember thinking when I tell my mates back in Devon they won't believe a word of it.

There used to be a big pub down Deptford way called the Montague Arms, where they used to have talent nights and the pub was a favourite of lorry drivers. Six or seven of our company drivers would go there - if they could, in a new Artic unit. There would be delays at red traffic lights as the driver were changed. Every one wanted to have a go at a new lorry. I never bothered as I was never going to get a new lorry. Remember Peters and Lee? Blind Lenny Peters playing the piano and lovely Diane Lee singing, *Welcome Home'*. I saw them first at the Montague Arms, long before they appeared on 'Opportunity Knocks' on the television.

Another trip would be to the cinema in the West End where the tractor unit would be parked on the pavement outside the cinema.

One late afternoon I was in the London depot with a driver known as Big Jack who lived in Bampton, Devon. Graham called Jack into the office. After a minute Graham came out shutting the door behind him as he did. He told me something had happened back in Bampton and there is a relative on the phone speaking to Jack about it.

Eventually Jack came out and told us that his son had been killed in a tractor accident a few miles from his home in Bampton.

'You can ride back with the Night Trunk,' Graham told Jack.

'That would get me back in the middle of the night and I wouldn't want to wake the wife,' replied Jack. 'I'm loaded for home so I'll leave early and can be in the yard, at Wiveliscombe, for eight o'clock'

'If you're sure,' said Graham.

Some time later Jack and I went to get some thing to eat. We came out of the café and understandably Jack didn't want to go for a drink. We started to walk the streets of London while Jack tried to make sense of it all.

'Children shouldn't die before their parents,' he kept saying. He was distraught with grief - something I would also go through a few years later. I can't remember where or how far we walked but I remember it was about one o'clock in the morning when we got back to the yard.

At 8 am Graham asked how Jack was the night before. I told him we'd walked a lot and, although I never heard him go, Jack had apparently left before six o'clock when the fruit shunter arrived.

Graham appreciated the fact that I had kept Jack company and I was given a morning job to do and I just messed about in the yard in the afternoon. Probably making tea.

Once, I did a trip to Penzance with Big Jack. We were both driving Reivers and got to Penzance too late to unload that day. We went for a pint and travelled from pub to pub and ended up at the Old Barn Club, on the campsite on the outskirts of town. This is a place that I had stayed a few years before. It was like a village hall with dancing and, more importantly, a bar. They used to have groups singing so it was very popular with locals and holiday-makers alike.

When it came time to go back to the lorries there was no sign of Jack so after a quick look around I went back to the lorry park and went to bed. The next morning I got out of bed and seeing no sign of my comrade I went to the nearby café for breakfast. Whilst I was partaking of my meal Jack rolled in looking slightly dishevelled and damp from the early morning dew. He told me he had left the club to get some fresh air and while walking along a path had tripped over something, possibly a dog. He'd woken up in the morning on one of the campsite lawns. With a wash and brush-up and a good breakfast inside us we were ready for whatever the new day brought.

In London, one morning, Graham told me to ride with Jack down towards Southampton and collect an Artic unit that had been repaired. We took one of the ERF LV tractor units coupled to a forty foot trailer, with Jack driving. We got to the garage in quick time with Jack coaxing the ERF up to 85 mph on the M3. After collecting the repaired Leyland tractor unit we made our way to the nearest café for refreshment. A driver walked up to us and asked if we were from Tone Vale Transport. We told him we were. He said he was also one of the company's drivers and the Leyland I had just collected was the lorry he normally drove. He asked if he could have it back by changing it for the one he was driving. Neither Jack nor I knew the man so we suggested he telephone Graham and ask the boss if he could swap. He was reluctant to do this so I took the lorry back to London and Jack went off somewhere to load his trailer. I never did see that driver again.

It wasn't always London or the West country. One trip was to Thetford in Norfolk, driving an Artic. On the return journey I was being followed by a very small sports car. I came to a long left hand bend in the road and I could see that there was another car approaching from the opposite direction. As it got closer I checked my mirrors as I always did when a vehicle came along and, as they pass, check that they have judged it correctly. This time, to my horror, the sports car had decided to overtake on a bend even though he could not see very far. There was no point in me braking as we would all end up in the same spot at the same time. I moved over to the left as far as I could and carried on at 40 mph and waited for the bang. I gripped the wheel and as the car passed in the opposite direction I looked in the mirror. Where had the sports car gone? Then I saw it, coming out from under the trailer. The landing legs are fitted about five feet from the front of the trailer and the first axle about twelve feet from the rear of the trailer. That did not leave a lot of room for a car between them. If I had altered my speed there would not have been much left of the sports car. I hope that the driver realised how close he or she had come to either being killed or at least seriously injured.

On a happier note I once took a load to King's Lynn, also in Norfolk. This time I had a Reiver loaded with two old tractors for the docks. The tractors were exported to so called 'third world' countries where they made work a bit easier for the poor farmers.

After unloading I telephoned Graham in London, as instructed, and was told to make my way to the London depot.

'I'm in Norfolk' I said.

'Yeah, I know' he replied. 'I'll see you tomorrow some time,' and put the phone down.

I jumped into the lorry and drove nine miles to RAF Marham, found the married quarters and parked the lorry. My eldest sister had a pen-friend who at the time lived at Marham with her husband Peter.

Her sofa was going to be a lot softer than the cold metal of the Reiver.

I found the house and went to the side door and knocked on it. A female voice from the bathroom window shouted 'Who is it.'

'Snuffy' I shouted back (Snuffy is the nickname I've had since birth).

'Let yourself in love,' came back the voice.

I went in and sat down in the front room and a couple of minutes later Margaret came in. She is about five feet ten inches tall and her shoulder length hair was wet and she was wearing a dressing gown.

'What are you doing here?' she asked

I told her that I was on my way to London and asked if I could kip on her sofa for the night.

'Of course,' she said. It was not the first time one of the family turned up like this. A few years earlier my eldest brother Jimmy had done the same thing.

Margaret told me that she would not be home that evening as she was going down to the R.A.F.A. club to play Bingo.

Not wanting to miss the opportunity to catch up with what she and husband Peter had been up to for the last few years I asked, 'Do they have a bar there?'

'Yes, they do,' replied Margaret.

'Then Bingo it is,' said I. 'Where can I have wash?'

'The bathroom is at the top of the stairs, help yourself. I'll just see to the dinner'

Up stairs and washed I went to get a clean pair of trousers from my overnight bag only to discover there were no trousers in there.

I went down stairs and told Margaret that I had no spare trousers and that during the day I had split my jeans. 'No problem,' she said. 'Take them off and I'll sew them up for you.'

Picture the scene, me on the sofa in T shirt and underpants and Margaret sitting opposite in her dressing gown and not a lot else, sewing my jeans. It was at this moment husband Peter walked into the room. The last time Peter had seen me I was a scrawny fourteen year old and he obviously didn't recognise me this time. The expression on his face said it all and when Margaret looked up and saw him in the doorway and that expression she just burst out laughing, which didn't help matters at all.

He stood there frozen in time looking at me and then at Margaret. Eventually she stopped laughing, wiped the tears from her eyes, looked at Peter and said, 'You remember Snuffy, June's young brother from South Molton.'

I said to him 'You last saw me in the summer of '64 when you had the old Humber Super Snipe.'

Luckily, he remembered the holiday and driving around North Devon.

Margaret told him about my ripped jeans and then he too saw the funny side.

We went to the club, Margaret, two of her friends and myself, and all of us played Bingo. One friend won a hundred pounds, the other twenty five pounds, I won fifty pounds and Margaret won nothing, although we did buy her a few drinks. The next morning we all had breakfast together and then I left for the long drive to London. Since that day I have always carried a sewing kit in my vehicle.

One day I was heading East along the M4 and decided it was time to eat so I pulled into Leigh Delamere services. In the early seventies microwave ovens were becoming popular and most Service Stations began to serve frozen meals which you put in the microwave and heated it up. Meal purchased and heated for the recommended time, I sat at a table and stuck my plastic fork into the centre of the meal. I must have been a bit enthusiastic as the fork disintegrated; not the first time this had happened. Although heated for the recommended time the food was piping hot on the outside and still frozen in the middle.

That day I was Mr Miserable and I took the food back to the counter. Rather loudly, I told the woman that this sort of food is the best way to catch food poisoning and she could either get a frying pan out and cook me something or give me my money back. Immediately three or four other drivers got up and also complained about the food. Then a few more did the same. She sorted some food out for us which calmed us all down.

A few weeks later I went into the same Services this time just to get a paper and have a cup of tea. The freezers and the microwaves had gone and new cooking equipment had been installed. I do not know if this was repeated at other Services as I did not use them very much.

Remember motorways were built for the fast movement of goods. Some had separate areas for lorry drivers, who also had priority when being served. Lorry Parking was free. Good old days.

Graham's café near Bridgwater used the same system for main meals. I always had a fry up or a salad. One day I was in the café and a large driver from Bideford told the owner that he wouldn't give the food he he'd been served to his dog. He got a salad for free.

Unfortunately many places used to have these machines in the cafés and canteens. The chipboard factory in South Molton had them for a few years but eventually went back to cooking meals in the traditional manner.

Talking of food, Tone Vale Transport used to collect new cardboard boxes from Ashton Containers in Bristol. These boxes were stored at and distributed from the Norton Fitzwarren Stores, near Taunton. There always seemed to be a Tone Vale lorry loading in Ashton Containers and usually two or three parked on the road outside the factory. The reason for this was that the food was very cheap in the works canteen and they would serve anybody. By the time we had driven from Norton Fitzwarren to Bristol we were ready for some food.

Fertiliser was collected from ICI at Avonmouth and was also stored and distributed from the Norton Fitzwarren stores and of course great use was again made of their works canteen.

I used to load bales of waste paper at a company in Great Dover Street, Newington, London. The company there used to get a lot of what is known as 'girlie' magazines, of which there was always an ample supply, for drivers. These bales were taken to the waste paper mill at Watchet. At Watchet paper mill were always a massive stack of old books, I used to help myself and when read I used to bring them back and swap them for different ones. They never seemed to have road maps though.

I climbed into the cab of the Badger one morning and looked at the delivery notes. Three deliveries, fertiliser to Kingswear in Dartmouth and Constantine Bay in Cornwall; and some wooden cases of semi-precious stones for Helston. All of this was in a single axle box trailer.

Bear in mind there were no satnavs in those days and no mobile phones. First stop Dartmouth, South Devon. It took a couple of hours to drive to this very popular tourist town and when I arrived I stopped and asked a policemen were Kingswear was.

He pointed across the river Dart and said, 'It's over there. There is a ferry across the river but it won't carry anything this size.' Looking at the amount of traffic in the town there was going to be a major problem turning around to go back the way I had just come. Then I had a brain wave.

'How far does that slip way go out into the river,' I asked the policeman. He had a think and replied, 'The tide is still coming in so it should be a couple of hundred yards'

'If I back down there to turn around could you stop the traffic for me for a minute.'

'Of course,' he replied.

You would think he was asked to do this all the time

The trailer was reversed into the river far enough for the trailer wheels, that were at the rear of the trailer, to get a wash. With the vehicle turned around and a wave to the bemused tourists and the nice policeman I set off to find a telephone box. I told Prickle that the first delivery was awkward to get to with an Artic and he told me to take it to Bell's Transport at Plymouth and he would get them to deliver it.

The first delivery was left at Bells and I set off for Constantine which is near Helston and everything was looking great.

At the Saltash toll bridge I was asked to pay the toll for an Artic, prices were on a board next to a picture of a four axle vehicle. I pointed out that my vehicle had three axles and I should pay less, in fact the same amount for a six-wheeler. After some discussion, during which time the queue behind me was growing quite rapidly he gave in and charged me the lower price. This meant I would make a small profit from Tone Vale every time I drove the Badger across the bridge in the future.

I got to Constantine in the afternoon, went into the Post Office and asked where the bay was.

'What bay?' asked the lady.

'Constantine.'

'Constantine Bay is the other side of Cornwall, near Padstow. About forty miles from here.'

I thanked her and started off for Padstow. On the way I decided to buy a new road atlas at the earliest opportunity. This trip was starting to annoy me even if it was my own fault. I left Constantine Bay around six pm. There was now a bungalow with a large amount of fertiliser on his drive. Tone Vale has just started doing house calls!

Time for a beer.

It was just a few miles out of my way to Stonegate Eggs at St Columb Major. They have a big yard on the outskirts of the town which is ideal for an overnight stop. After eating, the Red Lion was the pub of choice. The Air Force lads from RAF St Mawgan used to drink there and I was guaranteed to get a couple of games of pool. Also one of my brothers had just been posted from St Mawgan to Berlin and was well known to them which meant that they were not adverse to buying me the odd beer or two. As you can see when you are on the road you have to live off your wits a bit.

The next morning it was on to Helston. What *were* those semi-precious stones? Diamonds, pearls rubies? No, they were pretty coloured pebbles from South America and were used to make costume jewellery.

With the trailer empty I went back to Stonegate Eggs at St Columb and swapped the empty trailer for a loaded one to take back to Wiveliscombe.

One Friday afternoon I found myself and a few other Tone Vale lorries and drivers at Sharpness docks a few miles north of Bristol. We were there to load fertiliser from a ship. The four-wheeler Ford was loaded but the dockers were about to go home, so no more lorries were to be loaded that day. We were told that if we lined up the lorries by the ship they would be loaded in the morning, even if the drivers were not there. That sounded like a good idea but there was a problem, a Commer Artic parked in the way. The driver could not be found but as the keys were in the vehicle it was moved and parked safely in a narrow gap between two sheds. Who knows, it may still be there!

We sheeted and roped the four wheeler and all piled into it for the trip back to Wiveliscombe. There were five of us in a three seater cab. I sat between the seats and did the gear changing. There was a large amount of holiday traffic on the roads and the more knowledgeable drivers were getting fed up by the time we got to Bridgwater. They directed our driver around the back streets of Bridgwater and across 'the hills' to bypass Taunton and the traffic queues.

Friday night was spent at home but as the vehicles were away from the depot we all got paid our 'night out' allowance.

The next morning I was at Wiveliscombe at six am, no other drivers were in sight so I walked the few yards to the main road with the idea of hitch hiking seventy five miles to Sharpness. There was no real rush to get to Sharpness as the other drivers would sheet and rope the lorries.

If you held up a log book in those days a lot of different people would stop and give you a lift. I was only at the road junction for a couple of minutes when a car stopped. I actually knew the driver who came from Barnstaple and was on his way to Cardiff, Wales. He stopped on the motorway hard shoulder, beside a bridge that carried the A38 past Sharpness and, thanking him, I got out. I was stood on the A38 for just a few minutes when an old van stopped and gave me a lift straight to the docks. Since Wiveliscombe I had walked thirty feet.

Eventually all the lorries were sheeted and roped and we left in convoy for Wiveliscombe. Going through Bristol was an experience as there were policemen at all the major road junctions. We went into Bristol in a convoy of seven lorries. We were all together and we were waved through at every junction, the fastest time I had ever driven through Bristol. Once we were on the A38 the situation completely altered. The amount of holiday traffic was horrendous. Broken down vehicles were everywhere, and one side of the dual carriageway into Bridgwater was full of overheated cars.

Somewhere along the way, Martin and myself picked up a couple of hitch hikers. Some miles south of Bristol we came to a stand still and I turned off the engine to keep it cool. When the traffic started to move I went to start the engine but the starter would not work. I managed to let the lorry roll down hill and bump-started the engine. At the next three lane section I pulled alongside Martin and my passenger shouted to him that the starter was not working and we would go in front in case the engine stalled. We were both driving Albion Reivers and these lorries were certainly getting past their sell by date. Eventually we all made it back to Wiveliscombe. The journey from Sharpness, had taken six and a half hours.

The stretch of A38 between Bristol and Taunton was not the best road for me. I often broke down while travelling along this road in a Reiver. The course of action was to get the lorry to the nearest café, of which there were many, and phone for recovery.

Next door to Tone Vale Transport was the premises of Ross Fish and they had a Leyland wrecker with an LAD cab. This vehicle would arrive and using a rigid steel bar pull the stricken vehicle back to the workshop at Wiveliscombe. The driver of the wrecker used to drive very enthusiastically when pulling a broken down vehicle and it was some thing that I did not look forward to. Some of the broken-down lorries were not repaired but kept for spares.

Travelling along the same stretch of the A38 one day I came to a three lane stretch of road. The middle lane was commonly known as the suicide lane. As I was moving faster than the lorry in front I pulled out into the middle lane to overtake, at the time there was nothing coming the other way although there was a slight bend in the road. As I got level with the lorry on my left, two lorries came the other way also side by side. At a combined speed of at least eighty mph the gap between us closed very quickly and even with emergency braking the outcome was inevitable. At the last moment I tipped my head forward so that if the windscreen broke no glass would go into my eyes.

The was a loud bang, no glass, so I lifted my head and looked around. All four lorries had come to a halt close together. I pulled in front of the lorry on my left and the other lorry next to me did the same to the lorry on his left. Nobody was hurt and the only damage seemed to be that there were only two wing mirrors left between all four vehicles. The two middle lorries had both mirrors ripped off and the two outside lorries lost one each. It was agreed that there was nothing that could have been done to avoid an accident. We swapped details, recovered our respective mirrors and carried on our way.

Prickle asked me one Friday if I would do a Sunday run. A Reiver loaded with eggs for Stonegate Eggs, Wye in Kent. This meant that I would not be able to work Saturday and I got double time, lovely. The trip would take around seven hours and I could start when I wanted as the load was booked in for delivery Monday morning at 8am.

I arrived in Wye early evening and was told that the only place to park was the car park behind the council houses. After a pie and a couple of pints down the pub and I went to bed. The next morning about seven o'clock there was a knock on the door. There was a gentleman there and he said a cup of tea was waiting for me and he pointed to a house with an open door. I got myself organised and went to the house.

'Come in,' said the man. He told me he used to be a lorry driver and now he was retired. He gave tea to the lorry drivers parked there. It was his way of keeping up with what is happening on the roads. This was the first time a stranger had offered me tea.

The following Sunday it was a Reiver loaded with eggs for West Molesey, South West London. The eggs were for a Chinese company and I had to be at a certain lay-by in East Molesey. The boxes of eggs were trans-shipped to a large van which took them to a storage place that was not accessible with a lorry. It took about ninety minutes to unload and then I parked in Kingston-upon-Thames for the night.

The next day I loaded medical Instruments from Everitt Medicals on Mitcham Common. These instruments were delivered to Bristol. I used to love doing this trip it was a nice easy run even if there were a lot of boxes to move and it didn't take too long if there were three or four people doing it.

One time a shunter loaded the lorry and I picked it up at the Silvertown depot. For some reason there were around forty boxes of tomatoes on the back for return to one of the numerous small wharfs that used to be along the south side of the Thames.

I got to the wharf just as the men were about to go home and was told that tomatoes would be unloaded in the morning. I had to think fast or miss my night in Bristol.

'Now we have a problem,' I said to the boss. 'You know there was an earthquake yesterday? [somewhere abroad]. It was in all the papers.'

'Yes,' he said.

I pointed to the boxes of medical stuff in the back of the lorry and said, 'All that stuff is to be flown out from Bristol airport tonight for that earthquake.'

He pointed to one docker and said, 'Get a pallet now! The rest of you start unloading these tomatoes.'

It was all done in five minutes and I thanked them for their troubles. Bristol here we come.

When loaded for home 'Colesy' who used to drive one of the Mercedes (Maurice Williams drove the other) was always out of bed at 4.45am. He would wake all the other drivers and then make tea for them all. Five o'clock we would all leave Silvertown and head west. The rules were that the last driver to Heston services had to buy the breakfasts for the others, at least four. The trick was not to stop at red traffic lights.

It was a Saturday morning in Silvertown and I had gone to bed in my lorry cab at ten the night before. As usual 'Colesy' was up first in the morning and off we all went at five. All the others racing to Heston for breakfast after which they would take the M4, drive through Bristol and then stop for tea somewhere on the A38.

I was driving an old Reiver and decided to take my usual route along the M4 to junction fourteen and then to Hungerford for breakfast. After eating I would follow the A4 to Beckhampton and then the A361 to Wiveliscombe. The café at Hungerford was cheaper and better than Heston services and was a regular stop for me.

All the other lorries soon left me behind, so I went along quite happily on my own. I was thinking that I should be back at home by midday. Then as I rounded a corner, somewhere in West London, I spotted Gordon Hartnoll ahead of me. He was driving his new Leyland Buffalo Artic and he was following behind couple of eight wheeler lorries. They were all slowing down to stop for red traffic lights. I kept going and as I got close to them the lights turned green. Using the outside lane, I passed all of them and kept accelerating. I knew that if I kept to thirty three mph the next set of traffic lights would be green, and they were. The little convoy behind was now just a dot in my rear view mirrors. The Hungerford Café would have to wait until next time.

When I got to Heston there was still no sign of Gordon behind me so I joined the others in the services for my free breakfast. When Gordon arrived a few minutes later the others pointed out to him that he had been passed, in his new lorry, by one of the oldest lorries in the fleet, driven by the youngest driver. He took it like the good sport he was and paid without any fuss. We all left the services together but it was not long before they left me behind again. The Reiver would do fifty three mph and all the ones in front would do at least sixty. I turned off at junction 14 and was still the first one back in the yard. No point in hanging about on a Saturday morning.

Arriving back at the yard one afternoon Prickle told me that the following morning I was to be in the yard at eight. The stores foreman would take me to Taunton railway station and I was to take a train to London. Then I was to catch the tube to 'East Ham' and catch a bus to Silvertown and then bring a lorry back to Somerset.

All went well, commuting to London to bring back a lorry was great. Unfortunately, I got off the tube at 'West Ham' only to discover that there was no bus to Silvertown so I had to walk a mile to the depot.

Prickle was obviously a better transport manager than I'd thought.

Taking my usual, M4, A4 and then the A361, it was a pleasant Saturday morning and I was heading home. I was driving through a town, getting half way around a right hand curve in the road when I saw a policeman standing on the white line in the middle of the road. I slowed down and stopped. He looked at me and waved me on. I was driving an ERF at the time and pulling a thirty-three foot, double axle box van and I hesitated as the road wasn't that wide. The policeman was now waving me on more vigorously so I started to move forward keeping as close as I could to the kerb. The policeman was now looking in the opposite direction. The ERF edged passed him with the wing mirror just missing his helmet, I looked in the mirror and the wheels of the trailer were now on the other side of the white line and the side of the trailer was getting very close to the back of the policeman who was still looking in the opposite direction. Then the trailer came into contact with the policeman and as I crept slowly forward, the policeman was slowly guided across the road. He moved I couple of steps away from the trailer and as he turned to see what was pushing him I accelerated away. I put my hand out of the window with my thumb upright and took off as fast as possible.

To buy diesel the firm supplied the driver with an Agency card which is basically like a plastic credit but one can only buy diesel or oil. This particular Friday I was driving home along the A4 and needed fuel. There was no diesel tank at our London depot so I drove as far as I could before getting some more. With the fuel gauge registering nearly empty I pulled into a garage, stopped the lorry and walked to the kiosk so that the garage could check that my agency card was valid. Garages have a 'naughty book' containing a list of companies that have not paid their previous bills. Tone Vale Transport was on that list. The garage man said that if I wanted diesel then I would have to pay for it.

I bought some diesel, only it being Friday, I didn't have that much money; but at least it would get me to the next garage. I got to Shepton Mallet, again with very little diesel left and the only garage I could see was the same company as the one that I had just left. I pulled in and showed the man my agency card, he looked in the 'naughty book' and went past Tone Vale Transport.

'That's ok mate,' he said. 'How much do you want?'

I was really annoyed that I had already had to buy fuel so I told the man to, 'Fill her up.'

The ERF I was driving was equipped for Continental work and had an extra fuel tank fitted, it took ninety four gallons. Even better I also got quadruple green shield stamps, the roll of stamps was over six feet long. Green shield stamps were collected in a book and could be redeemed for various 'gifts'.

I arrived back at Wiveliscombe after the office had closed. I got the ERF ready for its next trip and put the paper work that I had acquired over the week in my pigeon hole. Home in time for a game of darts down at the pub.

As I had worked the Sunday before I didn't have to work the Saturday morning. I rang the office and asked Prickle what I had to do on the Sunday.

'Sunday?' he asked, 'Sunday! What about Friday? What happened? Ninety four gallons of diesel just to get back to Wivey. Twenty would have done!' (ERF tractor units did between five & six miles to the gallon of diesel).

'As you can see from my paperwork, I had trouble getting fuel, even having to use my own money to buy some. I thought if it was that hard to get it perhaps I should get as much as I can while I had the opportunity. Perhaps the company should consider paying its debts.'

That was the end of that conversation.

Arriving in Weston-Super-Mare one cold winter's evening, I found that the one way street in front of me was closed because of road works. My delivery point was the other side of the road works. I was freezing cold as I had just driven from London, in a Reiver, with no heater and a cold draught coming through the door. Whether the door would not close properly or if part of the door rubber was missing I cannot remember. I decided to go to the other end of the road and reverse up to the Chinese food store that was where I had to deliver, which is what

I did. After unloading, my back had warmed up a bit and I started to experience back pain. This pain I would experience for a few years.

One day someone told me that Tone Vale was getting a new AEC Marshall six-wheeled lorry. This was great news after months of driving the Reivers. Then he said that Prickle's son, who had just come out of the army, would be the driver of this new lorry.

I had been driving Reivers for more than twelve months and I wasn't too happy at the thought of some new boy having the new lorry. I went to see Prickle and asked if I could have an Artic unit of my own.

'Which one were you thinking of?' he asked.

'If possible, I would like one of the three ERFs please,' I said. The reason for wanting an ERF was that the cab was higher than the Leyland cab. Therefore the engine cover was a lot lower, in fact lower than the top of the seat. The seat was longer than my thighs so I had another seat back that I used as a cushion. Also the maximum speed of an ERF was faster than the Leyland. The Leyland had a strange hand brake which did not always work that well. I did have one runaway in the yard once, thankfully I managed to stop it just as it touched a new Leyland Buffalo

A few days later I was given an ERF LV. No more Reivers and I never saw a new AEC Marshall either. To this day I have no idea if there ever was one or whether someone was 'winding me up'.

Many of the companies I delivered to with the six-wheeler used to thank drivers with gifts. Wrigleys at Plymouth gave drivers a box of chewing gum; at Whiteway's Cider when a driver left the yard he or she was offered a bottle of Cydrax or Peardrax. At Stonegate Eggs, Bovey Tracey I used to get three dozen eggs.

'I gotta job for you,' said Graham one nice sunny morning in London, 'A load of eggs for Druid Street, near Tower Bridge.'

A nice short run, I arrived at Druid Street around twelve thirty. It was a street of old warehouses, I found the right one and knocked on the door.

'What you got?' asked the man who answered my knock.

'A load of eggs.'

'Right, lock the motor and give us the keys.'

'I can't lock it, the locks are buggered.'

'Just give us the keys then.' Which I did.

He went back through the door and then a few seconds later he reappeared, 'Have you had your lunch yet?' he asked.

I replied 'No.'

'Come with me.'

We walked to the end of a street and he took me into a café.

That is one thing that I used to love about London. There always seemed to be a café or a pub on every corner.

After lunch, which he paid for, we walked back up the road a little way and then he took me into a pub. He introduced me to his boss who brought us both a drink. We talked for a while and then the storeman said, 'I will just go and see how they are getting on with your lorry.'

A few minutes later he returned and gave me back my keys and a 50 pence coin.

'There you are driver: your keys and some money for a cup of tea on the way back. Have a safe journey.'

I thanked him and his boss for their hospitality and the boss replied, No problem driver, you're just like family.' In the pub I had told them that my mother was born in Bermondsey, not very far from Druid Street.

That has to be one of the best loads that I ever delivered as, when I got back to Silvertown, there was five pound note from Graham for delivering the load.

I was driving the ERF unit, no trailer attached, through Norton Fitzwarren one rainy day. As I went around one of the many corners in the village a bus pulled out in front of me. I stood on the brakes and the tractor unit did a one hundred and eighty degree turn. I just selected second gear and drove back the way I had just come. All the weight is on the front axle when there no trailer connected and even at small speed it can go into a spin. No harm done so carry on regardless.

One memorable trip in the ERF was to Falmouth Docks in Cornwall. It was a Friday delivery and I was told to start at four in the morning as the delivery time was 10 o'clock. The box trailer was loaded with ship's stores and shouldn't be too heavy. I arrived at the docks, on time, and asked where the ship was berthed.

'What's the name of the ship?' asked the gate man?

I told him the name on the delivery ticket.

He pointed to an empty area across from the office and said, 'Park your lorry over there.'

'Why is that?'

He pointed out to the bay and said, 'See that ship out there, that is the one you want.'

'When does it dock?'

'It doesn't. There are new owners taking over at six o'clock. After that a tender will take your load out to the ship.'

'You mean I have to stay here until six this evening?' I asked.

'No, you will probably be here a lot longer. Enjoy your day off in Falmouth,' he said smiling.

I phoned Prickle and told him that I was probably ten hours too early and I would not be empty until at least 10pm.

'Just wait there and when you are unloaded pick up a loaded trailer at Stonegate Eggs, St Columb Major and bring it back to the yard.'

I told him that it would be the early hours of Saturday morning.

He said, 'That's ok. Unless there's a problem carry on and I will see you Monday.'

They started to unload me at six thirty and, with two tenders (little boats) being used I was on my way by eight.

All went well and I got back to the yard at three thirty on the Saturday morning.

On Monday morning the hours I had worked Friday were discussed. Because I had been told to start at four in the morning and I had to stay with the vehicle all day in case things changed. I was paid for twenty two hours work. With time and a half and double time, the total hours paid were thirty three and a half hours. Not bad for a day's work.

The first time that I went to Stonegate eggs at St Columb it was in the dark and I had come from the West of Cornwall. When I left, in a different direction, I hadn't gone far when I found myself on a brand new road with no other traffic about. Time to put my foot down. After a few miles I came upon a pile of chippings in the middle of the road and then I realised why the road was looked so new. They were still building it.

After some inspection I found that I could get past the chippings and there was access to a small road a couple of hundred yards across some hard core. I drove along this road until I came to a sign post and found my way back to the A30 on my way home.

I was sent to ICI in Avonmouth to load twenty-one tons of fertilizer for the store at Norton Fitzwarren. Bags weighing 1 hundredweight were taken off a conveyor belt, by hand, and stacked on the trailer. Usually four people did this, including the driver. Once the lorry was loaded I set off to the store at Norton Fitzwarren, going down the notorious Redhill, near Bristol, and the journey was hair-raising, as the lorry suffered from brake failure. I was in second gear with the engine screaming. I thought of jumping out of the lorry, then I thought with my luck I would probably get run over by the trailer. Eventually the road levelled out; I was shaking but back in control.

The lorry was 32 ton *gross* weight and I calculated that the lorry had been overloaded by half a ton. I was sent back to ICI for a second load and I ensured that this was half a ton less - the legal weight. There was the obvious discussion at the store about the missing half a ton. I told them that I would not risk mine or anybody else's life by overloading especially as the brakes would not stop the lorry. I was given a different job to do.

A few days later I delivered a load from London to an animal feed store in Chard and again had problems with the braking of the vehicle. After I had unloaded I rang Prickle and told him the brakes on the trailer were rubbish.

'There is nothing wrong with that trailer,' he said. 'I had it on night trunk last night.'

'It was with me last night in Silvertown so how could you have it?'

'What's the number?'

'Twenty-three,' I told him.

'I've been looking for that one for a couple of months to give it a service. Bring it back to the yard. There is also a ton and a half of sacks to bring back.

I was really annoyed that he would say that. Because of bad record keeping peoples lives were being put in danger.

'I'm not putting anything on that trailer until the brakes are fixed,' I said and put the phone down. I returned to Wiveliscombe with an empty trailer.

The stretch of road from Barnstaple to Taunton was a challenging route. It had narrow bridges, steep hills and hairpin bends. It had the nick name of the 'Ho Chi Minh trail', named after the famous supply route the Viet Cong used in the Vietnam-America war. In the winter there could be three foot of snow on the hills.

One wintry morning I left South Molton in my car at 6 am and drove carefully along the snow-covered road to Wiveliscombe. The last mile included a steep hill which drops down into the town. Near the top of the hill is a right-hand hairpin bend before the road levels a bit and goes into a left-hand bend. After about two hundred feet the road drops steeply down into the town.

I managed to negotiate the first hairpin bend and the next bend and as I got to the steep bit I stopped the car. The road was covered in snow and a 'Marks and Spencers' Artic was trying to get up the hill. He would get so far but where the road steepened his wheels started spinning and then he would back down and try again. After about four attempts he gave up and flashed his lights for me to proceed. I stopped beside him and gave a report about the road conditions to South Molton but advised him not to drive up the hill until the snow melted a bit.

By the time I got to the yard, it was nearly seven o'clock. Surprisingly Prickle was there. He told me because of the bad weather things had changed. For me there was a forty-foot trailer in the yard loaded with two shipping containers full of timber for delivery to Shapland and Petter in Barnstaple. I told the boss it was time for coffee as the hill out of town is impassable so it was not worth trying to negotiate it for at least an hour.

Coffee drank I coupled up the trailer and checked every thing was ready to go. I got into my mini car and drove to the bottom of the hill to see if the 'M&S' lorry was gone. It was, so I went back to the yard and got into the lorry and set off for Barnstaple.

I managed to drive up the steep part of the hill but where the road started to level off I had to stop. There was a queue of lorries stuck on the hill. At least I was on a fairly flat bit, but it was covered in snow. As I stood there talking to the driver of an Electricity Board lorry in front of me I realised that my lorry was slowly sliding back down the road. Luckily I was able to borrow a shovel from the Electricity Board driver and cleared the snow from behind the axles of my lorry and trailer and that stopped it sliding.

Eventually I did get to Barnstaple but it took a long time as the lorry was fully loaded and had to be driven with care on the snow.

At Barnstaple I was told to drop the trailer as the front container was accessed from the front. I did as requested and was told it would take two hours to unload. I had a sister living in Barnstaple so I went and had tea with her.

I returned to the yard with the empty trailer. Prickle said there was nothing else to be done so I went home. A nice easy day. Normally one would have gone to Watchet and shunt trailers but that day the Brendon hills would have been impassible to an Artic lorry because of the snow.

When my first daughter was born I asked if I could have some time off. Prickle told me there were two new contracts starting and things were really busy. He said that I could do shunting for a week if that would suit me. I agreed with that as I would be home every night.

I had to start at six in the morning and take a trailer loaded with concrete beams to the new hospital in Paignton. There was usually an hour wait for the crane to start unloading me and then possibly another hour before the trailer was empty. Then it was just a few miles to the concrete works at Chudleigh Knighton where I loaded large concrete pipes. The pipes were about four feet high and chained to the lorry and then it was back to Wiveliscombe. I did this job for a week. Another driver complained to Prickle that the local work should be shared out. He told them he was the transport manager and they would do what they were told.

As you have seen some days things do not exactly go the way you think it should and this is a reason why a driver should always carry money with them, nobody had credit cards in those days.

At the end of the shift one evening I checked the delivery for the next day. A load of roofing sheets for Her Majesty's Prison, Princetown, Dartmoor. I connected up the trailer checked the ropes and the lorry was ready to go, in the morning.

The next day it was a six o'clock start and I decided to go to Plymouth, Yelverton and then to Princetown. This was not the straightest route and the A38 was in the process of being changed to a dual carriageway but I thought it would be the quickest route.

Despite the delaying tactics of the 'McAlpines Fusiliers' who were blowing up rock on the A38, I still got to the prison around ten o'clock in the morning. I rang the bell on the large double wooden gates. A little hatch opened and the warden inside asked me what I wanted. I told him that I have twenty tons of roofing for him.

'Just a minute,' he said.

In a little while he returned, opened a side door and invited me into a little office. He told me there were no builders on site to unload the roofing.

'You got loads of prisoners here, get them to unload it,' I suggested.

'We can't do that; we'd have every do-gooder in England complaining and whining if we had inmates unloading lorries in the rain. By the way, How long is your lorry?

'About fifty-feet in overall length.'

'That creates a problem. As you can see there are two pairs of gates. We like to let a vehicle through the first gates while the inner gates are closed. We then shut the outer gates and open the inner gates to let the vehicle proceed into the prison complex. Your lorry is too long to fit between the two pairs of gates. You will not be able to unload today as there are two things we have to sort out. Firstly, we have to make sure that the builders are on site to unload you. Secondly, we have to get more warders here to be able to open both pairs of gates at the same time. Go back into Princetown and park up and we will come and let you know when you can be unloaded.'

I telephoned Tone Vale and informed them of the situation.

I parked up in the town went for a walk and then waited for instructions from the prison. Eventually a warden arrived and told me to be at the prison at 10 am the following morning.

Meanwhile I was free to use the Prison Officers Club in the town. I went there and had a wash but I only stayed for one drink. There were only older wardens there and the atmosphere was terrible.

I went down to the pub and had a meal, after which I got talking to a couple of younger wardens. When I asked them why they didn't use the Club they answered, 'Have you been in there?'

'Yes I have,' I replied.

'It's always like that and the older wardens are always watching you. It is worse than being at the prison.'

I think I know what they meant.

The next morning I arrived at the prison at the allotted hour. I was informed that officers would block both sides of the road and as soon as the gates opened I was to drive into the prison. There would be a line of officer in front of me and I must not drive through that line. The outside gates will close and then I must reverse up to them.

This all went without mishap. Then an officer got into the passenger side of my lorry and after locking the cab doors I was directed to the unloading point. Some officers followed us. When we got to the unloading point I was told to stay in the cab with my own officer while the trailer was unloaded. The other officers formed a semi circle around the lorry. The officer in the cab told me that a few weeks ago some prisoners had stolen a petrol tanker and tried to drive it through the back gate. They succeeded in getting it stuck in the gateway which was slightly narrower than the tanker. This time they were making sure that a similar incident did not occur.

After unloading I drove back to the gates. I was told that the outside gates would be opened and a line of officers would stop any traffic on the road outside. When the inside pair of gates opened I was to drive straight out of the prison, turn left and park a few yards down the road. This I did and when I stopped the officer in the cab told me that he had never heard of both gates being opened at the same time. Extra officers had been brought in for more security and now that the job was done it was a great relief to all.

Like I say you never know what is going to happen next when you leave the yard with a lorry. Breakdowns, accidents, diversions, wrong directions, unloading/loading problems, the list is endless. The way to overcome it all is to have a kip, get a cup of tea or when all else fails hitch hike home.

One Monday morning I took a load of timber to Swansea and again on the hills of South Wales there was difficulty with the brakes. After I unloaded I phoned the office and told Prickle that the brakes were rubbish and he came back with the usual crap. Telling me he was driving the lorry the Saturday before and there is nothing wrong with it. He told me to go to the steel works at Gorseinon and load plate-steel for Heinz in London.

'I'm not loading this vehicle until the brakes are done,' I told him.
'There's nothing wrong with it,' he said.
'I am not arguing with you. I quit,' I answered.
'You cannot quit, it is after twelve o'clock.'
'If I had a decent lorry I would have arrived here before twelve.'
'I'll ring you back in a minute' he said and put the phone down.'
He rang back and told me to go to Silver Roadways depot at Swansea and they would check the brakes.

I was driving an ERF but not the one that I usually drove. It was found that the front brakes of the tractor unit were completely worn out and new brake shoes were fitted. Again some irresponsible driver had not bothered to report it. This was just the start of a bad week.

I loaded steel plate for Heinz foods at Park Royal, London. I was in a queue in Heinz yard in London waiting to be unloaded when the gate man came around and told us all lorries have to go outside the gate as the shift was changing. After the new shift started we were allowed back in. So much for drivers hours; how do you explain to the ministry man that you were told to leave a factory?

A Friday my last day, I was returning from Exeter with an Artic and decided to take the road that goes from the A38 through Bradford-on-Tone, to the A361. As I reached a narrow railway bridge there was already a lorry crossing it. I checked my rear view mirrors and seeing nothing there I reversed a few feet and let the other lorry continue on his way. I then crossed the railway bridge and a few minutes later I notice a Ford Popular car trying to pass me. His driving was a bit erratic and in the end I slowed down to let him pass before he killed us both. He pulled in front of me and stopped. A man got out of the car and walked back to me.

'You just backed into a car,' he told me. 'At the bridge.'

'I didn't see any car.'

'There was a mini-van behind you and you backed into it.'

'It must have been very close to the trailer.'

Then a woman arrived driving a blue mini-van. She jumped out and started shouting at me, claiming that I had backed into her.

I told her she must have been very close to the back of the trailer. I had reversed very slowly so I asked her why she hadn't put her vehicle in reverse and just backed-up a little, as there was no one behind her.

I checked the mini for front end damage and all the I could see was a small dent where the bonnet badge should have been. I gave her my name and the address of Tone Vale Transport and told her to get in touch with them.

A few weeks after the incident I received a letter from an insurance company claiming that I had reversed into a vehicle whilst driving a long-load lorry. I replied that I had never driven a long-load vehicle and that was the last I ever heard of it.

So ended two years with Tone Vale Transport. The last two years had been a real eye-opener and certainly an education, but I had gained valuable experience.

5

The Ulster Chipboard Company

The Ulster Chipboard company had just built a new factory on the outskirts of South Molton. They also had a factory in Coleraine, Northern Ireland.

Geoff Barker was the only other HGV driver employed at South Molton. There was a Commer Artic unit and a forty foot box trailer which was fourteen foot three inches high. The trailer was fitted with a large electric fan on one side. Pipes, carried on the trailer, were connected to the fan which sucked up wood shavings like a massive vacuum cleaner. There were double doors at the back of the trailer and a single door at the front.

After I had been there a couple of months a brand new trailer was delivered to the factory but this one was lower at thirteen feet six inches.

The trailers were loaded with wood chips at saw mills and any other establishment that planed timber. We travelled all over Devon and West Somerset but were always home every night.

At first Geoff and I took turns driving the Commer with both of us going out to load it. Then it was relegated to shunting as it was found to be worn out.

One job was in Bideford, loading shavings at a company called Bardev Pallets. A low railway bridge near Bardev meant that the trailer had to be reversed down two streets and then around a ninety degree bend. The bend was so tight it used to take about twelve shunts to get around the corner.

After we stopped using the Commer, Smythe's Transport pulled the trailer. Their MAN Artic only needed three shunts to get around the corner because the MAN had power steering.

After 12 months the bridge was raised and we could drive straight to Bardev pallets.

Torridge Transport units were also used to pull the trailers, although one of their drivers failed to see a forecourt canopy sticking out, in Mary Tavy on Dartmoor. Fortunately there was not any serious damage caused to the canopy or the trailer.

It was quite nice being driven around by other drivers, all I had to do was load the trailer when we got to our destination.

In the early days machinery was still being fitted in the factory and German engineers had to be collected and returned from Heathrow airport and various train stations. This job always seem to be given to me and the Range Rover belonging to the boss was used as transport.

One day I had to take one of the Irish bosses to the railway station in Exeter and make sure that he got on the train. The train was delayed for four hours, which was spent in the bar of the hotel opposite the station. Needless to say he was very happy when he left Devon.

After a few months the company was taken over by another company called Aaronson Brothers. One morning Mr Allan, the boss, came up to me and asked me what Artic unit I would recommend as the company was going to buy a new one. I told him that I liked the ERF, a unit that I had driven for the last company that I worked for.

Around two months later two new AEC Madator tractor units arrived at the factory. I was told that an ERF unit was £5,000 and an AEC unit was £3,000, so we got AEC Mandators

It was a few days later that Mr Allen came over to me and said that the AECs were to be used and which one did I want. The registration numbers ended 513 and 514. Geoff was superstitious so I had already agreed with him that I would take 513 if I had the choice.

From then on Geoff and I each had a unit of our own although we did not have a dedicated trailer. We agreed that we would take it in turns to do the longest trip and the other driver would do what ever else was needed. If there was only one trip to do then the other driver usually ended up helping out in the factory yard. Either unloading wood chips or help in the log park, at the chipper, turning wood into wood chips.

A long trip would be to Plymouth where there were four different saw mills were we loaded from.

It could be that both of us went to Plymouth on the same day but not to the same place.

There were some places that we went with both lorries on the same day. These companies had large storage areas and only needed to be cleared at least once a week. The places that come to mind are Staverton and Totnes both in South Devon. I loved Totnes, after loading we used to sit on the river bank and eat freshly made pasties from the local bakers.

To stop us getting bored we used to take one route on the way down and then come back a different route. We did this one day on a trip to Totnes and we headed back through Newton Abbott. When we got to a certain road in Newton Abbott we discovered the it had been made into a one way street and not the way we were going. There was no alternative route so I had to stop. I walked back to Geoff who was following me.

'What have we stopped for?' he asked.

'The road we normally go along is now a one way street and there is no alternative route,' I replied.

We abandoned the lorries and walked up the street where we found a traffic warden. After some discussion the warden went to the other end of the street and stopped the traffic. Then we drove the wrong way along the street with a promise that we would not go that way again.

We had to take turns working Saturdays and Sundays but we did get overtime rates. Usually we did not have to unload the trailers this was done on the night shift along with trailers from other companies.

To get to Plymouth we used to drive to Okehampton and then across Dartmoor and come into Plymouth from the North side. There used to be a little prefab café, on the outskirts of the city, that did wonderful fried breakfasts. Some times there would be a wait as the café would be full of Royal Marines from the nearby Crownhill Barracks.

One problem with the moorland route was that in the summer hundreds of Plymouth residents left the city to spend the day on the moors. The River Walkham near Horrabridge was a favourite place for families to go to. The problem was that the early visitors used to park neat and tidy but the ones that came later used to abandon their cars anywhere ignoring he fact that they were on a major route to Tavistock. This meant that in the morning the drive to Plymouth was fine but the return journey was fraught with danger as one had to pass cars that were parked on blind bends and on the brows of hills.

There was a saw mill at Exbridge, West Somerset, now an agricultural merchants. I was loading there one morning and the trailer fan stopped working. The factory sent out an electrician and he checked various electrical connections and it seemed to me the problem was not going to be an easy fix. As there wasn't many wood chips left to load I decided to call it a day and I would take the trailer back to the factory to be repaired. As I bent over to pick up one of the six inch metal pipes my forehead came into contact with the bare wires in the cable that had been disconnected from the fan. I got a lovely electric shock so I went and found the electrician and enquired if the power was on.

'Why?' he asked

I told him that I had just had an electric shock from the cable. I must admit that he was very concerned about my health as this was three phase electric (what ever that means) and five hundred volts.

I said that I was feeling fine and I will take the trailer back and it can be fixed in the workshop.

It is not only driving on the roads that are dangerous!

Richmond Walk, Plymouth, was quite a narrow road with parked cars on the pavements. Reversing into the saw mill there was impossible. I used to drive in and the side-loader would pick up the rear of the empty trailer and lift it around 90 degrees so that I could turn around. One day I went there and was told that the side-loader was broken and I would not be able to turn around. The sawmill was an oblong shape with a long shed either side. I drove very tight to the shed on the left then turned right at the end of the yard and drove into the right hand shed. Then I reversed out of the shed and into the opposite shed. I came out of that shed, turned right and parked alongside the right hand shed. The side-loader driver came over and said, 'You made that look easy, driver.'

'It was a lot easier than messing about with a side-loader,' I replied.

'Your other driver, Geoff, told me he couldn't turn around in here.'

'Perhaps you had the doors to the sheds shut at the first time he came here and he never thought of using the shed area to turn.'

'He can do the same as you did the next time he comes and I won't have to stop doing my work to sort him out.'

One morning Dave Priscott, our transport manager, told Geoff and I that there was one trailer to be taken and loaded at Bideford and also an empty trailer, which was parked in the log park and owned by a company in Swindon, that may have to be returned to Swindon and a loaded one brought back to South Molton.

As it was Geoff's turn to do the long distance run we decided to wait a while and see whether the Swindon run materialised. While we were waiting Geoff's tractor unit was coupled to an empty trailer and the trailer checked, ready to go. It would be a couple of minutes to swap units if necessary but Geoff didn't really want to go to Swindon. I didn't really want to go either; I had something on in the evening, probably a pool or darts match, and I liked to get down the pub early for a bit of practice.

With time moving on it was decide to let Geoff go on to Bideford and I was then left to do the Swindon job, if necessary.

While I was waiting I went off to check the Swindon trailer. It was a twenty foot single axle trailer and on inspection it was found to have no rear light bulbs or lenses. It also had a bald tyre.

I went back to the transport manager and told him that the Swindon trailer was not roadworthy and the reasons why. He told me that he would inform the owners of the situation and they would have to sort it out. He told me to forget about going to Swindon and go and find something else to do.

When Geoff returned from Bideford I told him what had happened about the Swindon trip.

'You didn't want to go anyway,' he said.

'Geoff, it is my job to go wherever I am sent but it is not my job to maintain vehicles,' I replied.

He laughed and said 'What you mean is, you didn't want to go.'

At the time many hauliers used to remove the bulbs and lenses from the trailer lights to stop them being stolen. The problem with this was if a driver was sent to pick up a trailer but had no spare bulbs or lenses he had the option of leaving the trailer or 'borrowing' bulbs and lenses from someone else's trailer. This led to all sorts of problems. On our site all trailers had to be fitted with working lights or they were not allowed to park.

A decision was made, by management, to teach all the weighbridge staff to drive heavy goods vehicles. I think that the idea was that they would be able to move lorries around the factory if necessary.

So yours truly was elevated to the dizzy heights of HGV driving instructor probably because Geoff didn't want to do it.

I was twenty four at the time and had been driving HGVs for less than three years.

The first pupil, I will call him Bob, was about thirty five years old and had no interest in driving lorries. He climbed into the lorry which was parked outside the weighbridge. At that time the weighbridge was situated a lot nearer the factory. He drove the lorry to the end of the drive, stopped and got out.

'I'm not doing this,' he said, got out, and walked back to the weighbridge.

I went back to Dave, the transport manager, and told him Bob wasn't going to drive the lorry under any circumstances. He literally seems to be terrified of the vehicle.

'Okay, try Geoff Miller,' he said.

I had known Geoff for a couple of years, we drank in the same pub and got on well together.

So the next day Geoff Miller drove the lorry up the drive, turned around and drove down again and parked outside the office block.

'How do you feel?' I asked. 'Confident enough to go on the road?'

'Yeah, I'll give it a go.'

Geoff drove up and down the drive a few times. Gear changing was practised with the unit stationary and the engine off. This was to get the feel of where the gear lever should be in any given gear. The next lesson was to familiarise himself with the vehicle controls. When training for the day was done I told him tomorrow we go out on the road. My idea was to get Geoff used to where everything was so he would be able to concentrate on the road at all times.

The next day we went to Bideford, to a company called Laminated Wood, on the western edge of Bideford. Here, the 'cyclone' as the machine that sucked up the shavings was called, was only turned off for one hour, at lunch time. Allowing a few minutes for the dust to settle there was around fifty minutes to load as much of the wood shavings as possible. It was impossible to load with the cyclone operating and there was no warning as to when it would be turned on again. There would be a whining noise and a few seconds later shavings and saw dust would be flying around the shed. Geoff Miller and I always had this job as there were two of us to load the trailer which did give us a chance to load the majority of the shavings. There were odd times when they delayed turning the cyclone on. Usually when they were gluing (laminating) timbers or bending timber. We would have one of the pipe sections inside the shed and as soon as the cyclone started we lifted off the pipe and threw it out the door; and we swiftly followed. Then we had all afternoon to have a late lunch, pack up and return to the factory and usually had time to empty the trailer ready for the next day.

When we returned to the factory the boss, Mr Alan asked Geoff how he had got on.

'Ok I think,' said Geoff.

I said, 'You actually went through a red traffic light and the trailer also caught the wall at Devil's Elbow (a notorious hairpin bend near the village of Swimbridge.'

I left Geoff unloading the trailer on the excuse that I was going to the canteen to get us a couple of coffees.

I went to Mr Alan's office and I told him that going into Barnstaple Geoff had stopped a bit close to some parked cars and had to work a bit hard to go around them. I claimed responsibility for that and had told Geoff to leave a bit more room in the future.

'The red traffic light was at temporary road works and it was just approaching them a little too fast for a loaded vehicle. There was no real danger to any one and the wall at Devil's Elbow again was some thing and nothing and all these thing I will go through with him later. All in all I believe he did well for his first time out.'

I then told Mr Allan what I said at the weigh bridge earlier was to stop Geoff getting over confident, and that I was sure he will make a good lorry driver.

One has to remember when driving a lorry the weight of the vehicle and load has a direct bearing on the stopping distance when braking. While watching the vehicle in front, one has to be aware of what is happening further down the road. Is the traffic stopped? Are there traffic lights? Is there a pedestrian crossing with someone near it? Are there small children on the pavement? In the countryside look out for agricultural vehicles, emergency vehicles, other large vehicles, animals especially horses, who seem to hate lorries. Be prepared to slow down and even stop if necessary.

The most dangerous person on the road is a car driver. Car drivers do not seem to realise that a lorry cannot stop in ten feet. They will cut in front of you and then brake, indicators appear to be optional extras. Indicating at roundabouts is non existent or they continue to indicate right when they turn left off the roundabout. The latter is very annoying when you have stopped, waiting for them to go past and they leave the roundabout just before they get to you. Car drivers seem to hate being behind a lorry, they will pass you even if they are turning off at the junction fifty metres in front of you.

This happened to me on the M2. I was fully freighted and travelling at 60 mph in the middle lane. A car passed me, pulled in front of me to exit the motorway only to find there was another lorry on the inside lane which was passing his exit. Did he carry on to the next exit? No he braked hard, causing the car wheels to lock. Fortunately for him, in the mirror I saw him passing so at least when he pulled in front of me I was aware of him. He braked hard and I had about forty feet to stop. Luckily I was driving someone else's Volvo F10 which seemed to have the best brakes in the fleet. The trailer wheels locked up and using the engine brake as well, I managed to slow the lorry just enough for the car to tuck in behind the lorry passing the exit. He came within about three seconds of dying needlessly - a long blast on the air horns signified his escape from a serious accident. The car driver gained no time at all by his reckless driving and lost a good deal of rubber from his tyres. This type of incident is a daily occurrence for lorry drivers.

Lorry drivers drive for a living and should be totally aware of their circumstances. What other traffic is doing, whether their load is secure, straps, ropes are not flapping about, the condition of the road etc. Hopefully, totally concentrating, unlike many car drivers that have passed me over the years.

These are all the things that Geoff had to take on board. It is not just a case of pointing a lorry down the road and hope that everybody else gets out the way.

We never used to carry sandwiches but instead made use of the nearest café or pub. There used to be one at Lapford, called the Yeo Vale Inn. We would stop there on the way back from Exeter or Plymouth.

The pub was situated at the entrance to a factory and when we got there I used to get out and move an ornamental tree and then Geoff could park off the road without blocking the factory entrance. We stopped there one lunch time and the landlord said 'I don't mind you boys coming here, but could you park somewhere else as the trailer blocks all the light through the window.'

When we left I always put the tree back in its place.

Exbridge was our destination one sunny day and after loading at the sawmill we dusted each other off and Geoff Miller drove to the nearby

Anchor Inn. Now to say this was a posh pub would be an understatement. We parked away from the pub to leave plenty of room for other customers to park. We went in and purchased a drink and sandwiches. Having consumed the same we asked the landlord for another drink.

'You can have another drink but would you please take off your overalls first,' he said.

'I don't think you really want us to do that,' one of us replied.

'On the contrary,' said the landlord, 'I insist.'

So we did as asked and we stood there in our underpants, socks and boots. Where upon we were asked to leave and not return. I knew he wouldn't be happy and I was right.

As we left we waved to the old ladies near the door. I am sure they hoped we would be back, after all we were both a bit slimmer in those days.

There is a main road that leads to Exbridge from South Molton but I used to make Geoff drive across country to Exbridge. This route was country lanes and included two narrow bridges, I told Geoff that anybody can drive A roads. My route was challenging and included one of the bridges where one had to be perfectly lined up to get across it in one go; it did include using a field entrance to get the trailer far enough to the left to clear the end of the bridge.

Another reason to use this road was the Froude Arms at East Anstey, where we now went for our lunch after being unjustly excluded from the Anchor Inn. There were benefits: the sandwiches were better and cheaper and we could park outside the pub. When we left, the landlord always came out to make sure the lorry did not hit his pub sign. We actually never got near it.

On the way back from Plymouth one day we were about fourteen miles from the factory when a smell of burning permeated the cab of the lorry. Geoff stopped and we got out and investigated the source of the smell. It didn't take long: the front wheel bearing of the cab unit was very hot. We were carrying flammable material and I decided to call out the Fire and Rescue service to cool down the bearing. As Chulmleigh was only two miles away the fire service arrived in a very short time.

They cooled down the wheel bearing and the rest of the vehicle was checked. I knew some of the firemen and after a short discussion it was decided to park the unit in a nearby lay-by and get it recovered by the garage who had sold it to Aaronson Brothers. Also get Geoff Barker to recover the trailer. This was all done in an hour or so. Little did I know that this would not be the only time that I had to get the fire service out during my driving career. The next time would be a much more serious situation - but more of that in a future chapter.

Back at the factory Geoff Miller and myself thought we would get Sunday off but no such luck. Bardev Pallets agreed to let us use their Ford D series Artic unit. This was only allowed to a gross weight of twenty four tons where as the Mandator was thirty two tons. With the load and trailer weight it meant the lorry and would be close to its gross weight.

Sunday morning we set off with me driving as there were no learner plates for the tractor unit. The trailer number plate of the Ford did not fit the Irish trailer so we wrote the registration number in the mud on the trailer door and left the Irish registration plate still attached to the trailer.

I had no log book as I had left it in the Mandator which was now in Exeter. I suppose I could have gone to Plymouth via Exeter but I thought as I never get stopped by the Police then there would be no problem.

All went well until we set off back from Plymouth docks. While going slowly up Tavistock Road we were passed by a police car who then proceeded to drive along in front of us, obviously checking the vehicle. At the top of the hill on went the blue lights and I pulled over. I told Geoff to leave the talking to me and I got out of the lorry to talk to the two policeman.

Geoff got out of the lorry and came round to join us.

'Can I see your log book?' requested the policeman.

'I don't have it with me', I replied.

'Why not?'

'I don't need one as I am driving less than four hours.'

'Where have you come from?' he asked

'South Molton.'

'You can do South Molton to here and back in four hours?'

'Yes'

'You were only coming along there at 20 mph'

'That's because you were in front of me and I couldn't pass you.'

'I stopped you because you have an English number plate on the front and an Irish one at the back. Why is this?' asked the policeman.

I told him that there had been an overheating problem with the normal lorry and we had to call the fire brigade out to sort it. Then the lorry had been taken away for repair. 'The Ford is a borrowed lorry but the trailer number plate would not fit the trailer so we wrote the number in the dirt on the doors.'

'What are you carrying?' he asked.

Remember this was in the days that the Irish Republican Army was active in the UK blowing up various buildings. Maybe he thought we were possibly carrying illegal arms or explosives.

'We are carrying wood chips that we loaded at Millbay docks,' I replied.

'Open the door please, I would like to have a look.'

'If I open the door then wood chips will fall out and there is no way of picking them up. If you want to have a look then you open the door, then it is your responsibility to clear up any mess.'

He started to gently open the door and wood chips started to come out, so he shut the door.

'You're welcome to follow us to the chipboard factory at South Molton and we will get it unloaded in your presence if that would settle your curiosity,' I offered.

'How often do you come to Plymouth?' he asked

'We have two lorries collecting wood chips with this type of trailer. At least one, sometimes both come to Plymouth every day of the week.'

'Alright,' he said, 'carry on your way.'

The police car pulled away and we continued on our way to South Molton.

Going down the steep hill just to the West of Okehampton I had some difficulty in slowing the lorry. I drove very slowly down the hill into Okehampton as I knew there were traffic lights at the bottom. Fortunately the lights were green so we didn't have to stop. At the next hill the brakes seemed to be worst so I decided not to drive any further. I didn't think the vehicle would stop if we had an emergency situation, so I parked in the next lay-by and telephoned the factory. I was told to stay where we were and they would send someone out. Around an hour passed and a van turned up driven by Willy Sanders who worked in the log park at the factory.

'What's going on? asked Willy

I told him the brakes were crap and I wouldn't drive it any further. Also Geoff and I hadn't eaten for a few hours and we were starving.

'No problem,' said Willy. 'We'll stop at the pub near the village of Copplestone.' Which we did.

We eventually arrived back at the factory about eight thirty in the evening and then went home.

The next morning I went and saw the boss and told him what had happened and where we had left the lorry. The trailer was recovered by a tractor unit from Smythe's transport. I went along to show the driver the location.

Tuesday I was called into the office to see the boss. He told me that there had been a right row about the Ford. Bardev pallets had it on contract from British Road Services (BRS) and it seems it should not have been used by another firm. Also BRS had, apparently, been out to recover the Ford but they could not find the lay-by where I had left the unit. I had to telephone BRS and give them directions to the lay-by which was on a major road and should have been easy to find.

During the week the Mandator was returned to the factory with a brand new wheel bearing fitted.

Sunday saw Geoff back in the driving seat and once again we were heading toward Plymouth. As we got to the outskirts of the city we spotted a police car parked in a side street. We hadn't gone far before the police car passed us and indicated for us to stop at the entrance to the marine barracks.

The police man asked me for my log book and I gave it to him.

. He looked at it and then said, 'You *have* got one then?'

'Yes,' I replied.

'You told us you'd lost it when the lorry caught fire. They soon repaired it, considering it was burnt out!'

'It was not burnt out. The offside wheel bearing overheated and I left the log book in the lorry when it was taken to the garage.'

'You've filled it out for the whole of last week. Why have you done that? And it took you nearly four hours to get to Bow, which is a fair way from South Molton.'

'I've filled it out as that is the easiest way for the company to monitor what I'm doing daily. As for just getting to Bow, the brakes were getting worse and worse as we drove home and at Bow I decided to park the vehicle up as I deemed it unsafe to drive any further.'

'Come with me,' he said. He walked to the boot of his police car, opened the boot and inside was the thickest book that I had ever seen. He turned to a page with a marker in it and pointed to a paragraph.

'It says here that a log book does not need to be used if the vehicle stays within 25 miles of base nor exceeds fours hours driving.'

I said, 'In my Road Haulage Association driver's handbook it says "or" not "nor".'

'Then that's obviously a misprint.'

'When I get back I shall write to the RHA and tell them of the misprint and tell them that they are obligated to inform all their members of the same.'

'Ok. Get on your way and don't give me an occasion to stop you again,' he said.

I replied, 'If you stop me again I shall report you for harassment, PC; and I read out his number.'

Then I said, 'Thank you for pointing that out.' And I got back in the lorry and we drove off. Of course I knew he was right, he had done his job and I had done mine. He never stopped me again and the next Plymouth policeman that did, led to a much different outcome. Of course that is in a future chapter. Keep reading.

I suffer from vertigo so to try to get over it, every evening I would climb the ladder on the outside of the left-hand side wood-chip silo. Every time I would go a step higher than the night before and then just stay there looking all around and getting used to the height.

One evening, around five thirty, I clocked off and then went up to the silo and climbed up to a height of around thirty feet. I was doing my usual one hand, one foot swinging around when there was an almighty bang. It came from the factory a couple of hundred yards to my right. Before I could do anything I was surrounded by a wall of flame. I have always had a slight fear of fire, from something that happened when I was boy.

The wall of flame was only a flash-over but by the time it had passed I was on the ground. I took both feet off the rungs and used my hands to control the rate of descent by gripping the steel sides of the ladder. As I was wearing leather gloves there was no damage to my hands although they were a little warm.

The flame was followed very quickly by thick black smoke. I ran across the log park, passed the weighbridge, climbed over the chain link fence, slid down the grass bank and jumped across the open drain. It was a small climb up to the drive and I was pleased to see that the drive was clear of smoke. I ran to the offices that were situated a couple of hundred yards to the south of the factory.

Although the office staff had gone home the offices were not locked. I went to the telephone switch board, it was a bit bigger than the one that I had used at North Devon Farmers. After flicking a few switches I got an outside line. I dialled treble nine and when the operator asked which service I required I said, 'All three.'

I told her that I was speaking from the chipboard factory at Hill Village, South Molton. I said there had been an explosion and there was also a fire. As I talked to her I could see thick black smoke pouring from the factory but no flames. I also told her that I had no idea of casualties at that time. I gave her the telephone number and said I would stay in the office to relay any more information when I had it.

It wasn't long before Mr Alan appeared through the smoke. Followed by one or two others. When they entered the office I informed Mr Alan of my actions and that the phone was switched to an outside line. I noticed Geoff Miller was one of the people who was with him. Mr Alan told Geoff and I to go and shut the factory gates and let no one in and then stay at the weighbridge until further instructions. The weighbridge was a lot closer to the factory then and the gates were next to it. By now most of the population of South Molton were aware of the fire as the factory was on top of a hill and the smoke was easily visible from the town.

It wasn't long before we heard the South Molton fire engine approaching, Geoff and I went out and opened the gates to allow the fire brigade access. The fire engine passed through the gates and we closed them. We had already been told that the only casualty was a young lad who appeared to have a broken arm. He had been hit by a steel door that had been blown off from one of the machines.

By now people had started to gather along the fence concerned about their relatives who worked at the factory. We reported that there was only one casualty and we would update them as time went on. We had already phoned our wives and said that we may not be home for a while. The sightseers were asked to keep the drive clear for emergency vehicles.

In a few minutes more fire engines arrived from nearby towns and villages. In total seven engines and a hose layer attended along with two ambulances. Two Police cars arrived and remained at the top of the drive to stop unnecessary vehicles entering the factory.

The casualty list remained at one broken arm. Reg Hunt was a bit bruised, he was just about to enter the factory through the steel workshop door when the explosion blew the door shut and propelled Reg back into the workshop at high speed. As one of his work mates later commented Reg had never moved so fast in all his life.

After about thirty minutes a black Morris Minor car arrived at the gate. The driver was wearing a dinner suit and informed us that he was the fire chief. We asked him for identity and after searching his pockets he told us he didn't have any on him. We told him that we were not allowed to let him in. He then got a bit annoyed and we said that we were only following orders. It was then that I had an idea.

'Would leading fireman Hill know you?'

'Of course,' the man replied.

'I will go and get him and if he agrees with what you say we will let you in.'

So off I went in search of LF Hill, he lived at the end of our street and I had known him all my life so I trusted what he said.

A few minutes later I returned with him and when he saluted our car driver I knew the man in the dinner suit was telling the truth. I told him to park his car outside of the office and we would keep an eye on it.

We found out later he was off to some posh dinner and as he knew an explosion at the factory would be a large job he had to attend. In his hurry to get to the incident he had forgotten to pick up his wallet.

A couple of hours after the explosion workers started to leave the factory which meant that only the night shift remained to assist the fire men. The crowd at the fence started to thin out so one of us went to the canteen to get some food and drink. The food was in machines and one had to pay for it then put it in one of the microwaves to heat it. As the evening dragged on, and to stop us from getting bored, we took turns to get both lorries ready for the morning. Then around midnight we decided to have some more food but someone had altered the machines to give free food and the firemen had ate the lot. Well I suppose they deserved it. There was still tea and coffee available.

We sat in the weighbridge until eight o'clock in the morning when we were told to go home and the weighbridge operator would take over our duties. We were given the day off. We had both been at the factory for twenty four hours. My longest working day, beating the one at Tone Vale Transport by half an hour.

The loaded trailers used to be unloaded in the log park opposite the 'chipper'. There were two silos that contained woodchips. Between them and slightly closer to the 'chipper' was a large fan similar to the ones on the trailers but a lot bigger. It was also not fitted at ninety degrees to the curb - more like one hundred and fifteen degrees. Originally a flexible nylon pipe was connected to the fan so it did not matter if the trailers where not parked square with the fan, they could be easily unloaded.

A few months after the big fire the nylon pipe was taken away and replaced with a rigid metal one as it was thought that it may create static electricity and cause another fire [it did not cause the first one.]

I used to work Sundays from eight in the morning and stay there until midnight and do the same Mondays. This used to give me a good start to the week, wages-wise. After about twelve months everyone was informed that all overtime work had to sanctioned by a supervisor. That led to a serious cut in my income as I was no longer allowed to work sixteen hour days.

One evening I was about to clock-off when Geoff Barker came up to me and asked me to see him back-on to the unloading fan. As it was a dark winter's evening it was not easy to see where the fan actually was and the trailer had to be parked in line with it as the unloading pipes were now rigid.

So I went up to the log park and we got the doors of the trailer opened and the trailer backed on to the fan ready for the guys to unload it. When I got back down to the factory entrance to clock-off the Transport manager, Dave Priscott, was there. I clocked-off and was about to leave when he asked me why I was clocking off twenty minutes after I should have. I told him what I had been doing and he replied that I did not have permission to work overtime and he took my clock card and wrote some thing on it. I used to have a bit of a temper when I was younger and we had a bit of a row about what he had just done. In the end I gave up and went home.

The next day I went into work and asked Dave Priscott if he was going to stick with what he said the day before. He told me he was. I went and saw his boss Cecil O'Connor and told him what had happened and Cecil said that he had to support the actions of his manager. I went back to Dave Priscott and told him that Cecil supported his action. I threw him the keys to the lorry (I had already taken my belongings out) and told him that he could drive it himself.

That must have annoyed him slightly as he did not hold a Heavy Goods Vehicle licence.

In line with company policy I was escorted off the premises and told to return at eleven o'clock when I could pick-up my pay and empty my locker. That was that, as they say, and two years of employment at the chipboard factory ended. I was still friends with Dave Priscott until he died in 2019.

To me, rightly or wrongly, it was a matter of principal.

Geoff Miller did pass his HGV test. I knew he would.

The wife was not too pleased, to say the least, but she knew I was not happy working for Aaronson Brothers, coming home every night covered in wood dust.

The rest of the day, Tuesday, I didn't do much. Wednesday it was off to Barnstaple, the biggest town in North Devon and see if I could find employment. The only success I had was with Shapland & Petters. They said that if I did not get a job within a fortnight they would take me on, working in the factory until a driving position came up.

This was a fall-back situation but it wasn't going to convince the wife to give me money for Friday night darts down the pub. Thursday I bought a local newspaper. There were a couple of HGV driving jobs in the situations vacant column.

The first was a timber company at Chivenor, about fifteen miles from South Molton. I telephoned them and the fitter answered the phone. He told me that the boss wasn't there and he took my name, address and phone number.

The next company was South Molton Concrete Works owned by Bill Rumsam, someone that I knew from playing darts, although he played for a different team. I phoned him up and he said come down for an interview. I went down straight away and being a local man he already knew a bit about me.

Usual interview stuff, working hours, overtime, wages etc. After talking for about fifteen minutes, ten of them talking about the darts league and other sports (Bill was sports mad) he said that he would take me on and asked when could I start?

'When do you want me?' I asked.

'Seven-thirty tomorrow morning would be good'

I said, 'That's fine by me.'

6

South Molton Concrete Works

The Concrete works were fairly new, with two tipper lorries: a G-cab Leyland Clydesdale and an old Ford D series. The Clydesdale was driven by Alan Bouchers and the Ford by George Roper, who was also the shop steward. A Leyland Bison, long-wheel base, six-wheel ready-mix concrete lorry driven by Ralph Binding and two ancient, well worked, short-wheel base, six-wheel Foden S20 ready-mix concrete lorries. One of those I was to drive, the other one was for spare parts.

Christine, my wife, was well pleased that I'd landed a job and even more surprised that I was to start the next day. That released some funds for the Friday night dart match.

Friday I checked out the Foden. It had a glass fibre cab with coach built doors, a big towing eye at the front which may come in useful off road. The diesel tank had a gauge on the side of it instead of one in the cab (it was stuck on half-full - or half-empty). The Foden was fitted with a four and a half cubic yard mixer drum powered by a separate engine. This engine is known as a donkey engine and was positioned between the drum and the back of the cab and fitted across the chassis. There was a large water tank above it. The controls for the mixer were three levers: one for throttle, one to put the drum into gear and one for the clutch. The drum also had a large lump of concrete inside left there when some one didn't clean out the drum properly a few years ago. This made the lorry rock when it was loaded.

When everything was filled and checked, I was ready to go. I reversed under the plant to load, climbed up the ladder fitted at the rear-end of the lorry and made sure that the large rubber tube, hanging down from the plant, was correctly positioned in the chute at the back of the lorry. It is wise to do this very time you load.

Start donkey engine, make sure the drum is rotating in the right direction. Start loading.

The mix is loaded with the drum turning at high speed and when loaded the speed was altered to slow.

Ready to move off. The Foden gear box was like no other: there was a plaque mounted on the dash board to help drivers.

Fodens had a four speed gear box with the lever coming up from the floor. The was also another lever on the dash board and this was for selecting low, normal or high range.

This is the gears from low to high:

One, two, three in low range.

One direct range.

Four low range.

One high range.

Two direct, two high range.

Three direct, three high range.

Four direct, four high range.

One could pre-select the required range on the dash board lever.

The gear would not change until the clutch pedal was depressed.

Gears one, two and three were so low that they were never used in normal road work

Gear box sorted, although I did look at the plaque quite a lot for the first few days. Off we go.

A serious problem was found. The engine smoked quite a lot, so bad in fact I christened the Foden, 'Thunderbird Two' after the space ship on the television programme.

I drove it for a couple of days and thought maybe it smoked because the vehicle hasn't been used for a while.

Friday went fine and Saturday was a day off. I was still in bed when there was a knock at the door. Christine came in and told me that there was a man to see me.

He told that me that he was the man who owned the timber company at Chivenor and he had come to interview me for the driving job. I told him that I'd already got a job and had started the day before.

He wasn't very happy and said that the fitter should have taken me on, I could have been sacked at a later date if I wasn't any good. With that attitude I'm glad I didn't go to work for him.

Hi-Temperature Engineers had just moved to South Molton and built a factory next to the Concrete Works. They also built some houses at

North Molton and Alswear, for key workers. North Molton is situated 3 miles from South Molton and on the top of a hill. The road to North Molton is twisty and goes through a wooded valley with the road rising up to the village after about two and a half miles.

The Hi-Temperature site was at the South Molton end of the village and overlooked the valley.

The first time that I went to the site the men were stood ready and waiting for their load. They told me that when they saw the smoke coming up through the trees they knew I was on my way and went and fetched their shovels.

The mechanic rode with me for a day or so playing with the diesel pump and other bits as we went along, but did it not improve the situation. The engine was totally knackered.

'Park it up,' Bill Rumsam said and go and find some thing to do in the shed.

The next thing that I know is the Foden is off to Lex Tillotson, a commercial garage in Taunton. A few days later it was back having had a second-hand Leyland engine fitted in place of the old Foden engine.

The engine was from an eight wheel tipper and had a lot more power than the old Foden. It would now go up a one in three hill fully loaded, in third gear. The problem was the steering was now so light, with the front wheels practically of the ground, that to go around a bend I slid along the hedges to steer the lorry.

I soon discovered that it had limited slip differentials fitted which means that when one of the drive-wheels starts to spin, the differentials lock and all four driving wheels then turn at the same speed. It was amazing. It would go anywhere, but only in a straight line. It also cornered like a rally car. It may look old but it could be fun to drive.

I took a load of concrete up to the log park in the chip-board factory one day and while I was unloading a lorry tipped twenty tons of wood chips in front of the Foden. When I was ready to go one of the builders said, 'You'll have to wait a bit to get away. The loader driver has gone for his lunch.'

There was no way around the wood chips. I said to the builder, 'Watch this.'

I got into the cab of the Foden, selected third gear, low range, and drove straight through the pile of wood chips.

Another day I arrived at a farm and the site was perfectly level but seriously muddy.

'Where do you want it?' I asked Farmer Nichols.

'Back over there,' he replied but I don't think you'll get there, the mud is pretty deep.'

I reversed across a concrete area, pointed the rear of the lorry in the direction it needed to go and very slowly got there. Ready mix unloaded the farmer said, 'I will go and get a tractor to pull you out.'

The glutinous mud was up to the top of the rear wheels. 'I don't need a tractor. Watch this.'

I got in to the cab, started the lorry and put her into low first gear. Then I let out the clutch. One rear wheel started to spin and then without touching the throttle 'Thunderbird Two' slowly advanced until she had got onto the hard concrete where I stopped and washed the wheels. As I left the farmer was still looking amazed, a lorry that is nearly as good as a Land Rover off-road.

On the old A361 there was a lay-by separated from the road by a grass verge about two feet high and two feet wide. There used to be a converted bus parked there which sold very good food. One day I pulled in there for lunch. When I came to leave I was boxed in by two lorries.

'You'll have to wait 'till we're finished,' said one of the drivers.

'No I won't,' I replied. I got in the lorry turned right and drove straight over the grass verge and on down the road. You can't stop a Foden.

The Concrete Works consisted of a massive agricultural shed with an office block, workshop, toilets and canteen attached to one end. This shed was known as the block shed used, as it was, for making precast concrete blocks. There was a separate area for the concrete plant and storage bins, as well as a large outside area to one side of the block shed where the new blocks were stacked and a large area at the front where the precast concrete products were stored.

Bill Rumsam, beside owning the Concrete Works, also owned a building company, as well as North Devon Scaffolding. If there was no concrete to deliver then I helped out in the concrete works, the building firm or drove the scaffold lorry. Helping out somewhere else was not my favourite job but at least I was getting paid for it.

If I was in the concrete works, in winter, I used to start work a bit later as I wasn't going to stand around a fire of pallets waiting for the weather to warm up to start work. You can't make precast in freezing conditions and the shed had six large entrances and no doors. The lower walls were nine inch blocks stacked one on top of the other. It was a very cold place to work in the winter

When I first started, the block yard was still being built and Saturday mornings were spent concreting parts of the yard.

The building foreman was Merv Crook who had been with Rumsam Builders for many years, 'Rumbo' had total confidence in him. One Saturday it was time to concrete another strip of the yard and all hands were called in.

Ralph's lorry was the one that would be used as it carried more concrete than the Foden. Ralph would start at seven thirty in the morning and load the concrete so it would be ready to spread about seven-forty. I arrived at seven-forty-five and Merv Crook asked, 'Were have you been, you were supposed to have been here at seven-thirty.'

'The concrete would not have been ready at seven thirty, so to get here at that time and sit around for twenty minutes would have been a waste of my time and Rumbo's money. 'What have you done since getting here? I asked. 'Nothing.'

I said all this as I stood in the door way of the canteen.

I could see that Ralph was now backing down to the site and Merv said to me, 'You can operate the controls and the rest of us will spread it.'

I stopped Ralph at the appropriate point. I told him that when I waved, keep moving forward at tick over and I would put the drum in high gear and then control the flow of concrete using the throttle.

'Come on!' shouted Merv. 'Let's get on with it.'

I climbed the ladder to make sure that the concrete was nice and wet as Merv had asked for.

'Do you want it fast?'

'Yes,' said Merv.

He didn't know, or had forgotten, about the high gear and he was stood close to the end of the chute.

I put the gear lever into high gear, put the throttle to maximum and let go of the clutch lever.

The concrete poured out of the drum, shot down the chute, hit the ground, bounced up and went all over the front of Merv. He jumped back a couple of feet and then described me as an 'uneducated, love-making, illegitimate person.' Or words to that effect.

Ralph's lorry was high geared and would not go up a hill anything steeper than a one in five hill. As North Devon is quite hilly it was not the best vehicle for the job. Therefore the Foden did the bulk of work across Exmoor.

I had a load for a farm just off the A39, between Lynmouth and Porlock. I decided the quickest way would be through Lynton, down Lynmouth hill into Lynmouth and up Countisbury hill. It would be slow, as Lynmouth Hill is a one in four, down and Countisbury hill a one in four, up. The highest point of Countisbury hill is two hundred and forty-five and a half metres above sea level. All went well until I came out of trees at the bottom of Countisbury. Seeing the grass on the left sloping down to the cliffs kicked-in my Vertigo. With the Foden in low gear I didn't relish going up this hill at all. Drastic action needed to be taken. There was no other traffic on the hill so I put on the head-lights and drove up the hill on the wrong side of the road. Near the top the cliff goes away to the left to make a headland, at this point I crossed to the correct side of the road and carried on. With the concrete delivered I decided to go through the Brendon Valley and across Exmoor to get back to South Molton. It may be narrow lanes but at least there were no steep cliffs.

The concrete works supplied a lot of concrete to Devon County Council, for their farms as well as their roads and one trip I did had a completely different ending to what I expected.

'Devon County Council, Brendon' it said on the delivery ticket. Their delivery tickets were often a bit vague and I just kept driving until I came across a yellow van or lorry.

The valley is deep, and a couple of miles long, with the village of Brendon in the middle. The roads are narrow and the West end has a very steep hill going down into it. If I hadn't come across the council men by the time that I got to Brendon I would ask at the shop. Village shops always knew what was going on and where people were.

The East Lyn river also flows through the valley.

On this occasion I didn't have to ask at the shop, I came across the council workers a few hundred yards from the foot of the steep hill. The foreman was looking a bit worried when I got to them.

I stopped the lorry and walked across to where he was stood by the river.

'Morning,' I said. 'Every thing alright?'

'No,' he replied. 'I was hoping you would be a bit late. The river has flooded overnight and we can't concrete the bit we wanted to.'

'We do have an alternative place that you can deliver it though. There's a farm at the top of Beggars Roost where we can put it.'

Beggar's Roost was about three miles away.

'There are a couple of problems with that,' I said. 'The first is if you redirect the load you will have to pay extra for doing that'

'That's ok,' said the foreman. 'What's the second?'

'I won't be able to drive there out of this valley. The hill is too steep and twisty and the steering won't grip. I will have to reverse up, so you will have to send your lorry up to the top of the hill and stop any traffic coming down. Also there might be a problem at Hillsford Bridge, at the hairpin bend. We will have to see what happens when we get there.'

'Fine,' said the foreman. 'Let's give it a go.'

So off went the council lorry, then me, reversing the Foden, and finally the foreman's van bringing up the rear. We all got to the top of the hill where I turned around and then set of for Beggar's Roost. We got to Hillsford Bridge and the lorry in front went on up the hill to stop traffic coming down. Then I started to go up, the hairpin bend is almost at the beginning of the hill. I got to the bend, selected first gear and using all the road started to go around the bend. I got just over half way around, selected reverse and let the lorry go back very slowly on opposite steering lock. With the lorry pointing in the right direction I proceeded to climb the narrow hill to Beggar's Roost. All a bit of a challenge but the concrete was safely delivered.

Another job for the County Council was concreting gulleys along the edge of roads. It meant driving slowly along while the council man, directed the chute and pouring a small amount of concrete along the side of the road. The Foden's low gearing was ideal for this job as I didn't have to slip the clutch. After about a hundred yards unloading was stopped while the council men shaped the concrete into a gulley and then we poured out a little bit more concrete and repeated the process.

The gulleys that were formed in the 1970s are still along the side of the Black Cat Hill on what was then the old A361 but is now the B3227.

When I first went to work for South Molton Concrete the sales of ready-mix concrete was spasmodic and I spent a lot of time on hire to Rumsam Builders doing various jobs. Also working in the concrete works supposedly helping others who seemed to disappear after a short while - something that really used to annoy me and led to many rows. On hot days I used to get my own back by climbing the ladder up to the top of the cement silo, which had a flat roof, and do a bit of sunbathing.

As time went on the sale of concrete blocks rocketed with house building increasing. Although this didn't have the same effect on ready-mix. There was also demand for insulation blocks. These were made of pumice and the nearest supplier was in Avonmouth so it was decided to purchase a new eight-wheeled ERF. Alan Bouchers was allocated this vehicle and the Clydesdale was kept as a spare vehicle.

All of the tippers were fitted with dropside bodies so that they could be easily loaded with concrete blocks. There were three other tippers that did work out of the concrete works: Freddie Isaac, an owner driver, David Horseman who drove the family Commer lorry and Dick Snow, who drove a Commer for Watts, the local firm that did mostly cattle haulage.

There was Bill Mahoney, Mervyn Way, Bill Hocking and Richard Jennings who all drove flatbed lorries and delivered pallets of blocks, many of which went to the Plymouth area.

Blocks were also delivered using the Ford and the Clydesdale. These loads were usually delivered in and around Barnstaple. After delivery we would drive to Nott's Quarry near Brayford and load chippings for the concrete works. The chippings came in different sizes depending on whether they were for blocks or ready-mix concrete. At the concrete works there was a large storage area for all the different types of chippings. Sand was also collect by various tippers.

Sometimes lorries would just go straight to Nott's Quarry to load chippings, ten tons per load. A round trip of one hour. Eight trips a day meant a total of eighty tons of chippings delivered.

To get to the Quarry meant driving along the old A361 toward Barnstaple. There is a long straight piece of road just outside of South Molton. This stretch of road is known as Aller Cross Straight and at the western end is the junction known as Aller Cross. Here the main road turned quite sharply to the left and the B3226 forked slightly right to Brayford and eventually to Blackmoor Gate.

115

One morning I was following Dick Snow and we were both driving along Aller Cross Straight, heading for Nott's Quarry. Dick got to the fork, slowed down, and turned right toward Brayford.

I looked across the low hedge, and seeing no traffic, I followed Dick. As I crossed the white line I saw a low sports car approaching me at high speed from the Barnstaple direction. It was so close to the ground that it was lower than the hedges which were about five foot high.

I had no choice but to accelerate hard. An empty lorry has reasonable acceleration, and an empty tipper lorry will also corner like a car.

I caught up to Dick very quickly and then had no choice but to go around him as well. The road curved to the right, narrowed considerably, and went uphill to a narrow hump back bridge, all in a few hundred yards.

Fortunately for me Dick was concentrating and seeing me overtaking he slowed down and let me pass. Needless to say, when we got to the Quarry, he had some choice words to say about my driving. I'm still not sure that he believed what I said but he never mentioned it again.

He was a really nice person and a couple of years later he moved away to live in Wiltshire. I hope he had a happy life there.

In the seventies Nott's Quarry was split in two by the B3226. There were three quarries on the South side of the road, with the main quarry being the middle one. Opposite the middle, and main quarry, on the other side of the road was the weighbridge, a large area where chippings were stacked and another area where lorries parked waiting to load.

After weighing to get the tare weight (the total weight of the vehicle when empty) a lorry was reversed under one of the storage hoppers on the Quarry side of the road. Care had to be taken as the B3226 was narrow here and some drivers were too busy looking around to watch were they were going.

The hoppers held different-size stone and had a hinged cover on the bottom. This cover was operated by pulling a lever. It was better to reverse in and start loading the rear of the lorry first. Once the chippings got near to the top of the body sides one reversed a bit further in until the lorry was loaded. The lever was pulled and the cover closed. Then the load was levelled a bit with the shovel that hung on the back or the cab. Then it was back onto the weighbridge to get a gross weight figure and collect the delivery ticket from Derrick Brooks, the weighbridge operator.

No need to sheet the load in those days so it was straight back to the Concrete Works to unload, thirty minutes later.

On tipper duties one morning I was sent to Nott's Quarry, but not for chippings. Today would be a first for me, today we are hauling tarmacadam (tarmac). Somewhere near Torrington a road was being resurfaced and Nott's had the contract to supply the tarmac. Every spare lorry was called in. Most tippers in the seventies were four-wheelers (two axles) most with a ten ton carrying capacity.

I duly arrived at the Quarry around seven forty-five and was told that I was slightly too early (that's a first for me) to load tarmac. I was given a tarpaulin - for the tarmac, later on - but first I was told to deliver a load of chippings to a farm the other side of South Molton near the village of Alswear. Chippings loaded and the tarpaulin sat on top I went off to Alswear, a round trip of about seventy-five minutes. Chippings delivered, I set off back to the Quarry and was travelling along a nice flat straight road just outside of Alswear when I suddenly remembered the tarpaulin. I had tipped with the chippings, normally I didn't use one so I didn't even think about it when tipping. I did a quick U-turn and drove back to the farm where I saw it sticking out of the chippings. With the tarpaulin safely in the back of the lorry, I set off back to the Quarry again. As I passed through South Molton I noticed a fire engine was catching me up, its blue lights flashing in the morning sun. As I got to Aller Straight, with a clear road ahead, I indicated left and waved the fire engine past. Life got even better when the fire engine took the Brayford road. I thought, if it goes to Brayford I will get back to the Quarry in no time, all I had to do was stick to his rear end.

We got to the Quarry in excellent time and I turned right and drove onto the weighbridge. What I hadn't noticed was that the fire engine had stopped beside the tar plant. Yes, you guessed it, the tar plant was on fire.

I was redirected to Venn quarry at Landkey, where the tarmac would now be loaded. By the time I got to Venn there was a long queue of lorries in front of me all loading for Torrington. One of them gave me an old washing up liquid bottle full of some unknown liquid which I was told to spray on the sides of the tipper, apparently it stops the tar-mac from sticking to them.

The tarmac was eventually loaded and when I got to Torrington there was another long wait to unload. Later - much later - it was back to

Nott's just in time to get a load of chippings for the concrete works. I vowed that the next time I do tarmac I will take a book. I never did do another load.

Ralph's ready-mix lorry had to go back to the dealers, I can't remember why but I do recall that the oil dipstick was the wrong one for that engine and had to be changed. Whether this had messed up the Engine in some way, I do not know.

A concrete mixer was hired and given to Ralph to drive. This lorry was a Guy and known as a 'Big J'. Ralph drove it for a few weeks until the Bison returned. The Guy had to go back to Harrow in North West London and Ralph said that he wasn't going to take it back.

I volunteered, I thought it would make a change and could get a bit of overtime as well. As it was I got more than I expected, The top speed on the Guy was 51 mph - even snails were passing me on the motorway.

The route I took was to junction three on the M4 and then across to Harrow thereby avoiding the busy routes of London. I delivered the Guy, then I made my way to Paddington Station and caught a train to Exeter. The plan was to catch another train to Eggesford and telephone from there and someone would pick me up with a car.

I just managed to catch the train at Waterloo and as the train pulled out of the station I decided it was time for lunch, it had been a few hours since I had breakfast at one of the service stations on the M5.

The only other occupant of the compartment was a lad, about seventeen years old. He didn't take the sandwich I offered. I told him that I had stared work as five that morning so this was an early lunch.

I told him that I came from North Devon and that I had delivered a lorry to Harrow in North West London and now I was returning to North Devon.

'That sounds like a good job,' he said.

'Unfortunately, it's a one off, the lorry was on hire for a few weeks and I had to return it to its depot.'

I got to Exeter and then caught the Barnstaple train that would take me to Eggesford station. I decided to go on to King's Nympton station and get off there as it was a few miles closer to South Molton.

I got off the train at King's Nympton only to find that there was no telephone. Plan B - I went out to the road and within five minutes I had a lift from Dezzy who drove for M. Way & Son Transport. Twenty minutes later I was in South Molton square where there is a telephone box. I phoned the Concrete Works and told them that I was back in South Molton and therefore did not need a lift and I would see them in the morning.

A few weeks later I was working in the block shed when Bill Rumsam and another man came up to me. 'Snuffy (my nick name) do you think you can help this man?' he asked.

'I'll try. What's the problem?'

The man said that his firm was erecting an agricultural building at a farm and they had been getting their concrete from Ready-Mix South West. The problem was that the drivers would not go into the farm yard where the building was being erected. This meant that a dumper had to be used to get the concrete on site. This was slow, and awkward to get the concrete into post holes. Would I be able to get the Foden onto the site? I told him that I had been on that particular farm with a tipper lorry a few weeks ago and there was no problem at all.

The next morning I took a load of ready-mix concrete out to the farm. I drove down the farm lane and into the sloping yard, parked the lorry and went look at the site. It's always a good idea to look first and see where you are required to get to. In this case it was through a gateway and on to a hard cored area about fifteen feet wide and situated at one end of the shed. The shed was on the right and on the left was a steep grass slope. The foreman asked if I could get into the shed. He would like some concrete put around the base of each of the vertical steel girders. A long job at the best of times, with a dumper it would be a nightmare.

'Is it ok to drive up the grass slope?' I asked. 'That way I can point the lorry in the right direction and reverse right down through the shed.' The floor of the shed was hard cored.

The foreman gave me a funny look, like most customers do when I suggest something that most other lorries would never be able to do.

'Drive where you want as long as you can get in the shed. We thought we would have to use the dumper from this point.'

'No, I think that I can get to all the steels. You should be able to fill the pits straight from the chute.'

'That would really save us some time if you can do that,' he said.

'Let's have a go,' I replied as I went to get the lorry.

I drove through the gateway and as close to the shed as was possible. I selected low third and proceeded to drive up the slope. When the rear of the lorry was pointing at a gap between the steels I stopped and reversed back beside the first steel. As the floor of the shed was sloping it was decided to start at the top and work down the slope. With me doing the reversing and the foreman working the drum controls the lorry was quickly unloaded. To get out of the shed it was necessary to drive up the slope again and reverse down and back along the hard core, as the ground was dry very little damage was done to the slope.

The foreman was delighted and said that they would get the rest of the concrete from South Molton Concrete Works. True to his word the foreman got all the concrete from us as long as the Foden delivered it.

It also cheered up 'Rumbo' as Bill Rumsam was known. There is a lot of concrete in an agricultural building and this firm would now get it all from us, also the concrete for any future work that they did in North Devon. Another success for 'Thunderbird Two and International Rescue'.

The mixer on the Foden was made by Stothard and Pitt and was a different make than the one fitted to Ralph's Bison and they revolved in opposite directions. I never realised this until Ralph was on holiday and I had to drive the Bison. I reversed under the plant and put the drum turning and went up the front of the lorry to fill the water tank. There was the sound of rushing water as Ern Dennis, the batcher, put some water into the mixer. Thankfully water was always put in first. I ran to the back of the lorry, wading through gallons of water. At the same time as Ern poked his head out of the shed door.

'What's going on?' he shouted.

'My mistake, I didn't check that the drum was revolving in the right direction. It works the opposite way round, to the Foden.'

All this took place as Bill Rumsam walked around the corner showing the new manager around the operation.

I put the mixer going the right way and carried on regardless as Bill gave me a very questionable look.

North Devon Scaffold had a Commer Pick-up; a Simca van for Des Goldsworthy the manager, and a Dodge 500 series four-wheel lorry. The Dodge was unusual as it was a long-wheel base vehicle but was fitted with a tipping body and low wooden sides. Most tippers are short-wheel base.

The driver's name was Roland and he suddenly left the company.

It was decided that George Roper would drive the Dodge. George was getting near to retirement age and didn't like that idea at all.

The steel scaffold tubes had to be loaded by hand and in a certain order, to avoid over-loading the rear axle. The scaffolders, who were on target work (a type of bonus system) liked to have the different lengths of tubes unloaded and stacked in their own stack.

The first couple of loads George just tipped out all the tubes and drove back to the yard. The danger of this is that the longer lengths of tube could easily be bent. Needless to say the scaffolders were not happy and complained to Des Goldsworthy.

Des, not the most diplomatic person I have ever met, told George he had to unload the tubes by hand.

George did this for a week and then refused to do it any more.

I was then sent down to Barnstaple where the scaffolding company was in the process of moving to new premises.

Life wasn't too bad, I was a lot younger than George so the work wasn't too hard for me.

The day started with driving the Dodge to Nott's Quarry and loading with quarry rubble (a mixture of rocks, stone and mud). Then it was off to the new yard where the drive needed to be hard-cored. As I drove slowly down the drive, tipping the body as I went. The result was a line of rubble spread along a length of the drive which Les, the yard man, and myself would level off. The rest of the day was spent delivering and collecting scaffolding at various sites around North Devon and West Somerset. In the afternoon, if there was time, I would collect a load of chippings either at Little Silver Quarry, North West of Barnstaple, or at Nott's Quarry and deliver it to the Concrete Works.

The company started to expand and took on more scaffolders and it wasn't long before I started to help put up and take down scaffolding.

Needless to say this led to a row with Des. I told him that if I was doing scaffolding then I wanted extra money. He got a bit excited, caught hold of my collar and then - after a row - he sacked me.

I drove the lorry to the High Street in Barnstaple where the lads were scaffolding one of the buildings and needed some more tube. As I was unloading I spotted Des Goldsworthy's van coming around the corner. I had already told the lads what had happened in the yard. I shouted to them that Des was coming and I put on my miserable face and started unloading the smaller tubes one by one, and waited for the fun to begin. Normally I would pick up 5 or 6 at a time.

Des got out of the van and walked over to me.

'What are you doing?' he asked.'

'Unloading the lorry.'

'You need to unload more than one tube at a time. you'll be there all f***ing day.'

'Why should I work my arse off for you? I asked. 'You just sacked me.'

'Yeah, I'm sorry about that. I didn't mean it; I just lost my temper. I will pay you extra money when you are actually scaffolding and not just driving the lorry. You happy with that?'

The scaffolders were my witnesses to what he said. So I looked at Des, said that would be fair and accepted his offer. I turned around, picked up 6 small tubes from the bed of the lorry, and saw that Des was smiling.

I said to him, 'There is actually one small detail: you can't sack me anyway. I'm not employed by you, only on hire.'

The scaffolders laughed, Des stopped smiling. but he did keep to his word.

A few weeks later we had to scaffold the front of an empty block of old flats in Westward Ho!

I drove the lorry down there with two scaffolders as passengers and we started to build the first lift. Each level is called a lift. By the time they had that up the long tubes were leaning against it for the next lift. Then I carried bags of fittings - and the short tubes - up the stairs of the flats and put them in the open windows on each floor. Then I parked the lorry alongside the scaffolding and stood the boards upright ready to pass up for the last, and top, lift.

We arrived back in the yard about two-thirty and Des asked what we were doing. When he was told that the job was finished he told us that he had allowed all day to do it. I had proved that I was worth the extra money.

Scaffolding is not without its hazards. In the winter the tubes freeze so hard that they stick to your hand. Removing the tube can result in loss of skin. I was fortunate to have a friendly Policeman who used to give me his worn gloves. Leather work gloves were not available in those days in the shops.

I was driving along in the Dodge one day when it suddenly turned right for no apparent reason. So I stopped, checked the wheel nuts were tight and that none of the tyres were punctured. The front wheels seemed tight, with no wobble on the wheel-bearings. No obvious defect found, I carried on driving. Over the next couple of days it did it a couple of more times, so I reported it to Des - there was no vehicle defects book in the cab to fill in. Over the next couple of days nothing was done about it and Friday night at the dart match I mentioned it to George Roper. I have an idea, he said and Sunday night we were both in the house of Mr Hockaday who worked for the Department of the Environment as a vehicle inspector. He said next time you are stopped somewhere give me a ring and I will come and issue the vehicle with a GV9 notice. Vehicle inspectors were not allowed to stop a vehicle but could check it if it was already stopped. A GV9 notice prohibits the movement of a vehicle until the listed defects are rectified.

On the Monday the Concrete Works had a phone call from the General Workers Union who wanted to know why the company's drivers were driving defective vehicles. On the Tuesday the Dodge went into Cox's garage and the steering joints were found to be worn and were replaced. The lorry drove perfect after that. Thursday morning I was driving through South Molton and Mr Hockaday, who was travelling in the opposite direction flagged me down.

'When are you going to phone me?' he asked.

'I was going to ring you tonight.' I replied. I told him about the phone call from the Union and that the lorry had been in the garage for the last two days to have the steering problem sorted out. I also thanked him for his time.

It was only a few months later that the Dodge was sold and a new Leyland Terrier was bought to replace it. The Terrier had a seven-ton payload and could be driven by anyone with a car licence. The Commer was also sold and replaced by a Leyland FG pick-up that could carry more weight than the Commer pick-up.

The amount of work for the scaffold firm was increasing and more men were employed and trained. While the training was taking place I stayed on hire to the firm.

Scaffolding bridges for the County Council was one of the contracts Des picked up. These were not the easiest job to do. Often you would be up to your waste in cold water and, although waders were provided, it was still pretty uncomfortable.

Barnstaple long bridge was the worst job and much of the work had to be done at low tide. When carrying the scaffold materials one had to dodge the pedestrians on the foot way. The bridge parapet is quite high and wide so that I had to lie on my stomach to pass materials up and down to the scaffolders. A most uncomfortable job.

A bridge at Beaford had scaffold put up on both sides so that the stone work could be repointed. When the job was finished I took the Dodge and two scaffolders. Billy Chugg and Peter Cobley, out to Beaford to take the scaffold down.

I parked on the single lane bridge and Bill and Peter started to dismantle one side, passing each tube up to me as they unclipped it, I stacked it on the lorry. Bill and Peter were both experienced scaffolders and I had to keep moving to keep up with them. One side finished we stopped for something to eat and then started on the other side. All was going well and the lads had got down to the lower lift, which meant I had to reach further over the bridge to reach the tube that they were passing up.

It was, lean-over, take tube while standing on the parapet, turn around at the same time as lifting the tube or plank. Then step across to the inch thick side board of the lorry and stack the item that I was carrying. Spin back around step on side board, onto parapet and lean over for the next item. Doing this one gets into a rhythm and one can also get complacent which is not a good idea.

I remember hopping from the side of the lorry onto the bridge and then I went right over the parapet. I missed the scaffolding and did a lovely dive into the River Torridge. Fortunately it was deep enough to break my fall. I surfaced and stood up and checked every thing. Arms, legs, every thing seemed to work. Five minutes later, if you had happened to pass by, you would have seen a man in the back of a lorry, stood in his underpants and big boots, stacking steel tube, while his clothes dried on the cab roof in the afternoon sun.

A few months later I took the Leyland Terrier to a bridge near Bampton, Devon. With me was Martin, a lad who had been with the firm for about eighteen months and another man, about twenty-five who had started that morning. The job was pretty straight-forward: take down the scaffolding on both sides of the bridge and load it onto the lorry and take it back to Barnstaple. Martin and I stood in the river and passed the new man the boards, fittings and tube, instructing him how to stack it. The job finished we got ready to start back and the new man said that Des had given him permission to drive the lorry. I questioned that but he assured me he was telling the truth. So off we went, with him driving and Martin and myself sat on the double passenger seat.

I could tell straight away that he hadn't had a lot of experience driving small lorries. It was just a few minutes before we started up the twisting Black Cat hill. Rather than settle for a slow slog in second gear the driver decided to rev the engine to maximum and then do a quick gear change to third gear.

This is something that you cannot really do, even in a small lorry, but he went for it. At maximum engine revs he pushed down the clutch pedal, jammed the gear lever forward, for what was only his second attempt to change into third gear. Gear selected, he released the clutch pedal. There was a screaming noise from the engine, followed immediately by a loud bang from the rear of the lorry. His three-second gear change had resulted in the differential, in the back axle, disintegrating into several small pieces.

The lorry rolled to a halt and we all got out to inspect the damage. It was pretty obvious that the Terrier was going no further. I told our new recruit that there was a phone in the café at the bottom of the hill and that he had better go down, phone Des and tell him what happened. Also, he should request a breakdown lorry to recover the Terrier. A car stopped to see if they could help, so 'Wreck-it-Ralph' got a lift down to the café.

Martin and I directed traffic and in a few minutes our new recruit was back with us, he had flagged down a car and got a lift back.

'What shall I do now?' he asked.'

'Martin is down that end directing traffic and you can take over from me.'

'What are you going to do?'

I pointed down the hill to where Geoff Barker was approaching in his lorry from the chipboard factory.

'You see that yellow lorry down there, that is the one that is going to take me home. There is no reason for me to stay here, you and Martin can wait for the recovery vehicle.'

I stopped Geoff and told him what had happened and he told me to jump in the other side. Geoff dropped me off in the Square in South Molton where I used the telephone box to phone Des back at the yard.

Des was not happy after I told him what had happened. I told him that there was no need for me to stay with the lorry and so I'd got a lift home. The next morning I got a lift to Barnstaple with my Uncle Arthur who worked there.

Des had me, Martin and the new boy in the office. I told Des that the new bloke had said he could drive the lorry and Martin verified it.

Of course he hadn't been given permission to drive the Terrier and Des was not happy.

I said, 'If you employ liars it is not my fault. I'm on hire to you and have to do what your men tell me unless you have said different.'

He turned to the new man and said 'You are sacked for gross misconduct, now piss off out of my yard. Your money and cards will be sent to you.'

He told Martin to go out in the yard and help the other scaffolders.

He knew I was not happy about the situation and he said 'I know it's not your fault. Get in the van and I'll take you back to the Concrete Works.'

A valuable lesson was learned here; next time someone said he could do this or that they were ignored until I was told different by someone in authority. Des didn't really blame me for anything and we had a drink or two together over the next couple of years.

As the scaffold lorry didn't need an HGV driver I never went back to the scaffolding as a driver but I did a few stints as an extra hand when needed. A few times myself and another lad would be sent out to take down a small scaffold and leave it for collection.

Life went back to a variation of work. At least I didn't get bored. Proper vehicle maintenance was not the top of the list in the 1970s as already has been pointed out. There were many occasions that I had time on my hands so I looked after the Foden myself. My father was an engineer on air-sea rescue boats and from a very young age I practiced a bit of back street mechanics. But the tippers were different, as anybody might be driving them. I went out one day with the Clydesdale and returned with a bent bumper and a dented wing. I had to put her into a hedge to stop her at a cross roads. When the rear brakes were checked there was practically no brake lining left.

A few weeks later George hit a stone wall outside a well known manor house near Bideford. A couple of days later found George and I rebuilding the wall, a skill that I had recently acquired while working for Bill Rumsam's building firm.

One day I was told to go to Little Silver Quarry, between Barnstaple and Ilfracombe and to be there at eight o'clock. Me and Thunderbird Two were going on hire to Pioneer Concrete. This was the start of a happy period in my life.

Arriving on time I was met by the dispatcher, Ian. He told me that Pall Europe were having a factory built at the Old Station in Ilfracombe.

All of the Pioneer lorries were delivering concrete to the site and my job was to stand-by in case anyone else wanted concrete.

Needless to say it was a quiet morning, spent making tea for the other drivers and keeping the pasties warm. The pasties and tea were supplied by Pioneer. There was some concrete for me to deliver in the afternoon and as the week went on there were more and more as builders wanted site deliveries. Also there were a couple of days that I also had to go to Pall Europe's site. There were deep pits for foundations and two or even three lorries would be needed to fill them up. At first the Pioneer drivers used to take the mickey about Thunderbird Two:, she was around ten years old and had been worked hard all those years.

But respect was soon earned by the speed that the Foden could do the journey from the Quarry to Pall Europe. From the Quarry it was uphill for a couple of miles and then down a steep hill into Ilfracombe and then up a steep hill to the site. Thunderbird Two used to romp up these hills and soon gained time on the slower six-wheeled Leyland Super Mastiffs of Pioneer Concrete.

I spent many days at Little Silver on hire and on call. In fact I was there so much that Pioneer put a very large Pioneer door sticker on the vehicle which up until then was not sign-written.

At times, being at Little Silver, was a bit boring but I always found something to do. One day Ian, the batcher - who also held an HGV licence - and I were talking and I said I wonder if the Foden would drive up the Quarry face. So we decided to try as the lorry was empty. The Quarry face was a very steep slope, but not vertical, with a lot of loose stone at the bottom. We got fairly upright and were looking at the sky. Then the limited slip differential kicked-in and we started to go up the face, Ian was slightly sweating when the rear wheels started to dig in and spin on the loose rubble. We gave up, backed down and went for a cup of tea.

The adventure at Little Silver Quarry reminded me of another challenging load. This one was to Farmer Hayze at Sheepwash farm, near the old Molland station. I arrived at the site and went to see where the concrete was required. There was a fairly level concrete yard and another yard beside it. This is where the concrete was required. The site was six inches lower than the concrete yard and on a steep slope. I told the farmer to go and get his biggest tractor and chain. I backed up to the edge of the concrete yard and the farmer reversed the tractor up to the front of the Foden. I chained the tractor to the tow bar of the Foden and told the farmer to stand back. As I reversed over the six inch drop the front of the Foden may well come up in the air and possibly tip over - I hoped the tractor would hold it down. With the tractor hand brake in the on position I started to reverse onto the site, dragging the tractor behind. With the chain under tension all the time there was no lift on the front end. When the front-wheels had come onto the site the Foden was stable and the tractor was unchained and moved out of the way. I was able reverse back to the area they were to concrete. They used a tracked digger to spread the concrete which was fairly dry so it did not all run down the slope. Driving off the site was no problem to the Foden with its double-drive axles.

A week later I took another load out to Sheepwash to finish off the job. I stayed on the concrete yard as they were able to spread the concrete from there.

A couple of weeks later I met Farmer Hayze in the Black Cock pub, which was a few hundred yards from the farm. He bought me a pint and told me he hadn't expected me to drive into the yard to unload the concrete; they were going to do that with the digger.

'There you are,' he said, as he gave me another pint. 'You deserve that you saved me and the boy a lot of work.' God bless our farmers.

Rumsam Builders had a tracked-loader and one day I was asked to go to Barnstaple and help Norman, the driver, with a repair. The track did not steer in one direction, which meant that the vehicle could go straight or left, but not right. Everything on these types of loader is heavy as it is made using thick steel. We got the covers off and then worked out how the brake and clutch system worked. The steering lever is pulled and a clutch on the appropriate wheel disengages the drive and then applies the brake; the track stops working and the other track turns the machine. Norman's problem was the clutch was not working correctly. The problem was put right the next day and he was back in business. Norman was levelling a site for a factory and in the near future it would need a lot of ready mixed concrete.

A few weeks later we started delivering concrete to Pottington trading estate, Barnstaple. One delivery had a problem. A narrow trench had been dug across the site and the steel plates to bridge it hadn't been delivered.

I looked at the trench and had an idea. I told the builders to stand back, drove the lorry back across the site and then reversed as fast as I could. I drove at an angle across the trench and, as I hoped, the lorry crossed the trench with no problem at all. Because it had a short wheel-base the axles were close together and because of the angle there was always five out of six wheels on the ground. To get back again I did the same in reverse. When Ralph arrived he was told about the lack of plates and asked how I had got across. 'Don't ask,' said the builders.

Pottington Estate is on the Braunton road going out of Barnstaple. Supplying concrete to this site took several weeks. During those weeks the bridge, in Barnstaple, across the river Yeo, was closed for repair. This meant that all traffic, including holiday traffic was diverted along one street. This caused a lot of traffic congestion and put extra time on deliveries. It took the Foden about ten minutes less time to do the run to Pottington and back to South Molton than the Bison, in fact Ralph falsely accused me of going across the closed bridge. The truth is that the Foden just went up hills better than the Bison. It would go up Swimbridge hill, a one in eight, in top gear, at about 40mph. Also the hairpin bend known as Devil's Elbow was taken flat out at 53mph - faster than most cars.

Running empty back to South Molton I had a problem at the bottom of Swimbridge hill. I knocked on the door of a bungalow and asked if I could use their telephone. While I waited for a mechanic I was given tea and cake by the elderly couple. There really are some nice people about.

Ralph also had a few days out. He used to go to Pioneer at Exeter where the roads are mainly flat and there is also some dual carriage-ways and motorways. Much better suited to Ralph's high-geared Bison.

I also had a day out at Exeter, alongside Ralph. A new brewery was being built at Honiton, just a few miles from Exeter. A very large floor was being laid and it had to be done in one piece.

On this job I had one Pioneer driver complaining that I was holding him up and he was losing money because Pioneer drivers got paid by the load and not the hour like me and Ralph, so I let him load in front of me. When I went into the restroom lunch time to get a cup of tea the driver was sat there, so I asked him why he had stopped. He told me that he had blown up his engine and the lorry was off the road. As I went out the door I couldn't resist shouting back, 'I bet you wished you had a Foden now. They may be slow but they keep going.'

Pioneer Concrete also had a Newton Abbott depot to where I would often be sent. It took one and a half hours to drive from South Molton to the plant at Newton Abbott and the same time to get back. Three hours overtime before I did my eight hour normal day. Often the batcher would give me a load back towards Exeter so that I could wash out my mixer drum at the Exeter depot and the delivery tickets for the last load would be left at the Exeter depot. I remember the directions to sites that I was given at Newton Abbott. As I did not know the area very well I was instructed thus: 'At the main road, turn left, straight through the town to the Penn Inn roundabout, straight across, up to the Jolly Miller, turn left, third right past the Blue Boar Inn and the site is just down the road on the right. I never failed to find a site. Once I was in a town, I was directed by various pub signs to the site - easy.

Mervyn Mock was a contractor who concreted a lot of farm lanes and yards. He was known for his Triumph Stag car with a silver stag on the bonnet. He always looked a bit grumpy and late one Friday afternoon I was given a load of concrete to a farm about six miles from South Molton. Arriving at the farm around five thirty in the evening I was met by Mervyn and the farmer.

'Alright?' he said to me.

'I'm fine thank you Mr Mock although I do not like working late Fridays,' I replied.

'Take it back if you like; I don't give a shit,' he said.

'No, I'm here now; where would you like it?

He pointed to a big pit beside the drive, 'Tip it into that big pit over there.'

I backed up to the pit, unpacked the chutes and poured out a bit of concrete.

'Is that wet enough?' I asked.

'Yeah, let it go,' he replied.

As the concrete was pouring into the pit he asked me why I didn't like being late Friday nights. I told him that work does come first, but Friday nights I play darts and I like to get up to the pub early for a bit of practice. Lord knows I needed it.

Concrete unloaded he signed the ticket and then he said I appreciate you coming out this time of night, have a drink on me,' and he passed me a five pound note. In 1980 that was more than a FEW of drinks. Perhaps he wasn't such a bad chap after all.

The concrete works had a customer that started building houses in Bishop's Lydeard in Somerset. The village is a few miles from the old

A361, the 'Ho Chi Minh trail' (as it is commonly known) and the customer decided to get his pre-mix concrete and his blocks from South Molton Concrete Works. It took around an hour and a half to get to the village with the Foden loaded and around an hour to get back.

One day, on the way loaded with pre-mixed concrete, just before I got to the site, the Foden started to make a bit of a rattle from the engine. I got to the site and discharged the concrete before telephoning the office. I told the manager that Thunderbird Two's engine had developed a bit of a rattle. The manager said bring it back to the concrete works. I told him I didn't think it would get that far and perhaps I should take it to Lex Tillotson, six miles away, in Taunton.

The manager said, 'I have a better idea, take it next door to them.'

'What's next door to them?' I asked.

'Their bleddy scrap yard,' he answered and hung up.

I'll take that as a 'yes' then, I thought. So off I went to Taunton trying to avoid revving the engine too much. I had only gone a couple of miles when the engine made a massive rattle and then a loud bang. Immediately I pushed the clutch pedal to the floor, at the same time I put the lorry into neutral. As I did this the engine stopped but I managed to steer the lorry into a pub car park.

I got out and looked under the lorry, there was oil dripping onto the ground and creating a growing pool of black liquid. I thought to myself this is terminal.

I used the pub phone to ring the office and give them the good news. They arranged for a wrecker to collect the lorry and take it to Lex Tillotson, also a car to collect me from Taunton.

After checking the engine it was found that the big end had gone through the sump and made a big hole in it. The con-rod had gone through the side of the block and the piston had gone up and smashed into the cylinder head. The engine was scrap and, it was decided, so was Thunderbird Two.

I have to tell one last story about Thunderbird two. In Devon we don't talk about rain because it puts the tourists off. We say a 'heavy dew'.

We'd had a heavy dew for a couple of days, the third day was dry and a load of ready-mixed concrete was required in Torrington. The River Bray was in full flood and to get to Torrington I had to cross the river a few miles outside of South Molton. Fortunately, many years ago, some one had built a bridge over the Bray. There is now a wide, modern, flat bridge and the road has been raised, levelled and widened. The old bridge was a narrow hump-back bridge. The road at the east side of the bridge went down hill to the bridge and was about three feet higher than the road on the west side which was a very gentle slope that led up to a cross roads.

I arrived at the east side of the bridge and where there was a little water on the road. On the west side was a lot more giving the impression that the bridge was an island. I drove onto the bridge and stopped to assess the situation. The flood water went for about twenty foot and the fields either side were also flooded. There was also a red car behind me. I decided to drive forward a little and try to estimate the depth of the water. Selecting fourth gear I inched forward. As the lorry levelled off the water was over the top of the wheels. I accelerated and the bow wave was a few inches below the wind screen. After a few feet the level of the water reduced as the road was now rising up to the crossroads and I was soon on my way again. Looking in the rear view mirror I saw that the red car was stopped on the top of the bridge. Wisely he reversed back, turned around and went in search of another route. The Exeter road would also be flooded so he would have to take the road toward Barnstaple to find a way past the floods. I doubt whether he would catch me up.

If you do drive into a flood and stall your car do not panic. Put the car into reverse, let the handbrake off and turn the engine over. The starter motor should be powerful enough to wind you back out of the water. The best idea is not to go into it in the first place.

A few days after losing Thunderbird Two I found myself with the manager off to Somerset and the town of Somerton. Somerton Plant Hire were selling some concrete mixers. Whether you believe it or not throughout my life I have had premonitions and, yes, many have come true. On this day I was navigating and although I had never been to Somerton before I took us straight to Somerton plant hire. This sounds easy in these days of Satnavs but back then there was no such thing.

There were two vehicles that were of interest to us. An articulated concrete mixer which would be easy to get into tight sites and also could pull the tipper trailer when the ready-mix trade was quiet. The other lorry was a six-wheel Leyland Super Mastiff. For years Leyland had named their commercial vehicles after animals.

The Super Mastiff had a donkey engine to drive the mixer drum which held five cubic metres of concrete and water could be put into the drum from the front and the rear. There was a very large water tank fitted above the donkey engine. This tank held two hundred gallons of water, a massive amount of weight.

It was decided to purchase the Mastiff, a cheque was handed over and I had the honour of driving it home. It was very low-geared and I barely managed to reach a speed of 50mph. The low gears were ideal for the hills around Exmoor and the cab was a bit more comfortable than the Foden. The lorry was blue and white with Somerton Plant hire written on the door. The drum was white and had a blue thick stripe around it, like a screw thread. If the line 'screwed' toward the cab then it was in the loading/mixing direction. If the line was 'screwing' toward the back of the vehicle it was in the unloading direction.

The Super Mastiff was put to work the next day and I found that it was very good on steep hills. One of the first loads was to Torrington which meant one in four hills. The Super Mastiff had the same rounded Leyland G cab as the Clydesdale although the engine was bigger than the tipper. The first time going up a one in four hill I discovered the gear box was different. As I rolled to a stop on the hill I found that the reason I could not select first gear was that first and reverse was the opposite way round to the Clydesdale. I also discovered that the Mastiff would pull away on a one in four hill, although it was wise not to fill the water tank, to keep down the total weight of the vehicle.

On another trip to Torrington two men in suits were waiting for me. They were from Weights and Measures. The building contractor believed he was receiving short measures of concrete and he had called in the ministry men.

The concrete mix is weighed into a lorry therefore it should be correct if the weighing machine is set correctly. The ministry men took me to a weighbridge at the Torrington milk factory. It was found that the weighbridge was built for four-wheeler lorries and was too small to weigh my lorry. I was told that we would have to go to the village of Beaford a few miles away. I refused, as the journey to Beaford would take at least half an hour and the concrete would be deteriorating; the customer may then refuse the load. So unless the ministry man signed for the load I was going nowhere. It was decided to split-way the vehicle. This entails weighing the front half of the lorry on the weighbridge then, driving forward, and weighing the rear half. The two weights are then added together. This gives you an approximate weight but would not be acceptable in a court of law.

The lorry weighed, I returned to the site and the concrete mix was unloaded between two rows of steel road formers. After the concrete was levelled one of the ministry men measured the depth of the concrete in several places. It was found that at the edges of the concrete the measurement was an average of six inches, while in the centre the average was nearly twelve inches. The site should have been a regular six inches all the way across. It wasn't concrete that was missing it was hardcore. It was a very red-faced builder that signed the delivery ticket and written on the ticket was the fact that the ministry had taken me off site to check my weight. This could have been classed as extra time and charged to the builder who is allowed half-an-hour to unload. When I got back to the works I told the manager what had happened. I was asked if I had been given a copy of the weight and I said no.

No prosecution can take place if a copy of the weight is not received at the time of the alleged offence. We never heard another word about it.

Mervyn Mock had a concreting gang and the foreman's name was also Ern. He was a pretty nice chap and very hard-working, as was the rest of the gang.

They were tasked with concreting a farm yard, not far from South Molton. I duly arrived on site and started to pour out the concrete. There was a girl about sixteen years-old helping them and I assumed she was the farmer's daughter. I suddenly noticed that she was stood in the poured concrete in bare feet and told her she must quickly get out. I explained she was in danger of chemical burns to her feet as well as the sand rubbing between her toes. I used the hose on the back of the lorry and washed her legs and her feet. As she went off to get her wellies Ern apologised. The guys were so intent on getting the concrete laid they hadn't noticed her lack of footwear. There was no damage done and the young lady returned and continued to help spread the concrete.

It was straight back to the concrete works for another load for the same farm as the lads wanted to complete a large area that day.

By the time I got back to the farm the sun had come out and it was getting very hot. I was wearing shorts, socks and working boots. The young lady was not present so I asked where she was as she had seemed very keen to help earlier. Ern said that she was going out and had gone to have a bath.

As I poured the concrete the farm house was on my left and something caught the corner of my eye. I looked up at the middle bedroom widow and I could see the girl brushing her hair as she sat in front of a mirror. As I watched she got up and leant around the mirror and was looking our way. She was also revealing the top half of her naked body.

I can only assume that she thought that I had no clothes on as the concrete chute was hiding my shorts. Then she stood to the side of the dressing table revealing that she was not wearing any clothes.

I shouted to the lads, 'When I say "now" all look to the middle bedroom window and wave,' which they did. She waved back and then realised that she was totally naked. I think every bit of her went red as she quickly disappeared from view.

Talking about baths and water, in the summer I used to make sure that there was plenty of water in the tank. At the end of the day there were several gallons of warm water in the tank that had been heated by the day's sunshine. The hose at the rear of the lorry would be hooked-up to the chute, turned on, and one or two of us would have a nice warm shower, still wearing our clothes.

A couple of days later I loaded with ready-mix concrete. 'It's for Mervyn Mock,' said Ern Dennis, the batcher. So off I went to the same farmyard without looking at the delivery address. I got to the farm and Ern, Mr Mock's foreman, was not happy.

'I haven't ordered any concrete and if Mervyn is pushing like this then he can do the job himself.'

I checked the address and it was actually for a farm at King's Nympton. I gone to the wrong address.

There is an ancient ridge way that passes near farmyard I was at and goes to King's Nympton. The road is not that wide in places but at least it was going in the right direction. So that is the route that I took. Through King's Nympton, to the valley road and then a couple of miles back toward South Molton. Mr Mock was not happy that I was a bit late but accepted my apology and all was well in the end. I vowed in future to check the delivery address on every ticket.

To the south of South Molton are the villages of George Nympton and Alswear. From both villages leads an up-hill road to the south and both of the roads meet an East to West road creating a circular route. There is a farm situated practically half-way along the East-West road between Alswear and George Nympton. This farm required several loads of concrete to concrete the long lane. Ralph was on holiday and a relief driver employed for the week. He had the first load to that farm and after instructing him on the mixer controls he loaded and off he went. As the roads to the farm were narrow we decided to go to the farm via George Nympton and return via Alswear. The route was anti-clockwise because the hill out of George Nympton is not so steep as the one at Alswear (Ralph's lorry struggled to climb steep hills).

I loaded and proceeded to the farm. When I got there I saw that the farm was in a valley and the lane was about half a mile long. There was no sign of the other lorry and the first load of concrete had been spread. The concrete gang was experienced and worked the mixer while I drove steadily forward. By the time I had washed the back of the lorry and chute they had finished spreading the concrete and were having a fag.

Usually when some one is doing a farm lane they have a few loads and then have a break whilst they move the road forms along ready for the next loads, usually a day or so later.

This farm job went well the first day. The next day we did the same but I did the first load. The hired guy did the second. I did the third and there was a slight delay on site, for some reason. Whilst I was un-loading I noticed that Ralph's lorry was reversing down. He obviously had not looked to see if I was still there or his eyesight was not as good as it should be. He got within a few feet of me and stopped. When I was ready to leave there was no other way but for him to drive all the way to the road, let me out and then reverse down again.

The next day we were delivering to the same farm and I was going up the hill out of George Nympton and Ralph's lorry was coming down. There was no room to pass so he had to reverse up to the lay by at the top of the hill. When I got level with his cab I stopped.

'What are you doing?' I asked.

'I fancied a change so I decided to go the other way.'

'If you had told me I would have done the same.'

We agreed to now go clockwise to that site.

Over the week there were one or two other things that the hired drive did that seemed a bit strange.

When Ralph returned Monday morning all became clear. The cab of the Bison was full of empty cider bottles. He must have been sozzled half the day.

The rear of a concrete lorry eventually gets a build up of cement and concrete on it. The best way to remove it is use a mild acid which breaks down the cement. This job was done outside the canteen as there was a hose pipe there.

One quiet afternoon I decided to clean the back of the Mastiff. Remember, in the 1970s health and safety was practically none existent.

The back of the lorry was covered in acid using a small long handled broom and a rubber bucket to hold the acid. About an hour later I returned and putting on my safety glasses I washed the back of the lorry using the hose. I removed the safety goggles and looked at the back of the lorry. There was a small area of concrete on the side of the hopper at the top of the lorry. I picked up the brush and brushed some acid on to the concrete then, as a spray of acid descended, I realised that I was no longer wearing my goggles. Too late the acid hit my eyes and I felt a searing pain.

I shouted to Ern Dennis who was working close by. He grabbed my arm and I told him to take me into the canteen which he did. He ran into the Canteen and I ended up running into the wall beside the door-way. He manoeuvred me through and led me to the sink. My eyes were still closed and I filled the sink with water and stuck my head into the water. After washing my face I opened my eyes, one at a time and thoroughly washed them out. After drying my face it was decided to take me to see a doctor; in those days they would see emergencies straight away.

Someone led me into the surgery, I had tied a cold wet rag across my eyes. The doctor checked my eyes and told me that there didn't seem to be much damage and then put some drops in each one to neutralise any remaining acid. I have to say those drops made my eyes really sting and after a few seconds the doctor told me to open my eyes and asked me what, if any thing, could I see. Things were slightly blurry but better than I thought they would be. Off to the chemist for some more drops and after a few days convalescing I was back behind the wheel - with no permanent damage to my eyes.

'West Molland' I read from the delivery ticket. The route takes one out of South Molton, past the Black Cock Inn then turns ninety degrees right, goes basically in a long arc, through Molland village and out the other side. After a few hundred yards you come to West Molland Farm.

This was a distance of around three miles along narrow roads. After unloading I was told that if the lorry was empty I could go back through the 'cover' as a wood is sometimes called in Devon. I thought I would try the wood as it was summer. Every thing was fine, even driving at 20mph, through a ford at the end and back onto the tarmac. I had saved about ten minutes. After a couple more loads I was getting to know the woods and was getting faster and faster. I got up to about 25mph, bouncing all over the place; then I went around a corner and there was a horse and rider in the middle of the track. Fortunately the rider decided it was unlikely I was going to stop and rode off into the trees. The rest of the trips were done at a slower pace.

A few miles from South Molton, on the Witheridge road is a farm that was run by Exeter prison, with prisoners doing the majority of work. I delivered two loads of concrete to the farm. The first load went well and the warder in charge was a good friend of my brother Maurice. After the concrete was spread and the back of the mixer was washed I rolled a cigarette and put my baccy tin on the flat rear mud-guard of the lorry. Some of the prisoners helped themselves and also rolled a cigarette. Cigarettes lit I picked up my tin, got in the cab and drove off.

When I delivered the next load, the following day, there was a different warder - a right miserable sod. As the prisoners rolled a fag he started complaining, I told him that they had worked hard and deserved a smoke. He told me to get in the cab and drive off. He said that he was in charge of the prisoners and he would say when they could smoke. I bet he didn't get much respect from them. He didn't from me.

Working out of Pioneer Concrete, Paignton, I was sent to Channing's Wood, a category C prison at Ogwell, near Newton Abbott. This prison was a bit easier to get into than Dartmoor prison. The prison warder tasked to escort me to the site, inside the prison, opened the door, looked into the cab and said he would walk. Snotty git, I thought, I cleaned that cab nearly every day.

CARE Village was a complex that housed young people with special needs. They always wanted to join in and help when ever they could. The problem, when I was reversing the lorry, was there were always three of four of them stood behind the lorry, waving their arms. I always used to get out and check where I had to reverse to and at CARE I had to count how many youngsters were behind me. If I couldn't see one I had to get out and check where they all were. Which meant they were all shouting, 'Come on!' They really were an enthusiastic bunch. After getting them to stand to one side I could eventually back up to the site.

A lorry driver is expected to do minor repairs as the day goes on and another load was going to push that to the limit. A farm near the village of Knowstone required five cubic metres of concrete. When I got to the farm, a place I knew as I used to deliver there when I worked for North Devon Farmers, I got out checked and the site. I was concerned that the site was marked-out with steel pins hammered into the ground. Typical farmers job: use whatever is lying around. To me it looked like a maze. I got back into the cab and started to reverse. There was a strange noise and lots of shouting, so I stopped. One of the pins, which must have been at least a foot high, had gone through the oil sump on the bottom of the engine.

A container was found and the oil drained. The sump, which was held on by several bolts was removed and taken into the farm workshop. A bolt was found and the hole in sump was neatly drilled out. The hole was made very tight for the bolt. A steel washer and then a rubber washer (from the milking machine) was put onto the bolt. The bolt was put through from the inside of the sump. Another rubber washer and another steel washer was put on the out side of the sump and then a nut was put on the bolt and tightened up. A locking nut was added, the sump refitted and the oil put back in the engine. No oil leaks were visible. After checking for any more tall pins we carried on with the business of tipping the concrete. It was fortunate that the mixer drum was operated by a donkey engine which kept the concrete agitating while we fixed the leak. That repair was still going strong when I left the firm.

While working for the Concrete Works my brother Maurice brought F C E Moore transport, South Molton.

On Saturdays, when not wanted at the Concrete Works, I would drive one of Moore's spare lorries, usually a Commer. We would go to Taunton Cattle Market. Maurice's son, Alan, would ride with me and sometimes my brother Philip or one of my nephews.

One day we went to a farm and picked up a large pig. As the next pickup was a load of bullocks we partitioned off the pig, using the top and bottom gates to keep her safe.

At the next farm, I parked at the end of a lane that ran alongside a barn. We let down the ramp and opened the gates and Alan walked off to get the bullocks. There was no one else about and all was quiet. After a couple of minutes I heard a small sound and when I looked down a large white pig was stood beside me. The pig had escaped. Normally pigs are not easy to move, they always seem to want to go the opposite way to where you want them to go. I needed to get the pig back into the lorry, quick, before the herd of bullocks arrived. Talking softly to the pig I turned her around and she seemed happy to go back up the ramp of the lorry. Inside there was the partition looking fine but the gate was open. The pig was put back inside and the gate was tied up with some binder cord as well as the bolt put across. As soon as I started to walk away she gripped the gate in her mouth, shook her head and the bolt undid but the cord held. The bolt was also tied. I think the pig wanted some company.

Soon after, the bullocks arrived and were loaded and we set off for Taunton. Arriving at the market the lorry was unloaded and then driven to the lorry wash were the float was thoroughly washed out using a high pressure hose. A job Alan loved to do. After the lorries were washed and parked in the lorry park we walked a short way to Station Road and Maurice's favourite café.

After consuming a fried breakfast he would have up to three sherry trifles. We used to tell him that if he had any more he wouldn't pass the breathalyser.

After breakfast I was told that I could go home but I preferred to walk around the market stalls and then wait and see if there were any animals to go back home. I was happy to wait as it made a nice change and I was on a set amount of pay so it made no difference to the firm If I waited around for a while.

One afternoon Maurice had two loads of horses to take home from a gymkhana. The second driver had completed his working hours so I drove the second lorry. The horses were loaded in South Molton around four-thirty in the afternoon. There weren't that many so they had plenty of room in the lorries but were tethered. I arrived back at the destination, Knowstone, a few minutes in front of Maurice. When the ramp was dropped and the gates opened it was found that one of the horses had been kicked a few times by another horse. The owner was very loud in her accusation that it was my fault. Just then Maurice arrived and asked the owner if she knew that the stallion, on my lorry, was known to kick other horses. She said she did know. Maurice told her that she should have said something when the horses were loaded as that particular horse could have been partitioned off. As she did not say anything when she had the opportunity, Maurice said that Moore's did not accept any responsibility, in fact he was considering reporting the woman to the RSPCA for causing unnecessary suffering to a horse. That was the end of that complaint.

The winter of 1978 was a bad one, with a serious fall of snow in February, several feet deep, that blanketed the country. It had snowed hard on a Saturday night and Sunday morning when the telephone rang. It was Mervyn Crook, Rumsam's building foreman.

'We need men for clearing snow. Can you get to South Molton Pannier Market as soon as possible?' he asked.

'Yes, fine,' I replied.

After a quick bowl of cereal and a glass of milk I stepped outside. There was a wall of snow in front of me. To the right was a four foot boundary fence so I climbed on to that and walked along it to the footway. My experience in walking on scaffold poles had come in useful.

It was three streets to the town square and Pannier Market and I eventually got there after skirting several large snow drifts and deep snow.

There were a few other people there including the Police. We were given shovels and asked if we could dig a pathway from the Square to the junction of Barnstaple Street and West Street where the road to the hospital had less snow on it.

First we had to check all the vehicles parked in the square to make sure that nobody was inside them. As the vehicles were up to the roof in snow the quickest way was to walk across them from one roof to the other. Two of us set off, you had to clear a window either side of the vehicle to let enough light in to be sure that the vehicle was empty. Thankfully, we reported that all of the vehicles were empty.

Then we started shovelling, with two in front to make a path through the snow, and the ones behind to widen it. It was hard and awkward as the snow hadn't frozen and was still powdery.

When we got level with the King's Arms two of us dug a path to the front door while the others carried on toward our goal.

At lunch time we repaired to the King's Arms for food and drink as none of us had brought any food. The landlord and landlady, Dennis and Beryl Cross showed their appreciation for us digging them out.

After lunch we carried on snow moving and when level with the Barnstaple Inn we dug a path to the front door of that pub, well. . . it *was* owned by Bill Rumsam. It was still daylight when we got to the crossroads. It was decided that we would finish for the day and regroup the following morning.

The next morning we were split into groups and sent to various streets to make sure that the homes of the elderly were accessible. It was a bit easier to cut the now frozen snow into blocks and dig them out. There was also plenty of tea and biscuits from grateful residents.

Lunch time and it was back in the Kings Arms where I was talking to Ralph Binding. I told him that I was full up with tea and cake. He said that he hadn't had any. When lunch was over I told Mervyn Crook, who had also volunteered, that Ralph and I would do West street and Barnstaple street.

'Fine,' replied Mervyn, so off we went.

We cleared a path to the houses in Barnstaple Street and then went on to the bungalows in West Street. We started clearing snow and I tapped on the front door of one of the bungalows. A few seconds later the door opened and an elderly lady looked at us and said 'Did you knock on the door?'

'Sorry madam,' I said. 'I caught the door with the handle of the shovel (I had a long handle shovel).

'You look a bit cold out there, would you like a nice cup of tea?'

'We would really appreciate that,' I said. 'It *is* a bit cold out here.'

While drinking the tea Ralph said to me, 'You little shit. You banged on the door deliberately.'

'As if I would do such a thing,' said I.

After two more cups of tea Ralph said, 'Keep control of your shovel handle, I couldn't drink any more tea if I tried.'

The next day diggers had made their way to the town and were sorting out the roads. We were given a two-metre lengths of steel reinforcing bar each and told to probe along the edge of the streets until we found a road drain; then clear the snow away ready for the thaw.

By the fourth day the Concrete Works' big Weatherhill bucket-loader was being used to clear roads of snow and I was given the Leyland tipper and told to help clear snow. I worked with a tracked digger who loaded me with snow from the road and I would take it down to the old Council Works where I could reverse up to the edge of the yard and tip the snow down a steep slope, directly into the river.

Two weeks after the snow came we were clearing the old Alswear Road and a farmer arrived on his tractor via a couple of fields. His name was Bill Hill, a friend of my brother Maurice.

'I live over the other side of the hill and I want to go to the pub tonight and play skittles. The other side of the hill is snow-free as I have managed to clear it with my tractor. If you can get to the farm before you go home there is a crate of beer in it for you.'

We'll do what we can,' we told him.

So we got to work loading and carrying snow. While I was taking snow to the river the digger driver was dumping it over the hedge into Bill's field. We arrived at Bill's farm just after four and instead of a crate of beer, were given a glass of beer and some home-made cake.

That was the last of the snow clearing; the next couple of days I had off. I was suffering from snow blindness but after fourteen days of non stop work the bank balance was healthy. All over-time was charged at time and a half and the two Sundays, double time.

It was five years that I had been employed at the Concrete Works. The Ford tipper had gone and George Roper was driving the Clydesdale. Ready-mix sales had dropped and I found myself back on the building sites or working in the block shed helping with precast concrete. Occasionally two of us would be out in the yard straightening scaffold tubes using a special machine with long jaws that closed onto the pole, straightening it. One had to be wide-awake to use this machine for as the tube straightened the two ends were brought in line immediately. The end of a twenty-one foot heavy steel tube could travel quite a distance during this procedure as one labourer found out. As we straightened a twenty-one foot tube, he was stood astride it. The tube used his testicles as a launch pad and propelled him several feet in the air. When he landed he danced around the yard for some time using several words that are not found in the Oxford Dictionary. He didn't make that mistake again.

I was getting really fed up and so it was time to move on. Gregory and Son were looking for a new driver for long-distance work. The transport manager was one of the sons, Roger, who I had gone to school with a few years before, so I arranged for an interview.

A few days later Ralph went in to the Concrete Works' Office and gave in his notice - he had got a job with Devon County Council, driving a new eight-wheeler with a roll-on, roll-off, body. A little while later Ern Dennis, who was Bill Rumsam's father-in-law, came over and said to me, 'Ralph is leaving and now you will be the number one ready-mix driver'.

I replied, 'All drivers should be treated the same and the work shared. Ralph did most of the ready-mix because he wouldn't do anything else. I am fed up with doing other peoples' work here while some of them seem to disappear. I have just told Bill (Rumsam) that I will be leaving the same day as Ralph.'

And so South Molton Concrete Works lost two ready-mix drivers on the same Friday. Ralph and I enjoyed our beer at the King's Arms that night and toasted to a prosperous future for the both of us.

7

Gregory and Son - Part One

On the 5th of February 1979 I started work at Gregory and Son Transport, East Street, South Molton. The company was run by Reg Gregory. His eldest son, Roger, was the transport manager, Margaret Kingdom was the secretary and Michael 'Spider' Warren, was the fitter.

When I started there the company had eight lorries. One Scammell Crusader four-wheel tractor unit fitted with a two-twenty Rolls Royce Eagle diesel engine; four Volvo F88 four-wheel tractor units fitted with turbocharged two-ninety engines. Also a Volvo F86 six-wheeled tipper truck; two Ford four-wheeler flat-bed lorries - a seven tonner and a ten tonner. In addition there were two BMC mini pick-ups, Reg Gregory's Mercedes, Mrs Gregory's Morris 1000 convertible, a Range Rover and whatever car Roger had at any particular time.

There were two fridge trailers; one was a thirty-six foot York trailer with a fridge container bolted onto it. This trailer was over fourteen feet high and care had to be taken when going under bridges. The other trailer was also thirty-six foot long, a purpose built trailer and covered in a plastic coating - this was less than fourteen feet high and not a problem at most bridges. There was a few forty-foot long flat bed trailers used for general freight, and one tipping trailer. Others tipping trailers were hired, as required, to move various bulk loads.

The lorry that I was to drive was the Scammell. It looked like no other English lorry. It was very flat fronted with a leather cover that could be fixed over the radiator grill. It was often mistaken for an American lorry.

The whole of the front radiator grill lifted up to reveal the radiator, which itself was hinged and held in place by a large round handle, similar to many valves. When the handle was loosened the radiator could be pulled to one side to reveal the engine. The oil level dip-stick was easily accessible on the side of the engine, also the fan and belts were straight in front of you. It was recommended not to swing the radiator to the open the position while the engine was running.

The clutch pedal on the Scammell had a very strong spring and took a lot of effort to operate it. Most of the time I did not use it once the lorry was moving. If the engine revs were kept low it was easy to change gear. The trick when changing up the gears was to put it into neutral and after two seconds ease it into the next gear. When changing down neutral was selected, the throttle revved a little and then the gear lever was eased into the lower gear position.

Roger Gregory told me that the Scammell did the fridge work which involved loading and delivering chicken meat and fat to Shippams Meat at Chichester, West Sussex. There was a set rate of pay and a bonus calculated on the amount of money the vehicle earned, per week.

I gave the name 'Humphrey' to the Scammell.

One of the fridge trailers was loaded on a Friday and then brought back to the yard and connected to mains electricity. The load was then taken up to Shippams on the Sunday, ready to be unloaded on Monday morning. The trailer was then returned to the yard on the same day. Tuesday mornings I drove to Chulmleigh, a village consisting of single track roads. I had to manoeuvre up to the front of the factory, blocking most of the street. Robert Mortimer, who ran the Chulmleigh factory, loaded a few pallets of meat and some milk churns full of chicken fat. It was then off to Shippams in Crediton, a few miles further along the A377, to collect the rest of the consignment.

The Shippams factory at Crediton was a fairly new complex built alongside the main road with easy access. Live chickens were brought in, killed, cooked, de-boned, packed and loaded in the fridge for transportation to Chichester factory to be made into meat paste.

A couple of months after I started work for Gregory and Son the Chulmleigh plant closed and all work was transferred to Crediton along with the staff. Many of these girls knew me as I had married a girl from the same village, Chawleigh, that they came from.

The move was ideal for me, I used to get to the Crediton factory about ten past eight and the trailer was loaded by breakfast time at ten o'clock. Tea and a pasty were consumed during a friendly game of cards. At ten-thirty I would leave the factory and make my way further down the A377 to the city of Exeter and join the M5. Then I would cut across country from the Taunton junction to the A303, either through Ilminster or via Langport. There were no by-passes in those days. The Scammell and the newer plastic coated trailer were always looking really smart and was the set-up the boss preferred to have used for this run. There are two really steep hills on the A303: one at Chicklade and one at the junction of the A303 and the A36.

I soon discovered that the brakes on the newer fridge trailer were nowhere near as good as the York trailer. The hill at Chicklade is not very long but is pretty steep (twelve per cent) so what I used to do was slow down a bit before I got to the hill, get a bit of a gap between me and the vehicle in front and then let the lorry role down the hill under its own weight. One particular day I followed the same procedure and as I went along the piece of road at the bottom of the hill I saw that there was a car waiting to pull out from the entrance to a café. I was probably doing 45 to 50 miles per hour and as I neared the café the car shot out in front of me. I had no choice but to go around it and as there was a lorry coming the other way, I couldn't hang about. I passed the car and slowed down and stopped right beside the lorry coming the other way, who had also stopped. The driver happened to be Geoff Roberts from Bideford who was still driving for Taunton meat haulage.

I jumped out of the cab and walked back to the car. The windows were opened and rather than argue with the driver I suggested to the passengers that, in the future, they ride with a driver who does not have suicidal tendencies. The driver was quite apologetic and accepted that he was not concentrating as much as he should have been. Accepting his apology I walked back to the lorry and after exchanging pleasantries with Geoff, I climbed into the cab and continued my journey. A little further along, the road turns to the left and changes to a dual carriage way as it goes uphill. As I started up the hill I waved on a car; as it went past I waved to the lads and they all waved back. It could so easily have had the same result as in Cornwall. This time they all got away without any injury. What will happen next time? Because there *will* be one.

Not much further there was long stretch down hill and at the bottom I would leave the A303 to go through Salisbury and on to Southampton. Following the M27 and A27, I eventually reached Chichester and Shippams Meats at East walls.

Over the previous weekend I had talked with Francis 'Frank' Pidler who previously had driven the Shippam run. He'd given me plenty of information even down to which pub to go to.

East Walls is right in the town and covered a large area. The road in the late 1970s was quite wide and even though there were double yellow lines there was never any problem parking there.

I usually arrived around three-thirty in the afternoon and parked on the street until just after 5.00pm; plenty of time to do some shopping.

When the factory was empty, just after five, I was allowed to reverse into the yard and then alongside the back of the building. Opposite the building was a large boiler house. The boiler-man was called 'Tiger'. He used to make me a cup of tea when I got there and he allowed me to use his shower room. All very welcome.

The security company had consisted of three people: the boss and two others. The boss was a bit miserable. He would let me in the front door of the factory and escort me, through the dark, to my lorry. The other two would make tea for me while we ate our supper from the Chinese takeaway just down the road. One of them would always get me to bring him back a steak and kidney pie.

The first night at Chichester I went into the Cattle Market Inn, close to Shippams. While I was looking at the menu a man offered to buy me dinner. While he went to the toilets, I left. Further along the road was The City Walls pub. In there a school-teacher asked if I wanted to go back to his place. I was quickly discovering that Chichester had a lively gay community. The next pub was the Four Chestnuts, recommended to me by Frank Pidler, where I had a game of cards with some of the locals.

Seven o'clock the next morning a gang started to unload me while I went into the boiler room for a wash and a cup of tea with Tiger. Then it was back to the cab for a bowl of cornflakes. I'd decided that if I was going to do long-distance work I was going to be more organised than I was at Tone Vale Transport. I had a sleeping bag, two pillows, one hot-water bottle (there were no cab night-heaters in those days). One kettle, a saucepan, a tin-opener, a bottle-opener, matches, a lighter, a washing up-bowl, a water-carrier, a thermos, and china mugs x 2. Also washing and shaving articles, knives, forks and spoons; tea, coffee, various tins of food, breakfast cereal, bread, cakes and milk. Usually enough food for three days. Also a weekly spending allowance of £20 from a weekly wage of about £140.

About 7.50am I was empty and ready to roll. There was one time when a churn of fat fell over and the lorry was washed clean using a two inch steam hose which delayed departure. Usually I had to be out of the yard by 8 o'clock.

Mondays and Wednesdays I left Chichester and made my way back to South Molton with an empty trailer usually stopping for lunch before I reached South Molton. The afternoon was spent checking the Scammell and trailer, making sure to top-up the fuel ready for the next day. Sometimes I would take a trailer up to the chipboard factory ready to be loaded.

There was also times when I helped Spider. Spider once showed me how to adjust trailer brakes. There is a shaft that comes out of the rear of the wheel hub. This shaft is connected to the brake shoes. There is a vertically arm connected to the shaft. The arm is then connected to the brake actuator. A large round piece of apparatus containing the rubber bellows that fill with air when the brakes are applied moving the linkage and applying the brakes. On the shaft is a 10mm bolt that when turned in the correct direction takes up the slack on the arm. Spider said that if there is about twenty five millimetres of play on the arm then the brakes should be pretty good. Of course in the large workshop the axle could be jacked up and the wheels checked that they moved freely after adjustment. This never seemed to improve the brakes on the newer fridge trailer. It was rumoured that when this trailer was eventually sold, it was found the actual brake shoes were smaller than they should have been.

Tuesdays and Thursdays I would start about 7.15am and drive an empty fridge to Shippams at Crediton. Load the trailer and deliver it to Chichester. Friday I would leave Chichester and drive to Shippams at Crediton. In the trailer would be the same number of wooden pallets and some empty milk churns.

I would stop for a cup of tea on the way and arrive at Crediton around twelve-thirty. The empty pallets and churns were unloaded and a load of full churns and pallets would be loaded. Tea and pasty for lunch was essential and I would leave around three and drive back to South Molton where the fun would begin.

Gregory's yard was in East Street, the main street in the town. It was also on a slope. There was no parking in those days in East Street, which gave me about fifty feet of manoeuvrability. After finding someone, usually another driver, to see me back, the show began.

The trailer had to be reversed exactly ninety degrees to the driveway down to the yard. The gateway is ten feet wide. After about a hundred feet there was an S bend around a building. Here the drive widened slightly. Next to the building was the workshop. The loaded fridge trailer was parked in the bottom of the workshop and, as described plugged into an electrical connection. This would keep the fridge working until Sunday. The Scammell was disconnected from the trailer and after checking oil and water levels and filling with diesel, I drove it home and parked it in the car park near my house.

Sunday, after a roast lunch it was up to the yard, connect up the fridge trailer and drive to Chichester. The trip took around four hours, same as from Exeter. Sundays I usually stopped for a cup of tea at the Frying Pan Café at Sparkford. The garage is still there but the original café and a house have been demolished and a new diner built there.

After arriving at Chichester the lorry was parked up and then I would go for a drink and either a game of darts at the Forester Arms or a game of cards at the Four Chestnuts. Some times I would go for a walk.

On one of these walks I came across the Victoria pub. The Victoria was quite a large pub with a long reversed L bar. There were a lot of young people in there so I decide a pint was in order. There was no one behind the bar, but after a few moments I could here the jingle of chains and the barman arrived. Several strands of chain around his neck and standing about five-foot four with blue eye shadow. I was served a pint of beer and sat at an empty bar stool and studied the other customers, something people on their own often do.

I soon realised girls were sitting holding hands with girls and boys were holding hands with boys: another gay bar. But wait, what is this, another barman has just arrived from the other bar. He is over six feet tall, wearing a black vest and has a crew cut and the muscles of an American marine. He walks up to a male customer at the end of the bar and says, in a deep voice, 'I've got those records for you.'

Then he turns to the woman companion of the man and said, in a voice that had raised a couple of octaves, 'Oh I just love that dress!'

Another gay bar done, time to walk up to the Four Chestnuts. Now I do not have a problem with gay bars but I like to have a game of darts, pool or cards and in Chichester the gay bars don't seem to do any of that. There used to be a gay bar at the city end of the New Kent Road.

I've been in there a couple of times, the lads were sociable, the beer was good and they played pool - what more could a man want?

I'd arrived at Shippams, Chichester one day when, within a few minutes a lorry arrived from Newlyn Fish of Penzance in Cornwall. The driver, an elderly man, asked if I was going out for a drink later. I told him I'd be going out about eight o'clock where upon he asked if he could join me.

Just before eight he arrived at the front door wearing a blazer, collar and tie and polished shoes; he looked like he was going to a wedding. There was me in jeans and a T shirt.

Now the guys at the Four Chestnuts have a wicked sense of humour and would surely take the mickey if I took our Cornish comrade up there. I decided I would take him to the Victoria and if he appeared to be open-minded then I would take him on to the Four Chestnuts.

Arriving at the Victoria there was no barman in sight so I gently rattled the plastic ash tray on the bar. Again, you could hear the jangle of chains slightly before mine host appeared.

'Yes?' he asked.

'I'll have my usual - a pint of bitter please,' and I asked my companion what he would like.

'A light ale please,' he replied as he took in the gaily attired barman.

He quickly worked out that he was in a 'gay bar' as they were known in those days. He appeared slightly uneasy as we chatted away.

Why is it that men seem to get nervous in a gay bar? It may not be so in the present enlightened times, but forty years ago it certainly was.

After finishing my beer I asked 'Cousin Jack', as Cornish men are known, if he would like another.

He declined and said it had been a long day and he was going to go back and go to bed.

Outside the Victoria I pointed to another pub and said, 'We can go in there if you like.'

'No I'm feeling pretty tired I'll probably see you in the morning,' then he turned right and walked off down the street towards Shippams. I turned left and walked toward the Four Chestnuts. Cousin Jack had failed the test. In this world you have to accept people for what they are. Who are we to judge our fellow man or woman? I never did see that driver again.

The trip to Chichester was usually pretty easy, even during the holiday season, but there were exceptions.

At Landford about seven miles south east of Salisbury, along the A36, at a fork in the road was a transport café that sat on top of a small hill. It was a favourite stop for me as it would be around one o'clock when I got there - the prefect time for lunch.

Eventually the café was sold and changed to a restaurant, open evenings only. Lorry drivers continued to stop there, not realising it was closed. After a couple of weeks the new owners altered it to a café during the day and a restaurant at night.

Arriving there one day, there was an accident at the entrance to the café. It happened immediately in front of me. An empty car transporter had slowed right down to turn across the road and up the slope to the café and a Jensen Interceptor car had hit the back of the trailer.

The Jensen was of fibreglass construction and received extensive frontal damage while the trailer had scratched paint. With the A39 completely blocked someone decided to clear the road. At the time I was chatting to a blond lady driver in an RAF lorry behind me.

I saw the transporter drive up the slope and into the café car park and then I heard a shout. The Jensen Interceptor was on fire. Some people had decided to push it off the road and on to the grass verge. If you are going to move a vehicle that has been in an accident always disconnect the battery first. Those guys had not done that.

Myself along with the WRAF and one or two others ran across to the burning car which now had its tailgate open. The driver of the car was a salesman and his samples were in the back. We formed a line and the samples were unloaded and stacked on the grass verge well away from the burning car.

It took Romsey Fire Brigade twenty minutes to arrive at the scene where they very quickly dealt with the burning vehicle. While watching the fireman, the WRAF asked if there was an alternative route as she was going to be late at her destination. We all told her 'no' as we were enjoying her company too much to let her drive off. Of course she could have taken the right fork, driven a few miles and picked up the M27 at Cadnam. We just didn't want her to get lost. Perhaps the Royal Air Force should give their drivers maps.

Talking about the M27, I had a funny experience one day while driving on this motorway. The traffic was very heavy as I joined at Junction 2 and headed east toward Southampton. After a couple of minutes I got my speed up to around 55 miles per hour and the traffic in both lanes was doing about the same speed. Suddenly it was if I was mesmerised: the traffic seemed to be standing still, and the road speeding along underneath us. I knew that this was not good so I eased off the accelerator and the traffic on my right was now moving a little faster. The spell was broken and normality returned, I had never experienced it before or since and I reckon I have driven a million miles and then some. Tired I hear you say - I had only left the café about ten minutes before.

Ninety five percent of the time I did this run during the day so even in the winter there wasn't too many problems. The Ho Chi Minh trail (old A361, Barnstaple to Taunton) was a challenging road in the winter and so was the road from Taunton to Wylye, in Wiltshire. After Wylye, in Wiltshire, the road is pretty flat all the way to Chichester, the only real hill being Pepper Box Hill between Salisbury and Southampton.

There were a couple of times when I did the run at night mainly because of breakdowns. One time, in winter, I was heading to Ilminster and the lorry seemed have problems getting a grip going up the steep hill into the town. As I gingerly drove through the quiet town I saw a policeman standing in the middle of the road. I stopped next to him and climbed out of the cab. As soon as I let go of the grab handles on the side of the cab I slid across the sloping road. I went passed the policeman and stopped when I hit the edge of the pavement the other side of the road. I managed to walk back to the policeman and said 'I was going to ask you what the road surface was like but I have just found out. Is there anywhere in Ilminster to park for the night?'

'The only parking is at the bottom of the hill that you have just come up,' he replied

'I'm not driving back down there,' I said 'What's the road like to The Frying Pan café at Sparkford?'

'I've no idea but I suspect it won't be very good. I haven't seen much traffic since I came on duty a few minutes ago.'

Then we noticed that my Scammell and trailer was slowly sliding toward us only to be stopped by the 'cats eyes' in the middle of the road. Time to move on, I decided. I climbed into the cab and slowly moved forward. A little further on there was a bit of a dip in the road where a road branched off to the right. The road curved a bit and was also on a slope. The traffic on the other side was stopped with a Dutch lorry in front. I stopped at the top of the slope and got out. The road didn't feel so slippery as it was further back. I got back in the cab and flashed my headlights at the Dutchman. He drove across the junction on the wrong side of the road. I stopped him next to me and told him that the road further on was very slippery. Then I crossed the junction and stopped next to the lorry at the other side and warned him of the road conditions. I then drove carefully to the Frying Pan Café, a few miles further on. There I stayed the night and carried on to Chichester in the morning. It was the first time I had ever been late.

The next time was similar - a starter motor failure at Crediton. By the time 'Spider' was able to source a new one it was dark. The new starter motor was fitted but it still didn't work. We used one of Shippams Foden six-wheelers to pull the Scammell to start it. I decided to head for the Frying Pan Café and hopefully park there for the night. The West side of the lorry park was on a slope and so was the road so I would be able to bump start the lorry in the morning. Off I set but by the time I got to Taunton it had started to snow. The nearer I got to Sparkford and the café the worse the snow got. By the time I got to Sparkford the snow was around three inches but had stopped. I managed to park on a slope and turned off the engine. I tried to restart it but no joy so a bump start in the morning it would be but the snow would have to be gone.

As it was so cold I decided to book a room in the house at the back of the café. I was asked if I wanted a hot water bottle. I told them I already had one. I realised later they meant a female companion. My hot water bottle was a blue rubber one.

I had eaten my evening meal and as I was a bit fed up decided I would get some fresh air by walking down to the pub a few hundred yards down the hill from the café. In the summer, drivers used to walk to the pub in Queen Camel, a village about a mile from the café, down along the C road which backed on to the café. Too far to walk in the snow.

It was about nine o'clock and walking in the snow was quite nice. There was only the young barmaid in the pub and I chatted to her as I enjoyed my beer and chilled out. There is nothing worse for a driver than a breakdown causing a late delivery and aggravation for the driver. A change of scenery was definitely in order. About a quarter to ten the barmaid announced that she had to close as there were no other customers. She said that if I waited at the front door she would give me a lift back to the café. I did as I was told and waited while she locked up and got her vehicle from the back of the pub. I was surprised when she arrived out the front. I was expecting some sort of four-wheel drive and she had a Ford Fiesta, a very small car. She was a very good driver and a bit of snow was no problem to her. I did notice that the snow had started to melt.

The next morning I was out of bed at five, a swift cup of tea and I was on the road. There was no problem bump-starting the Scammell. At that time of the morning there was little traffic and with most of the snow gone I got to Shippams just after seven. The unloading crew were there ready and while they unloaded I had a bowl of cornflakes and a coffee supplied by 'Tiger.' The engine on the Scammell was left running and by eight o'clock I was back on the road. Back at the yard the starting problem was cured. In the dark 'Spider' had missed a black wire that should have been attached to the starter motor, easy to do in a pitch black lorry park. The load had been delivered just a couple of minutes late so there were no real problems and with the lorry now fixed and because I had started early, I went home early.

An annoying, recurring defect on the Scammell was a broken brake pipe. There was a small bore metal brake pipe that went from the back plate of one rear wheel across to the back plate of the other rear wheel. The connection on the near side came out of the top of the backplate, went up over the top of the chassis, then there was a ninety degree curve, the pipe then ran across to the other side of the lorry and after another ninety degree curve the pipe went down to connect with the other backplate via another tight ninety degree bend.

This pipe had a habit of breaking - right on the final ninety degree bend - it must have been a regular occurrence because there was a spare pipe kept in the cab of the Scammell.

The first time it broke was in a little village near Salisbury. There was a garage across the road and the spare pipe was quickly fitted. The old pipe was kept as a pattern for the next new one. A few days later a new one was made and put in the cab of the Scammell ready for the next time.

The next time, it happened in the centre of Southampton. The M27 east of Southampton hadn't yet been built and to avoid low bridges, with the fridge trailer, I used to go straight through the city centre. On this day I was running late and at ten to five in the evening the pipe broke at a set of traffic lights much to the annoyance of a traffic warden. After convincing him that I did not break-down just to annoy him I was left alone to fix the problem. A few minutes later I was back on the road and looking forward to one of Tiger's coffees at Shippams.

The next day after dropping the empty fridge trailer at South Molton I drove down to PM Clarke's garage at Barnstaple. Duncan was the fitter tasked with making a new pipe and he asked for the old pipe to use a patten for the new one.

'It's a waste of time making one exactly the same as it will only break again,' I told him.

'I have to make it the same as the original,' he said.

'It's obvious to me that the flexing of the chassis is causing the pipe to break. What I want is a pipe with a metre circle in the middle between the two chassis members, the backplate connections can be the same. Hopefully the circle will take up any movement in the chassis members. I am not going to accept a pipe that's the same as the original. I'll go somewhere else and have one made.'

After talking to Arthur, the workshop foreman, a pipe was made to my specification. A few weeks later I had the opportunity to look at a later model Scammell Crusader of Rich's from Crediton. On the newer model Crusader the pipe was routed along the side of the chassis to the rear of the vehicle, across the back of the vehicle and back along the chassis to the other backplate.

My design used less pipe. I never had that pipe break again. New addition to my curriculum vitae: 'design engineer'.

One day I asked why a return load was never looked for on the Shippams run. I was told the run was always done like it is and the Scammell is the unit that pulls the fridge trailers.

One day I was directed to Arundel after unloading at Shippams. I collected a large wood working lathe for North Molton. It was a challenge to tie it down inside a fridge but I delivered it safely, the same day. Plus I had a little more bonus that week.

After the lathe job I convinced Reg that return loads, even part-loads would mean a lot more profit on that run. This led to a few loads of bananas to be transported from Shoreham docks to places like Plymouth and Bodmin in Cornwall.

On a winter's day I had delivered one load of bananas to Bodmin, returned to Crediton and loaded for Chichester. By the time that I got to Southampton it was dark and the off-side headlamp was not working. Some thing that 'Spider' could fix the following day. The M27 had little traffic and I was enjoying the drive until I spotted a police Range Rover on a motorway bridge.

After going under the bridge I could see the police car coming down the off ramp. So I eased back on the accelerator and as soon as the blue lights went on I pulled over onto the hard shoulder and stopped.

While the policeman walked up to the passenger door I hastily covered the two boxes of bananas on the passenger seat. Although they were there legitimately it was better that they were not seen as it may complicate things.

The passenger door opened and a voice said 'Good evening driver, log book please.'

'Good evening,' I replied as I handed him my log book.

The policeman checked that the entries in the log book were up to date and then handed the book back to me.

'You only have one headlight working,' he stated.

'That is the least of my worries. I have eighteen ton of frozen chickens defrosting in the trailer. The fridge motor has stopped working.'

'What's up with it?'

'I don't know, it won't start up. It fired a couple of times but won't keep going.'

'I'll have a quick look at it for you,' he said.

I got out and joined him on the cat walk behind the cab.

The policeman pushed the starter button and the engine coughed a couple of times but would not fire up.

'That's about it.' I said.

'I was going to stop in Southampton for the night but because of this I decided to carry on to Shippams at Chichester were they can plug an electrical connection into the trailer or get a crew in and unload it.'

Not wanting to be responsible for 18 tons of soggy chicken the policeman decided to allow me to continue my short journey to Chichester.

I thanked him for his efforts and went on my way. Actually the chicken meat was chilled and not frozen and as long as the fridge doors were not open would remain at the correct temperature for several hours. The problem with the fridge? It had run out of petrol just after Salisbury. I gave 'Tiger' a couple hands of bananas, took the rest of that box home and the other box I sold to the local green grocer.

There was one driver form Barnstaple called Roger Squire and on the side of his lorry was written 'The Squire of Barnstaple.' Roger was an old-school driver and would help anyone. He also liked a prank. After a couple of drinks at the Compass Inn at North Petherton, we walked back to the lorry park at Graham's café. I gave him a large hand of bananas and he looked across the lorry park, 'Have you got another hand?'

'Are you hungry or some thing?' I enquired.

'Just give me 4 or 5 bananas and shut up.'

As he was bigger than me I gave him some more.

'Hold these,' he said, giving me back the larger hand.

Then he crept up to the back of an articulated cattle lorry and pushed the bananas through one of the ventilation slats. He then gently tapped on the side of the trailer and ran back to me.

All hell was let loose as the pigs woke up and found the bananas. A large amount of pigs were fighting over them and the squealing was deafening. Cab lights were coming on as drivers had woken from their slumber. The ones that had recently left the pub were getting out of their lorries to see what was going on. The driver of the cattle lorry had got out of his bed and started the lorry. He drove out of the lorry park toward the motorway and, leaving his trailer in a lay by, he returned to the café. While he was gone Roger and I got into our respective lorries. One could faintly still hear the pigs for a long while after.

Another time after a delivery of bananas, I was running a couple of hours late by the time I left Crediton. I called into a café at Clyst St Mary, near Exeter, for my lunch as it was a few hours since I had eaten breakfast. The café had a lorry park that would accommodate about 10 lorries that had to be reverse parked. When I finished my meal I went outside to find that an army lorry was touching the plastic coated fridge trailer. He had backed-up at an angle and reversed into the side of the trailer.

I went back into the café and approached the four soldiers sat in the corner. Their rifles stood in front of them and were quickly grabbed by them. I told them that one of them had reversed into my trailer and I need them to move the lorry before I could inspect the damage.

As the lorry was a four-wheeler I asked the driver to turn toward the Scammell and let his lorry run down the sloping lorry park a little way. This would take the over-hanging body away from the trailer. This the driver did and after inspection there was found to be no damage to the fridge trailer, the army lorry must have barely touched the trailer so all was well. The driver escaped a charge but I bet he took some ribbing from his mates for a day or two.

I even once had a load of hanging beef carcasses for a return load. My first hanging load but I did know you had to drive it very carefully to avoid damage to the carcasses and not turn the lorry over.

Loaded just outside of Chichester I set off for Exeter and, for some reason that I cannot remember, I took a southern route. All went well until I was going along the Ringwood bypass. As I was passing an eight-wheeled tipper lorry there was a bang and the offside windscreen disintegrated and fell into my lap. As soon as the windscreen went I closed my eyes and stood on the brakes. This particular day I was pulling the York trailer so the lorry stopped pretty quick. When it had stopped I shook my head to get rid of any glass on my head and then I took my handkerchief out of my pocket and dusted around my eyes. I looked to my left and the tipper had also stopped, The driver was giving me a quizzical look so I put my hand through the gap in the windscreen and waved to him. We both got out and walked around the back of our lorries to make sure that no one had driven into us.

I told him that my windscreen had shattered and gone all over me so I couldn't see. He said I was partially past him and when I braked so hard he thought perhaps something was coming across in front of us so he braked as well.

Nothing had hit our lorries but there were cars all over the grass verges behind us. We got back into our respective lorries and I pulled away first and drove into the nearside lane to allow cars to overtake. A couple of miles further on I pulled into the town of Ringwood and parked in the lorry park - this would not be the only time that I had a problem on this bypass. After about half an hour Roger Gregory rang back and told me that if I could get to Exeter the windscreen people would meet me at the cold store and fit a new screen whilst I was being unloaded.

I removed the windscreen rubber with broken glass still stuck in it and cleared the glass out of the cab.

I put the heater fan on to clear any glass from the heater tubes. Then I set off for Exeter. A few miles down the road was a sailor hitch-hiking. I stopped and offered him a lift which he accepted as it had just started to rain. Eventually I got to Exeter and unloaded and the new screen was fitted.

Next stop Shippams at Crediton for an extra night out and a lie in, the following day. On the way to Crediton I came across a minicar stopped on the straight road near Quicke's farm shop. I stopped to see if I could assist, and it transpired the lady driver also had a broken windscreen. After covering the seats in her car I put on a leather glove and put my fist through the windscreen. Then I removed the screen rubber and put it into the boot. I wrapped up the broken glass and put that in the boot. I told her not to use the heater but she would be okay to drive the couple of miles home to Crediton. I drove behind her until we got to Shippams by then she was nearly home.

The above is why lorry drivers were known as the Knights of the Road.

It was just a few weeks later that Reg Gregory asked Shippams for a raise in the rates that they were paying him. He was told that they had given the contract to a Somerset company who would do the job cheaper than the present rate paid to Gregory and Son. I can't help thinking that if they had been more flexible with vehicles that did the Shippam run and therefore getting return loads every time, things may have been different.

So ended what had been a long contract for Gregory and Son.

The next job that I did with the Scammell was removing quarry waste from the Devon County Council Quarry next Nott's Quarry at Brayford to three separate land fill sites. The sites were at Tiverton, Winkleigh and Deep Moor at High Bullen near Torrington. The Scammell was fitted with its own oil tank and pump for tipper work. The trailers were hired. The six-wheeler Volvo, driven by Jim White, was also on this job but at the time, as there was a lot of quarry rubbish to clear, I was sent to help Jim and his Volvo.

Winkleigh and Deep Moor landfills were not easy to get to because of narrow roads and steep hills, whereas the Tiverton site was on a main road. Winkleigh and Deep Moor were fairly level sites and gave me no problem but Tiverton was a different kettle of fish.

The trick, on this job, was to get away early and do two out of three tips, in rotation, in one day and try to get back and load for the next day before the Quarry closed at four-thirty. The land-fill sites did not open until eight in the morning, so it really depended on local traffic during the day as to whether this could be achieved.

Tiverton was basically a hill of mud, the entrance was uphill, from the base, running South to North and the tipping area was West to East from the base. One had drive across the side of the hill to the tipping area and then back downhill to tip. After tipping one had turn right toward the gate and attempt to make it to the exit. In the summer, when the land fill was dry, there was little problem. In the winter it was very challenging with soft mud and little grip.

The first trailer used was a high-sided one about thirty-six feet long. After tipping at Tiverton late one afternoon the tipper body refused to come down and the site operator was not prepared to stay on while I tried to fix the problem. It was either leave the site or get locked in. A tipper with the body fully-up is a very unstable vehicle and there was no way this one was going to be driven across the site without turning over.

I drove at a very slight angle to the top of the site, in front of the gate, and then reversed through the entrance to the large tarmacked area on the other side of the gate. After a quick consultation with Spider back at South Molton I managed to find a loose hydraulic pipe connection. With the connection tightened, the tipper body came down and I was on my way home. There were other jobs that I did with that tipping trailer, mainly woodchips from local sawmills.

Two other drivers did wood chips with the company tipping trailer, Tony Morrison and Francis Pidler.

I was following Francis (known as Frank) across some moorland in East Devon. We were travelling along a C class road, one of Frank's short cuts, when we came upon some commandos out training. Because of the gorse bushes growing on the moor they hadn't seen us coming, but they certainly heard us. It was a seriously uneven road and every time the trailers went over a bump there was a loud bang. The noise must have sounded like some invading army, with the trailers continually thundering like some artillery barrage. When they did see two red and white articulated lorrys bearing down upon them they took to the moorland. I think we can safely say that having routed the enemy Gregory and Son won that battle.

One Friday, nearing 5pm I tipped a load at the chipboard factory in South Molton and again the tipping body would not lower. I reversed back to the road fence and tried to convince the body to move by driving backwards and forwards but to no avail - it would not move. I telephoned 'Spider' who said he was going to play darts that night and he was just off home.

'I can't leave it here until Monday with the body tipped right up.'

'Telephone the tossers who hired the trailer to us and get them to come and sort it out'

The 'tossers' as 'Spider' called them, did not answer their telephone so I left the trailer where it stood away from any other machinery and there it stayed all weekend swaying in the breeze; I also played darts on Friday nights.

Monday came and by loosening some hydraulic pipes the trailer body eventually dropped. The trailer was then taken back to the owners with the comment that it needs to 'checked over.'

The next one was hired from Nott's Quarry. It was a low-sided forty-foot trailer and at the time was not being used by them.

One job was taking quarry waste to a site on the A361 at Bampton. A bungalow was being built on the western outskirts of the town. Between the site and the road there was a little valley that had to be filled in before building work could start and an access road constructed. To tip the quarry waste meant closing the main road for a few minutes sometimes three to four times a day. After a couple of weeks the road was constructed and a nice easy job came to an end.

To get to Tiverton land-fill site meant using the B3237 through Witheridge. This road is a mini version of the Ho Chi Minh trail, fifteen miles of hard work. With the Scammell in for repair I was given a Volvo F88 to drive. The weekend had been a very cold one and the wet, soggy, quarry waste had been sat in the trailer all weekend.

The Monday morning was bitterly cold and I was coming into Tiverton down a long hill, known as Long Drag. The exhaust brake was used to slow the vehicle down. A couple of hundred yards from the stop line at the bottom of the hill I pushed down on the footbrake pedal and nothing happened: the brakes had frozen coming along the top of the hill. With the T junction at the bottom of the hill approaching I pushed harder with little affect. The speed was now about four miles an hour but not decreasing, I needed a little help. There was a stop sign a few yards from the junction so I decided to see if it worked and it did. I slowly hit the sign and it bent over a little I applied the hand brake at the same time and the lorry came to a halt. I stopped the engine and then, after turning off the air supply to the individual pipes of the trailer I disconnected them one by one, turned the air back on and blew out any ice in the lines. I also partially drained the air tanks allowing pressurised air into them and hoped that this would help clear the ice from the air pipes.

It seemed to work and I was able to reverse away from the stop sign and check the damage. The stop sign sprang back upright and the only damage to the lorry was a cracked bumper. The brakes now seemed to work fine, probably due to warm air from the engine being introduced into the system. So off I went to the landfill site.

I entered the site and as I started to tip the trailer it started to lean. On further inspection it was found that one side of the load had frozen and if much more came out from the other side the whole thing would turn over.

I lowered the tipper a fair bit and then went and got the tracked digger driver. With the front bucket of the digger he pushed the trailer upright. With the trailer up as high as it would go we stood back and watched. After several minutes and a bit of sunshine, the remainder of the load finally came out. I decided never to leave the trailer loaded over the weekend again; at least until the Spring came.

Eventually the contract for quarry waste came to an end; I believe the Council then did it with their own tippers and maybe Gregory and Son six-wheeled Volvo. To be honest I wasn't sorry. I was taking home less money than the other Artic drivers mainly because they were paid subsistence money for nights away and the tipper work that I was doing was day work. With everyone sleeping in the sleeper cabs of their Volvos no money was needed to be spent on lodgings. So it was a bit extra money in their pocket.

One of the Volvos and the firm's tipping trailer was on weekly hire to Evans transport of Bideford. This job rotated around the Artic drivers who all drove their individual lorry. By this time I was also on long distance and my wife, Christine, was not totally happy with this as it meant I was away for three or four nights a week.

It eventually came round to my turn doing the Evans' work. To be honest I didn't like doing it. One minute you were white, covered in china clay dust and the next black, covered in coal dust.

On hire to Evans my week began with taking the already loaded tipper to Stoke on Trent with a load of china clay. Kevin Jury was also there unloading his Evans eight-wheeler. He asked me where I was loading coal from and I told him Burton-on-Trent. He said then I had better get a move on as that colliery closes at two o'clock. It would have been nice to have been told that from Evans before I started.

I got to the colliery about 1.40pm. The weighbridge operator pointed to a silo and said the coal that I wanted was in there. If there wasn't twenty tons then I would have to wait until six the next morning before any more was produced. I told him if there was not twenty tons then I would go with what I had. Actually, and luckily, there *were* twenty tons in the hopper.

By the time you have finished this book you will be able to come to your own conclusions as to the cause of the decline of the collieries and the docks of the United Kingdom.

Loads of china clay and coal were delivered by Humphrey Scammell and myself that week, as scheduled. The only thing that Mr Evans had not taken into account was that Humphrey was not so quick as Volvos. For example Humphrey had a less powerful engine than the Volvos and the three hour trip to Birmingham with a Volvo, took Humphrey at least three and a half hours. So each trip to the Midlands and back took at least two hours extra, therefore two trips put me four hours behind by Thursday night. So while the Volvos were back at base, Thursday night I was still in Walsall.

Mr Evans was not pleased; apparently one was supposed to deliver a load of coal Friday morning and then do one or two loads of chippings locally and then go the Peter's Marland and load china clay before the clay works closed, early Friday afternoon. I missed out on the chippings and therefore caught up the Evan's Volvos as they loaded their clay. Mr Evans decided that the Scammell was not the lorry for the job. Hurrah.

One Saturday morning I was given what appeared to be a real money-making job. Monday go to a cold store in Plymouth and load frozen fish for a freezer ship that was tied up at Plymouth docks. After unloading, go to where ever I was sent by a Plymouth firm and load more fish for the same ship. Then stay in Plymouth until the boat was loaded.

By eight in the morning I was loaded and at the boat just after nine. In front of me was a queue of lorries that had loaded Saturday. By mid morning I was on my way to the next cold store. Less than two hours later I was back at the boat and there was an even a longer queue.

The dockers had loaded the boat for four hours and then gone home saying they were too cold to continue working. Why they did not have a break every hour or so I do not know. I failed to get unloaded until Tuesday morning. I loaded and got back to the docks to find the dockers had gone home again. That night all the drivers decided to turn off their fridge motors as a dozen or so motors running through the night makes a heck of a racket. On Wednesday morning I was unloaded around ten o'clock. There was no point in staying in Plymouth; it was a complete fiasco. The lorry was not making any money so I decided to go back to South Molton. I went into the freight office at the docks and asked for five pounds. He gave me the money and asked what I wanted it for.

'I'm going home and that is going to buy my breakfast on the way.'

He was not very happy man and I reckoned there would soon be others doing the same.

Humphrey Scammell wasn't very well; his engine couldn't tick over. His accelerator pedal was pivoted a couple of inches from the bottom end, so to raise the revs slightly I would stick my two ounce metal tobacco underneath the end and that would slightly raise the revs and the engine wouldn't stall. I got back to the yard early so that 'Spider' could sort him out. Before we got Humphrey into the garage Roger Gregory came down to the yard.

'We've got a little job to do. There's a lorry from Somerset, broken down, at the bottom of Factory Hill and we have to recover it and take it down to the lorry park,' he said. 'We'll take the Scammell and the tow bar.'

I went and got the tow bar and tied it to the chassis, then I drove to the Scammell and Roger to the defective lorry. It was only a few hundred yards from the yard. We took the decision to drop the trailer and pull the DAF tractor unit to the lorry park and then return and collect the trailer. The trailer was disconnected and the tow bar, which was about ten feet long, was connected from the Scammell to the DAF tractor unit. I slowly pulled forward until the DAF and trailer were parted. Before I got out of the Scammell I put my tobacco tin under the accelerator to keep the engine running. I checked the tow bar and fixed an 'ON TOW' sign to the back of the DAF.

'Do you want to steer the DAF [no power steering, no brakes] or do you want to drive the Scammell?' I asked Roger.

'I'll drive the Scammell,' said Roger. Unlike many transport managers Roger did hold a Heavy Goods Vehicle licence.

'Take your time,' I said as I climbed into the DAF. I let the hand brake off and, as there was still plenty of air in the system, I waved to Roger and off we went.

We went up the hill past the yard and then it was a left turn into New Road, downhill for about three hundred yards then a right turn, past the Cattle Market and up to the lorry parking area.

All went well until the turn into New Road. We went around that corner a bit too fast for my liking and the same when we sailed into the back entrance to the lorry park. It was a bit slower when we drove around to the front and parked up. This last bit Roger obviously did with Humphrey in first gear.

I put on the hand brake and got out of the DAF and disconnected the tow bar. While I held the bar Roger disconnected the other end of the tow bar and we put it on the back of the DAF. We decided to go and get the trailer and then we would tie the tow bar to the Scammell and go home.

'I don't know what's wrong with the Scammell, it doesn't seem to slow down when you take your foot of the accelerator,' said Roger.

'Let's have a look,' I said and there was my tobacco tin still wedged under the pedal. I told him why it was there and apologised for not telling him earlier. To be honest I'd forgotten all about it.

'You can drive down and pick up the trailer,' he said. He came with me to make sure there were no problems. We had recovered the vehicle in less than an hour after receiving the initial phone call.

And Humphrey's accelerator was fixed by the end of the day.

Devon was in the grip of winter and there was snow forecast. Jim White and I were given the job of driving to Plymouth to load mackerel which was destined for a fertiliser plant in Hull. I was to change trailers with Frank Pidler the following day at Exeter Services and he would turn around and take the fish to Hull. I would deliver the load that was already on his trailer. This would be done early in the morning. Because of driving hours Jim White would drive as far as he was legally able when he left Plymouth; take a minimum break and continue on his own to Hull.

'Which way are we going to Plymouth?' asked Jim

'Straight across Dartmoor. Empty, it should take about an hour and three quarters.'

'Do you think that's the best way? They've forecast snow for tonight.'

'I don't think it will snow until midnight; by then we'll be safe in Plymouth'

'Okay, I'll follow you,' said Jim.

We left the yard at eight and via Dartmoor got to the docks just before ten that night. There were only a couple of lorries there in front of us. Apparently the ten o'clock arrival of the fishing boat had now been put back two hours - all the local hauliers had been told and they stayed home in the warm for a couple of extra hours.

What made it worse was that around eleven the agent, the same one as organised the great fridge boat fiasco a few months before, arrived with his girlfriend. Both of them stuffing their faces with fish and chips while they made light of the fact that we drivers would have to sit around for another two hours until the boat arrived. There were no toilet facilities and nowhere to get food or drink. Fortunately both Jim and I had some tea and sandwiches that we shared with the other drivers. When I got back to the office the next day, I told Reg that I would never do any work for the firm again.

Eventually the fishing boat had docked and we finally got loaded. We then had to park for half an hour with the butts tipped-up slightly and the little hatch at the back of the trailer slightly open. The fish were loaded using water and this parking for the half-hour allowed excess water to drain. A few vehicles had not previously done this and the weight of the fish sloshing around had caused their tailgate to burst open depositing several ton of fish all over the motorway.

In the early hours of the morning Jim and I set off for Exeter Services where I changed trailers with Frank Pidler and headed for home and an early finish - fish for dinner. While I had been loading I put a few mackerel into a new, unused, fertiliser bag with a lot of ice and hung it on the back of Humphrey. There is something to be said for night trunking after all.

Joe Penfold, a local scrap merchant, hired the tipping trailer to take a load of batteries to another scrap merchant in Leicester. Joe came with me and we stayed overnight; a boyhood friend of mine he treated me to dinner. After tipping the batteries we made our way to the steel works at Corby where a load of slag was loaded.

That evening we were back in South Molton and I parked the lorry for the night. The next morning it was off to a field at Alswear where the load was tipped into an agricultural machine that spread the slag over the field. This operation takes a couple of hours as the spreader only held about a ton. It was made worse because the butt was wet in places when the slag was loaded and the slag stuck to the wet sides and had to be scraped off.

I went home a very grey colour, covered in basic slag. Thankfully this was the last tipper job that I ever did.

Above: Aaronson Brothers chipboard factory at South Molton. Loaded trailers were parked on the right-hand side of the drive. The weighbridge and factory gates were at the end of the row of trailers. The factory is in the background. And the silos that the author used to climb are on the right in the log park.

Below: Another view of the chipboard factory drive, with four Torridge trailers on the right. A Torridge Transport lorry and trailer in the foreground. The wood chip drier and various silos in the back ground.

169

Above: A Ford tipper similar to the one run by South Molton Concrete Works.

Image by author.

Below: Foden S20.

Image by author

170

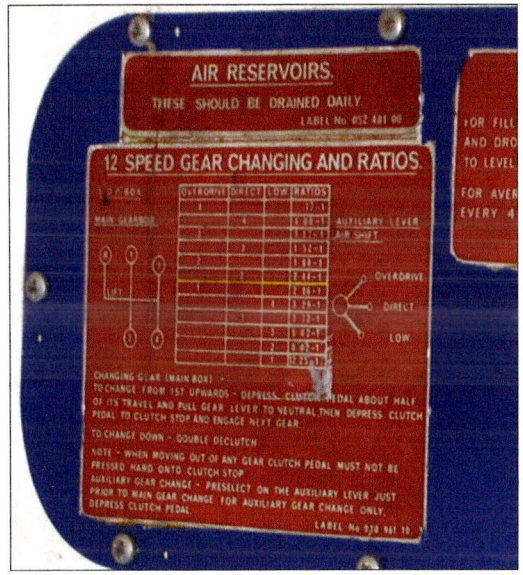

Left:

A Foden gear change plate as fitted to the dash board of a Foden lorry.

Below: A Rolls Royce Eagle diesel badge as fitted to the Scammell Crusader. Image by the author:

Above: The entrance to Gregory and Son's yard, East Street, South Molton. The widow on the left of the entrance was originally the office door. The entrance is 10 feet wide and the road is forty five feet.   Image by author.

Below: Humphrey Scammell, A Scammell Crusader fitted with a 220hp Rolls Royce Eagle Diesel diesel engine. Note the rolled up radiator blind. A rare accessory.   Image by Graham Roberts Autos

Geoff Miller with Gregory and Son's Ford which he drove after he left the chipboard factory. The Ford tractor unit is coupled to the York trailer with the fridge box and the newer white fridge is in the back ground.

Below: Gregory and Son HNX loaded with chipboard.

Image courtesy of Nigel Blunt

173

Above: Gregory and Sons PUN 903S coupled to a forty foot trailer. The last lorry that I drove for them. Taken at the auction where it was sold. Note the Kuhn farm machinery stickers on the front bumper.   Image courtesy of Marcus Lester

Below: A Volvo F88 Coupled to the white fridge trailer.

8

Gregory and Son - Part Two: The Flat Years

Flat trailers are just referred to as flats. These are the type of trailer that I was to pull for the rest of my time on Gregory's or so I thought.

The flat trailer were mainly used for the haulage of chipboard, loaded at Aaronson's, South Molton and delivered all over UK and also exported to Northern Ireland and the channel islands.

Smythe, Torridge, R&G, Pandoro, Crawfords, Tone Vale transport, Bill Hocking and Chris Leather were just a few of the hauliers that also worked at the chipboard factory, along with some owner-drivers who delivered and loaded there.

Pandoro did all the Northern Ireland work, Tone Vale stopped loading there after a few years when the company had a reshuffle and it was decided that running the forty miles from Taunton to South Molton empty was not cost-efficient.

Our loads were delivered mainly in England. Aaronson had four other depots in Leeds, Nottingham, Birmingham and in London, firstly at Rickmansworth and then at Bow, East London.

A large amount of loads that Gregory and Son did were to the West Midlands and Birmingham area. Return loads were mainly slab wood back from various sawmills, west of Birmingham.

Some trailers were adapted to carry wood using eight-foot long removable metal stanchions made from four inch box steel fitted to specially-made holes in the floor of the trailers. Some trailers had the same type of stanchions except they fitted into four inch bearers laid flat on the floor of the trailers.

Fertilizer was loaded at ICI and Fison's Fertilizer Plants at Avonmouth and Ellesmere Port, Cheshire.

From Leeds it could be garden concrete products from Southowram, near Brighouse. This was not a favourite load as it was awkward to rope and sheet and could also take several hours to load.

Other loads were to London but most drivers did not like driving through London, maybe this was because they did not know the city too well.

We had a young driver, Paul Bennett, join the company and he was given the seven ton Ford to drive.

Both Fords were used to deliver to the smaller DIY shops in London. These were usually converted cinemas and not the easiest places to get to.

His first trip to London was a real challenge to him, due to his lack of knowledge of the city. He was very concerned when told that his next trip was back to London. I told him to go into the services and buy an A-Z of London and if he got lost then just stop and check his position. I told him not to worry about blocking traffic, it is better to work out where you are than go round in circles looking for somewhere.

A few weeks later he was in the yard and was smiling as he came up to me.

'What are you so happy about?' I asked.

'Yesterday I broke down at the end of Kew Bridge'

'What did you do?'

'I left a note on the windscreen and went to the nearest café until someone came and sorted out the problem'

'How did that feel?'

'Great and the food was excellent.'

'The stores you are doing are done every week so you will soon find your way around. If you go into B&Q outlets there are little maps of the stores in that area. Really useful for directions.' He soon settled down to the job as his confidence grew.

One job I had was to take chipboard to a sawmill near Yeovil and Paul Bennett also had a load for the same place. When I got there Paul had already unloaded and he told me that I had to weigh before and after unloading. He said that he would show me the way to the weighbridge, about a mile up the road. I told him that eventually, as the newest driver, he would probably get the Scammell to drive. If he drove the Scammell to the weighbridge I would tell him how to change gear without using the clutch.

He found it very easy and gave me a smooth ride even though it was only a couple of miles.

It is strange, in transport, that I used to go to one area for a few months and I would then go to a different area.

One winter it was the Midlands and loading back from various sawmills mainly in Shropshire and South Wales. Just getting to the Midlands could be challenging. First one had to travel the forty miles of hell, the Ho Chi Minh trail. In a good winter there could be a foot of snow, in a bad one, drifts eight to ten foot high and plenty of ice although the 'Black Cat' area seemed to stay free of ice. Then there was the M5 where local, heavy snow storms often happened.

'Three loads for ABC Erdington,' said Roger Gregory one day. 'And two for Leeds.' I was still driving the Scammell at the time. Maurice and Francis were also going to ABC. We'll see you at Erdington they said, as they pulled out of the chipboard factory. They would be there half-an-hour before me but I was ok with that. No point in hanging around for me. The Scammell was fast on the flat but a bit underpowered on hills and often I would let more powerful lorries pass me - one day I may need their help. I got to the top of the M5 at Bristol and it started to snow; and it carried on snowing. Then the daylight faded and even more snow came. I started to pass other lorries parked on the hard shoulder. Little fires were burning under their diesel tanks. English lorries seemed to suffer from diesel freezing; it goes like jelly and won't flow to the engine. The only way to get it to work was to heat-up the tank. On Gregory's we used to put a gallon of petrol in the diesel tank before we filled up with diesel. That seemed to cure the problem.

The nearer I got to Birmingham the worse it got. The Scammell was pretty good on snow and with no major hills in front of me I was pretty confident of getting to my destination.

ABC Erdington was at the end of an L-shaped trading estate just off the Tyburn Road. A few yards from the end of the trading estate was the Tyburn pub and I imagined the others would be in there and a nice pint of Ansells would be on the bar waiting for me. In the morning there would be buttered toast and coffee while our lorries were being unloaded. The trading estate was far enough away from the noisy main road and a quiet night's sleep could be had. With a chip-shop just up the road it was an ideal place to park for the night.

The snow was getting really thick and my speed was down to forty as I passed Strensham services. I thought fifty minutes more and I would be parked up. I was listening to the country music on the tape player and some guy singing about Denver, Colorado. I wondered if it was snowing there. That woke me up a bit and I realised there was nobody else on the motorway; nothing had passed me for ages. I checked the rear view mirrors and there was a long line of vehicles behind me. I guess they were happy for me to be the pathfinder- not a gritting lorry in site but then virgin snow is pretty good to drive on.

As we got to junction 2 the snow was disappearing, the road had obviously been salted here and the cars behind started to speed up and overtake. For me it was the M6 down to 'Spaghetti Junction' then a couple of miles of ring road. The snow fall was lessening. At last I reached the Tyburn House pub, a left-turn and then a right and into the trading estate, down to the end, another left-turn and- there was no one there. At least Maurice and Frank should be there. I decided that a warm pub and a meat and teddy pie was too strong a temptation. So I left a cold cab and went off in search of sustenance and a game of pool at the pub.

Fed and watered I returned from the pub and the Scammell was still parked on its own. Into the sleeping bag with a hot water bottle and a mound of blankets on top, I slept like a log.

The next morning the other two arrived. They'd become fed up with driving in the snow and decided to park in the Services. Apparently there was a pub just down the road and could be accessed by walking down the service road. I did point out that they must have walked a lot further in the snow than I had, to get their libation.

After unloading we all left together and headed for South Wales. The snow had disappeared overnight and we made good time. While we were stopped for breakfast Maurice, who was following me, said that as we travelled along the Tyburn Road and hit a series of bumps, Humphrey Scammell had taken off and every wheel, unit and trailer, was off the ground. A real 'flyer'!

Strangely I remember leading the three of us through the large bollards of a single-lane road works on the M50. After that we probably split up. We collected slab-wood from Ross-on-Wye, Cinderford and a couple of other sawmills in the Forest of Dean. Also the old chipboard factory at Monmouth. These places were all in the same area.

Monmouth was a good place to park overnight. Close to the town centre there was a good size lorry-park with a pub attached to it and there was the Green Dragon pub, just over a little bridge.

The pub attached to the lorry park seemed to play country and western music every night. After parking-up Maurice and I decided to cross the bridge and have a game of darts at the Green Dragon.

Maurice was a lot better player than me although I did have my moments and that night I had a few. After about an hour of losing doubles matches our Welsh friends started to show their annoyance by speaking in Welsh. Maurice advised me it was time to go. As he walked out of the front door Maurice shout at them, 'No matter what language you speak you still effin lost!' I made a mental note not to go back into the Green Dragon for a few weeks.

The sawmill at Woofferton, near Ludlow, was one of the worst to visit in winter. Just a mile from the sawmill was the Trout Café, an ideal place to fill up with food before loading.

The yard of the sawmill was covered in large pits and in the winter was covered in slurry mud. I used to steadily drive out of the yard and onto the road to rope down. I didn't want to get my ropes all covered in mud. I passed the sawmill a couple of years back and the yard is all nicely concreted now, but the Trout Café has gone.

While passing Long Bridge in Birmingham the differential in the back axle of Humphrey Scammell disintegrated and I was towed to a garage in Aston. As it would be a couple of days for repairs to be done, the office advised me to return home. I took a bus along a route that would cross the motorway and got off at the stop just before the M5. It wasn't long before I was given a lift in a Cornish lorry and the driver dropped me off at Graham's Café in North Petherton. I could not get a lift to South Molton so Roger Squires, who happened to be parked at Graham's Café, said I could use the top bunk on his Volvo. The next morning I was dropped off at the office by Roger. Reg Gregory was not pleased. He asked 'Why should I pay for a night out?'

I said 'I took a bus to the M5 and you have incurred no other cost for me to get back here. If I'd taken a bus to New Street station, a train to Exeter, a train to Barnstaple and a bus to South Molton it would have cost you a lot more than a night out.'

'Put like that I have to agree with your actions.'

I was paid for the night out.

Mole Valley Farmers is an Agricultural suppliers that started in South Molton and has now spread nationwide. In the early 1980s they were confined to the South West of England with the most eastern branch at Yeovil. Kuhn farm machinery of Telford was one of the things we carried for them. The worst thing in the world to transport was a hay turner. It consisted of a metal frame connected to four wheels, the same style as a supermarket shopping trolley and no hand brake. To the frame was fixed circular bits of metal with sprung tines hanging down. When the machine was in motion these round bits revolved and the cut grass got thrown around by the tines. The only way to make this secure in the trailer was with ropes tied around the frame. The problem was that when you pulled on the rope the machine would roll toward you. So one side had to be tie loosely and then the other side tied down. Then back to the first side to take up the slack on the rope. While carrying out this operation the rope would get tangled up with the tines. It was a real nightmare. It was a good idea to also sheet the load so if a rope broke the sheet would stop it falling off the trailer.

'A job for Mole Valley tomorrow,' said Roger one day.

'What's that?'

'There's a ship-full of fertiliser at Exmouth docks. The fertiliser is to be taken off the ship and delivered straight to the farm.'

This did not cheer me up. I'd had this before. When you get to the farm the driver is expected to unload it on his own. Well this was not going to happen this time.

The next morning I arrived at Exmouth dock at seven thirty. It did appear that every transport firm in the West country was represented there. However loading was very quick and I was on my way to a farm in West Devon. As I neared the farm I came upon a narrow bridge just before a left hand bend. I got three-quarters of the way across and then needed to turn left. I reversed back on the opposite lock and after five shunts and continually jack knifing the unit, I managed to get the trailer off the bridge and could carry on my way. The farm was only a few hundred yards up the road. I stopped outside the gate on the right. On the left was a cottage, set back from the road, with a lawn that ran down to the edge of the road.

The farmer came out and congratulated me for navigating my way across the bridge, the first Artic to do so. He said he wanted me to back into the farm yard. I told him that I could not do that without driving onto the cottage lawn.

'No problem there - it's our cottage,' he said.

So I backed into the yard without any trouble and parked parallel to the farmhouse, which was separate from the cottage. I got out of the cab and the farmer asked if I could now back around to the right and park next to the shed.

The farmhouse had a similar layout as the cottage, set back with a lawn in front. I told him that I would have to drive on the lawn with the front wheel of the unit.

'It didn't damage the cottage lawn so it shouldn't damage the farm lawn,' said the farmer.

I shuffled the trailer about a bit and got it pointing in the right direction and started to reverse. The trailer went around the corner and I started to follow with the Scammell. I turned the steering wheel hard right to straighten up and as soon as the front wheel went onto the grass it sunk down up to the axle. That was it. The men unloading the trailer had to walk a bit further that they thought and of course it took a lot longer than expected to. After unloading and getting pulled off the lawn by the farm tractor, I turned right at the gate and found a different route back to the docks.

Gibbings and Son sold construction and agricultural equipment from their yard in the village of Chulmleigh. Today's load was a complete surprise not tractors like normal but two self-propelled Combine-Harvesters. After they were loaded on to a standard flat trailer the total height was checked. Normally something like this would be loaded on a low load trailer. The height was under sixteen feet which is the height of motorway bridges. The cutter bars were still fitted to the front of the combines but were within the legal load limit. With the Combines roped-down I set off, about 8.30am for Exeter to join the M5 avoiding trees with low branches on the way, and finally I was on the motorway - my ultimate destination, Boston Docks in Lincolnshire.

As I drove North the wind became stronger and stronger and finally got to around hurricane force by the time that I reached Bridgewater. The maximum speed that I could get out of the Scammell's 220 horse power Rolls Royce Eagle diesel was forty-five mile per hour. The trailer with its high load was getting blown all over the road as I tried to keep control. Then various panels started to fly off from the Combines and be hurled across the Somerset Levels like large frisbies. After what seemed hours I got to the Gloucester area and the winds subsided a bit. I finally arrived at Boston Docks and by 4.30pm and parked at the unloading ramp and the first Combine was unloaded. When it came to the second it was found that the ignition had been left turned on and the battery was flat. The bed containing the cutter bar had been lowered onto the sheets, and the deck of the lorry, to make the Combine more stable as it was transported, so dragging it off was not an option as it would damage the sheets. The Dock's resident mechanic had already gone home so it was a case of wait until the morning. This meant that the following day I would get back to the West Country few hours later than I had estimated.

It was a case of 'sitting on the dock of the bay; watching the tide roll away' as Otis reading sang, or maybe a cup of tea and a cake while watching Annie Jones, Mrs Mangle's grand daughter, on 'Neighbours', on the television I now had in my cab. Tea and cake with Annie won.

The lesson to be learnt here was always check that ignition keys were turned off or, better, removed and put in the cab of the lorry, when carrying machinery or vehicles.

It wasn't long before I was given a Volvo F88, with registration number HNX. Paul got the other N registered one, as Francis Pidler had moved on to an R registered one. I christened my lorry 'HNX'.

After the Scammell the Volvo was a luxury. Sixteen-speed gear box, a bigger engine, double bunks, meaning that my wife or daughter, Ann Marie, could accompany me on trips. An air-powered clutch made gear- changing was easier. It was heaven. It is easy to see why hauliers went for foreign lorries in the 1970s and 80s. American lorries had sleeper-cabs in the 1950s. English manufacturers were still bringing out non-sleeper cabs in the 1970s. Many good drivers left to work for firms which had these new sleeper-cab lorries and their powerful engines. HNX was rumoured to have a bus-differential and would do 80 miles per hour and was fitted with an American police siren. One of R&G's lorries also had one. Hank, on Torridge, had a two-tone train horn.

Ratchet straps had now become common to secure the goods, although I still used ropes to cross the front and back of a load. It helped to keep the sheets neat and tidy. Tachographs were now fitted in the cabs to record hours driven and the speed of the vehicle.

There was a company in Tipton, the West Midlands that used a lot of chipboard. The name of this company was C J Coffin and their yard had no gates. We used to use the yard for overnight parking. I was parked there one night and around midnight I heard a vehicle enter the yard. A transit van reversed up to the rear doors of the factory, one man got out and approached the doors. I turned on the headlights of the lorry, the man jumped back into the van and shot out of the yard as fast as his vehicle could go. There was no number plate on the back of the van. I waited until someone came to work the next day and reported what I had seen. They realised it was a good idea to let lorries park overnight in the yard.

Just up the road from Coffin's yard was a shop that opened at six in the morning and sold groceries, papers and cigarettes; everything one needed to start the day. Going North to the junction with East Tipton Road was the Dudley Port House Hotel.

North of East Tipton Road was a large trading estate where one company had a lot of chipboard, maybe five or six loads a day. Lorries used to park overnight in East Tipton Road but eventually the Police started to move them on. That was when we started to use Coffin's yard.

I had got used to running Sunday when doing the Shippams run. When I went onto flats I carried on running Sundays. It meant that I could tip and go to a sawmill, load and be back to South Molton Monday evening. If the load was further North than Birmingham it still gave me a chance to get back to the West Country by Monday night.

One weekend Frank Pidler asked where I was off to Sunday. I told him that I was going to Tipton and I would park in Coffin's yard. As I was not fond of night-driving I would leave at three in the afternoon and that would get me to Tipton around seven, allowing for a tea stop. Then I would go down the Dudley Port House Hotel for a game or two of pool. Frank told me that he was off to Manchester but would stop in Tipton with me. If he left Tipton at six-thirty in the morning he would be in Manchester by eight. From Tipton one could cut across and join the M6 at Junction 9.

About 8.30pm Frank walked through the pub door next to the pool table and asked what I would like to drink. When he came back with two pints on Ansell's bitter, he asked, 'What sort of pub is this you've brought a chap to?'

He obviously had not been in there before.

'What do you mean?'

'That barman. He's as bent as a nine-bob note.'

As he had not been in the pub before he had not met Dave, the bar manager. Unlike me who always frequented the nearest pub, some drivers preferred to go into pubs that they knew, or with other drivers that knew the pub. Like many males Francis was wary of gay men and Dave, the bar manager, was proudly gay. He wore make up and chains adorned his neck. The brewery thought he was good at his job, as a few months later, they offered him The Great Western over Wolverhampton way.

I said, 'Dave's all right, he's a nice chap.' By the end of the night Francis and Dave were arm in arm singing along with the jukebox.

'That's a nicer boozer,' said Francis as we walked back to Coffins Yard.

The barmaid at the Dudley Port House Hotel was called Sandra Bell and her husband Dennis, known as 'Ding-Dong' was always in the pub playing dominoes - I got to know them very well. When Sandra left the and went down the road to work at the Cottage Spring Pub I also went with them. Dennis was a fitter for a transport company and if work got really slack he could always find me a load from somewhere. If I got to Tipton early I would walk up to their house and have a cup of tea and play with the kids and their Alsation dog.

Just North of the pub was a large area of land where I sometimes used to park the lorry instead of using Coffin's Yard. Next to this waste ground was a chip-shop and I used to go in there and get my dinner and a gallon of hot water to wash in. Even though I always offered, the owner of the chip-shop never took any money for the water.

Round Oak Steel Works at Dudley was a massive place with its own railway lines and several different rolling mills. I used to hate to be near the train as it crawled along the tracks pulling large containers full of molten metal, swaying to and fro, as it passed by. I wouldn't have been able to outrun the molten metal if one ever fell over.

In one of the mills you could watch railway lines being formed. Red hot they shot across the floor, snaking this way and that.

In another mill would be plates of steel some times two or three feet thick, being made. The red-hot steel would travel along rollers through the press and come out the other side. Beside the rollers was a hut and when the steel plate stopped some men would come out of the hut carrying round steel plates fixed to a long handle. When the plate stopped moving these men would walk on it and use the handles and plates to flatten any small defects in the steel. They placed the plate on the defect and hit the handle with a large hammer. Eventually my load of steel would be ready to load. The trick in loading steel was not to go near it until it was hung just above where it is to be place on the vehicle. It would then be guided by hand, usually using a piece of wood or an iron bar, to the correct place to be dropped. You don't want six or seven ton of steel dropped on your head. Steel was usually loaded by the use of a crane fitted with an electric magnet fitted to it. There could be more than one delivery place so the load had to be made with the last delivery on the bottom and the first on top. Obvious you say, to most people, but not to everyone. I used to deliver steel as far South as Hale in Cornwall. Hale was a regular drop.

Steel was a more preferable load as the rate was a lot better than slab wood therefore a better bonus for me. Slab wood was always the priority as keeping the chipboard factory running meant many loads for us to deliver.

Graham's Transport Café and filling station at North Petherton was a popular place for drivers from Devon and Cornwall situated just a few hundred yards from the M5. It was a sort of gateway to the South West and a place where lorries turned off the M5 and headed for North Devon. It was also a good place for a dodgy night home. You could leave your lorry there and get a lift, not just back home but also back to your lorry the next morning; therefore sleeping in your own bed and beinging paid for it. If your lorry is away from home you get paid 'night out' money even if you are not with the lorry.

The downside to Graham's Transport Café was that the meals were frozen and heated in a microwave when purchased. This could end with red hot food on the outside while still frozen in the middle - the very thing I led a rebellion about when I worked for Tone Vale Transport. When eating at Graham's I used to either eat a salad meal or some thing that was fried and freshly cooked.

The girls who worked in the Café were brilliant. Early one morning I walked into the Café and asked Iris,' Have you got any Aspirin?'

'No, take my car and get some from the village shop. It's the red Ford out front,' and she threw me a set of car keys.

I caught the keys and went outside got inside the red Ford and found there was no steering wheel. I went back into the café.

'That was quick,' said Iris.

'I can't drive the car. Somebody has nicked your steering wheel.'

'Try the other side, it's a German Ford Taunus.'

When I returned the drivers in the Café gave me a round of applause - for finding the steering wheel.

A couple of hundred yards down the road, toward the Motorway was the Compass Inn, run by an older couple called Nora and Eddie. Many drivers were regulars at the Compass and even though Nora ran a 'tight ship' it was a very popular pub. Eddie was a little less strict.

Just before closing time someone would always get Nora into a discussion about trade unions, her pet hate, and at the other end of the bar Eddie would be pouring drinks as fast as he could. Eleven o'clock and that was it - bar closed.

I have known only once when this did not happen. I had my daughter with me and I wanted to meet a friend at the Compass but did not want to leave my daughter alone in Graham's lorry park.

We had eaten dinner earlier so when I got to the Compass I asked Nora if I could park the Volvo tractor unit in their car park next to the pub. I explained that I did not want to be too far away from Ann Marie. Nora said that would be fine so I dropped the trailer at Graham's and returned to the pub and parked in the corner. I put the television on for Ann Marie and made sure she had everything she needed. I told Ann Marie that if there was any problem just blow the air horns.

I hadn't been in the pub long when a furniture lorry pulled up and reversed into the car park next to the Volvo. Nora was watching this happen. The driver and mate got out and came into the pub and walked up to the bar.

'Is that your lorry outside?' she asked the driver.

'Yes,' he said. 'I saw the Volvo there and I thought that it would be ok if I parked next to it.'

'What is parked outside of my pub is my business. That driver has permission to park there, you do not. The lorry park is just up the road. If you park up there I will be delighted to serve you and your friend on your return.'

The driver left to move the lorry and his mate stayed and got the beer in. I told him why the Volvo was there and that normally there was no lorry parking outside of the pub. The mate apologised to Nora for not asking first, before parking. Nora accepted the apology and when the driver returned he was made most welcome.

At closing time most of the customers had left so I asked Nora if my daughter could use the ladies toilet while we finished our beer.

'Of course' she said

So I went and got her from the lorry and brought her into the pub. I pointed to the toilets and off she went. In a couple of minutes she was back.

'Thank you,' she said to Nora.

'What a lovely girl,' said Nora. 'Would you like a small glass of lemonade?'

'Yes please,' said Ann Marie.

Nora returned with a glass of lemonade and a bar of chocolate, 'The chocolate is for tomorrow.'

Then Nora looked at us, the few drivers that were still in the pub.

'I suppose you lot want a drink as well?'

'It would be wrong for a lady to drink alone,' came a voice with a Cornish accent.

Nora just smiled while Eddie poured the drinks. Someone offered to pay but she said it was after time and she couldn't take money.

The next day Ann Marie wrote a thank you letter to Nora and Eddie.

There was a friend of mine that I used to meet at Graham's whose name was John Kerrigan. John lived near junction 17 on the M6 and used to deliver soda ash in a powder tanker trailer to South Molton. He delivered near to where I lived and some times popped in for a cup of tea. He became a great friend of mine.

One Sunday morning Frank Pidler was in the New Inn in South Molton. I ordered a glass of Coca Cola, as I was driving that afternoon, and walked over to Frank.

'Did you read about John Kerrigan in the paper this morning?' he asked.

'No I don't have a Sunday paper,' I replied.

'He's dead. He was killed in a fire yesterday.'

I have to admit the news hit me so hard that I had to sit down. Ron, the landlord handed me a copy of the paper and I read the story a couple of times.

There was a wedding in John's family that weekend and when I had seen him the previous Wednesday he was very excited about all the family coming home.

The story said that it was believed one of the wedding guests fell asleep on the settee and dropped a lit cigarette which eventually set fire to the whole house, John got out, but two of the children didn't.

John went back inside to get them. None of them came out. John and his two small children died in the fire.

Through my tears I told Frank that I had seen John last Wednesday at Graham's and how John was so excited about the wedding. As for going back into the fire, it was just the sort of stupid thing he would do. He was always thinking of others and I don't believe he had a bad bone in his body, as my old mum would say.

John had a great sense of humour and was always up for a laugh. One evening we were in the Compass and Nora told us that the following week there was going to be a party put on by the ladies skittle team. John and I were ordered to attend. I can't remember the reason for the party but I think it could have been Nora's birthday. The following week, as ordered, John and I were propping up the bar of the Compass along with a lot of other drivers. At the allotted hour the ladies of the skittle team paraded out of the skittle alley. Nobody told us it was a pyjama party.

We were studying form, so to speak, agreeing that there must be some very lucky husbands in North Petherton, when the front door of the pub opened.

A Ferrymasters driver stood there in his yellowy brown overalls. His eyes were almost on stalks as he saw the ladies. 'I'll have some of this!' he shouted as he took off his overalls and stood in his underpants - which, by the way, were the same colour as his overalls. Ferrymasters must be the only company that issues underpants to their drivers. His actions did raise a cheer from several drivers.

It wasn't long before Nora asked me if I would like a free drink. Of course I answered yes. John's face was a picture as Nora walked off to get my drink as he hadn't been asked. He did laugh when Nora returned with a yard of ale and loudly announced, 'Here's your drink Stephen!'

The receptacle for a yard of ale resembles a large glass hunting horn with a glass bowl at the blowing end. One is expected to drink all the ale, non stop. When it gets to the bowl at the end the glass it has to be rotated to stop a sudden surge of beer. I have to say that I failed and got a face full of beer much to the delight of the rest of the pub. Never mind, it was free.

John was still laughing when Nora returned with another yard of ale. 'Here you are John; your go!' You did not say 'no' to Nora and I am happy to report John failed as well. We were cheered by the fact that you do not normally get free beer at the Compass. Dancing with the skittlers and a free buffet all helped to make it an enjoyable evening.

Another evening and John and I wee at the bar of the Compass. One of the Cornish tipper-drivers was there. He was a bit fed up as one of the wheel bearings had collapsed on his trailer and he was parked-up until it could be replaced. Not a good place to be if you were on a bonus scheme.

He left the bar and went over to join a load of drivers sat at a table. Among the drivers was a woman about twenty-five years old chatting away to them all. It did remind me of bees around a honey pot.

Eventually she made her way to the bar and started to talk to the two handsome men who were couple of years older than herself - John and me. She had obviously had a bit to drink and was in a very happy mood.

'What's your name,' she asked John.

He told her his name and then she asked me the same question.

'Stephen, although most people call me Snuffy,' I replied.

'Snuffy, Snuffy. . . little Snuffy. I like that name.'

We talked to her for a while. She was very pretty and had a large chest - John and I were alpha males in our prime. I can't remember who asked but we were told that her chest measurement was thirty-eight and a half inches. Does the half inch make much difference we asked and after some discussion we agreed it did. Eventually she went off and talked to someone else in the pub.

As soon as she was gone our Cornish tipper-man was back at the bar. He was having a go at John and I for talking to the woman. He was obviously in drink and wasn't really making any sense. He started boasting that his Scania lorry would run rings around my Volvo. He didn't mention John's DAF. Most West Country drivers knew who drove what as we saw each other quite often. Most Scanias would only do about 60 per hour and with HNX good for eighty, there was no way he would even catch me. After a few minutes he went back and sat down but kept looking at us.

Over the night we got the full story. Some driver picked up the woman near Brighton and she was on a week's holiday. She'd hitched a lift with a driver and rode with him until she got fed up and then found another driver to go with. It appeared that she was looking for a new driver and had promised the Cornish man a night of love. In his drunken state he was getting jealous of John and I.

John and I left the pub and decided to have a cup of tea before going to bed. John didn't carry a cooker so we sat in my Volvo, with the windows down enjoying the summer evening. We heard her long before we saw her.

'Snuffy! Where's my little Snuffy!'

John and I got out of the lorry and waited. As I was parked at the front of the queue it wasn't long before we saw her. We were amazed how well she was walking considering the time she had spent in the pub. She insisted that we both had a cuddle and good-night kiss before she went off with her new driver - not the Cornish man, we noticed. John and I went back to our tea.

We were sitting there discussing the finer points of ladies from Brighton when we heard a lorry start up. Then a Scania lorry pulled across the car park heading to cut across in front of us. It was the drunken Cornish tipper-man. I believe that he was trying to hit my Volvo with his trailer. He missed by several feet, drove past the petrol station and then up the main road and, I assumed, headed to the back of the lorry park. There was a long black skid-mark left by his seized trailer wheel. John looked at me and said, 'What a crap driver - he couldn't even get you when you were stationary.'

Early in November Bridgwater carnival is held. John and I arranged to meet Iris, from the café, in the Compass Inn at six in the evening and she would drive us into Bridgwater to watch the carnival. The day arrived and John and I went into the Compass only to be told that Iris was ill and would not be picking us up. As it was a nice evening we decided to walk the two miles into Bridgwater. We had not walked too far when we came across a queue of cars waiting to get into Bridgwater to park. John and I beat them. Iris had told us that we should go for a drink at a pub in St John Street after the carnival.

John and I found a spot near St John street to watch the carnival. It was a spectacular display, all the floats displaying numerous amounts of lighting. Near us there was a youth who decided to stick some thing into the rump of a passing police horse. He ended up with a kick in his stomach. When the rider was told what had happened he let the youth off with a warning - the horse having already dispensed its own punishment. Needless to say the young man left the scene very quickly.

When the carnival finished, we made our way to the pub. Maybe Iris had recovered enough to see the carnival and would be there. The pub was certainly crowded and it appeared most of the customers were local. It was made clear that we weren't particularly welcome. After enquiring if anyone had seen Iris, as we were supposed to meet her there the atmosphere changed. It seemed that any friend of Iris (she was well-liked in her home town of Bridgwater) was a friend of theirs.

A young lady started talking to us, apparently she had lodged with one of my brothers for a few months. I made a mental note to visit my brothers more often.

Closing time came and the young lady offered us a lift back to Graham's Cafe. She had not been drinking alcohol so we accepted, after all it was a long walk when you'd had a few drinks. After dropping us off she gave each of us a kiss good-night and drove off. As usual there were a few drivers stood around talking and asked us who she was but, of course, gentlemen don't tell. It is always good to keep other drivers guessing. John and I had enjoyed a wonderful evening and a kiss good night: cream on the cake.

Rest in Peace John

Jeffrey Binding, Ralph's son, told me and Francis Pidler that he would like to drive a lorry. He had already been out a few times with the local Heavy Goods Vehicle driving school but he wanted to get some experience roping and sheeting loads. He used to use the strap of his wife's handbag to practice tying 'dogs legs' (dolly) knots in the pub. His mum was concerned about him leaving his engineering job before he finished his apprenticeship. I told him that we would help him as long as he finished his apprenticeship. A deal was struck and we got a pint each from Jeffrey's mum.

Jeffrey would come with one of us up to the Aaronson's on a Saturday or Sunday morning and help us and anybody else who needed it. When getting ready to move off most drivers helped each other rope their loads. Then they would all drive off in convoy.

One Sunday all of Gregory and Son lorries, except Jim and the F86, left the chipboard factory and went in convoy to Gordano Services where we all stopped for a cup of tea. A little further up the M5 the convoy would split - some going toward London on the M4, the rest staying on the M5 North to Birmingham, Manchester and Leeds - apart from one. Somewhere along the trip from South Molton to Gordano Frank Pidler had lost two trailer wheels. He was stuck until he got two replacement wheels the next day. This was the only time in two and a half years that all the lorries ran together.

Jeffrey had a week's holiday and I convinced Reg Gregory to let him drive the Volvo up the road. L plates were purchased, put on the Volvo, and off we went.

The first thing you learn is that 8 foot x 6 foot sheets of melamine coated chipboard is like carrying blocks of ice. Once they start to move you are in trouble. Many experienced drivers have lost their loads on the Ho Chi Minh trail, so a learner driver has to take extra care, driving smoothly with no sudden turns on the wheel. It may take an extra five minutes to get to the M5, but a least you get there.

I noticed that when Jeffrey passed other lorries on the motorway he would get too close to the vehicle in front and then almost swerve around them. I told him that when he got close enough to see the rear of a lorry in front he should check his mirrors and get ready to overtake. When he could see the Long Vehicle sign on the rear of the lorry in front he should start to overtake; and if he could read the number plate he was too close to overtake. In that case he had to slow down and get a bit more room to overtake. He soon picked it up and gave me a smooth ride for the rest of the journey.

The first time we went to London, Jeffrey did fine. As I knew the roads fairly well I could give him directions well in advance. At Neasden, on the A406 North Circular Road, there is a long S bend on the two-lane carriage way and a bit further on a pretty sharp right hand bend, both of these needed to be taken with care.

A lot of loads went to a furniture factory at Edmonton. There was a short dead-end road and on the corner the 'Cart Overthrown' public house. There were two factories along that road and also a long lay-by. An ideal place for an overnight stay. There was a chip shop and two transport cafés on Montague Road, the main road that the pub fronted.

It was probably at one of these factories that we delivered. I do remember we had a return load from River Road, Barking.

Driving a lorry along the North Circular Road you were directed around Dagenham. I told Jeffrey to head for Ilford and keep on the centre white lines or else the buses will keep forcing you to stop and let them pass. From Ilford down the back of Ripple to the A13, straight across the roundabout and we were on River Road. Our return load was a load of reinforcing bar for Newton Abbott. A heavy load and low to the ground. Well-roped, one could corner like a sports car. It was ideal for Jeffrey. Now to go straight through the middle of London.

We headed West along the A13 until we came to the three bridges in a row. I told Jeffrey to turn left after the bridges and go along the Highway and East Smithfield. Tower bridge had a weight limit on it, so at the end of the Highway, we ambled across the road to the traffic lights next to the tower. The road curves around and down to Lower Thames Street and Billingsgate market.

'This corner is fourth gear in the winter and third gear in the summer,' I told Jeff.

'Why the difference between winter and summer?' he asked.

'See the grass on the right? In the winter there is no one there, but in the summer it's full of young ladies sunbathing and you don't want to miss anything.'

The road dropped down to Lower Thames St and we passed Billingsgate fish market, and went under London bridge. As we approached the Southwark bridge I told Jeff to straddle both lanes as we are going to turn left and cross the bridge. The road ahead was subject to a weight limit so all HGVs turned left across Southwark bridge. I told him to keep an eye on the nearside as motor bikes, scooters and cyclists would try to undertake. As he started to turn I shouted 'Stop!' A motor scooter undertook and a lesson was learnt with no one hurt.

After crossing the bridge I always turned right and followed the road along the river to Vauxhall. The reason for this was there was a newsagents on Southwark Street that we could park outside and I could buy my fags and a paper.

Other HGV drivers preferred to go to the Elephant and Castle and then along Kennington Lane to Vauxhall. I always thought that this option got pretty busy traffic-wise. Using the latter route, there was an option of three bridges to cross to the North bank of the Thames and the M4. The bridges were Vauxhall, Chelsea and Battersea. My preferred route gave the option of also crossing at Lambeth and Westminster bridges.

The rest of the trip to Newton Abbot went without any problems. If Jeff needed a break from driving then I would take over for a while. It is pretty tiring driving through a strange city when you are learning and the brain ends up working overtime.

We went into Heston services for some food, if I remember rightly. In those days, at Heston, you could actually get a half-decent meal. Another thing with Heston services was there were two lorry parks, one behind the other. The West Country drivers liked to park in the

South park. It was the furthest from the buildings, quieter for sleeping and a short walk to the nearest pub where lorry drivers could sit in the beer garden and watch Concorde fly past at five minutes after nine.

In the Autumn we hauled loads of straw mainly from Hertfordshire and Essex. The man who sorted the loads was called Jimmy. To say he was disorganised would be an understatement. Very often I would arrive at a farm to discover the load was not ready and had to wait, sometimes until the next day. This was wasted time and used to annoy me. I was given a load to collect and when I arrived at the farm the corn had not been cut. I told Reg that if I was not loaded the next day I was going to come home empty. I had booked a day off to go to the Commercial motor show and I was not going to miss it. I suggested that he forget the straw and I would get a return load from somewhere else. Jimmy assured Reg the load would be ready the following day. The next day came and no straw, at four in the afternoon, I set off back to North Devon empty. When I went into the office Saturday there was a row. I pointed out that in the two years I had been employed at the firm I had never refused to take any load, anywhere. I had booked a day off and it was up to the company to make sure that I was home at the appropriate time.

For the next load of straw I arrived at a farm about lunch time, only to be told that Jimmy was supposed to have arranged a crew to load the straw. The straw was in the field ready to load but no one had arrived to load it. I told the farmer I would wait. About four o'clock a friend of the farmers arrived at the farm. A few minutes later another friend arrived. It seemed that a trip to a pub was being arranged, although the men were concerned about me waiting to be loaded. They convinced the farmer to load me before they all went down the pub. In the end the farmer relented and work began. The straw was loaded using tractors with grabs, it was small bales in those days. By six I was in the yard loaded and roped all ready to leave the next day.

I had a wash in the dairy, no hot water, but it was a hot day. The farmer said they were off to the pub if I wanted to come along. I thanked him and jumped into the back of a pick-up truck with the others who had helped to load me.

It was a lovely pub and I ended up playing darts with a very pretty farmer's wife. We hadn't been at the pub long before Jimmy arrived. Jimmy said he had been at the races and had enjoyed a fruitful day -

some of his winnings must have been spent in the racecourse bar by the state of him. 'I'm so glad that you won,' said the farmer, 'as you owe me £140 for loading a lorry last week.'

Jimmy produced a cheque-book from his pocket and wrote a cheque for the same sum. Then the farmer said, 'Now you need to buy these lads a drink or two for loading the lorry today.'

Jimmy wrote a cheque for fifty pounds and said when was gone he would write another. I was nearly trampled in the rush to the bar. I thought it was time that I got a little back for all the times I'd waited for loads of straw. So I ordered my first pint and a packet of cigarettes.

When we got back to the farm, we were all invited in for supper - a monster fry-up. Food consumed, I went to sit down and some one said some thing to me. At the same time I swear that the heavy armchair moved sideways - of it's own accord. I missed the chair ended up sitting on the floor and discovered my leg muscles refused to work. As I was helped up there was a lot of laughing and some comments about the buggers from Devon who can't take their drink. Time for bed thought I and off I went to my Volvo cab hotel.

The next morning, when I woke up, the farmer was sat on the wall next to the lorry. I went into the dairy and had a cold wash which woke me up.

'When you leave be careful you don't catch the electric wire to the outside toilet.' said the farmer.

I had a bowl of cornflakes and then set off for Devon. As I got halfway out the farm gate I saw an electric cable drop to the floor. No toilet light now I thought; never mind, I never do the same farm twice.

Wrong. Wednesday found me at the same farm where the farmer told me that I had pulled down the light cable. I apologised and he told me he had refitted it, but now it was higher. The straw was loaded straight away as there was plenty of help; I've no idea where they came from. The load roped, I decided to head back toward Devon as I had a couple of hours left to drive. Graham's may not be possible - Portishead was.

At Portishead there was an old railway yard, with a hard surface, that we used as a lorry park - there was no charge. A lane ran alongside the yard and there was an entrance into the yard from this lane. We used to drive into the yard using this lane, then the lorry was facing in the right direction to exit through the main entrance in the morning.

There was the Red Lion for a drink and the Chinese for supper. There was also another pub if one wanted a quieter drink.

One time when Christine, my wife, and I walked back from the quiet pub in Portishead, I noticed what looked like a torch shining in an upstairs window of an office block. While Christine kept an eye on the office block I went and phoned the police. A few minutes later a police car arrived we told them that we saw a light. They had a look around and all seemed secure. So I went back down the street with one of the policemen and we both saw the light but the other two policemen didn't. They were a little further down the street from us. The mystery was finally solved, at a certain angle the window caught the reflection of a street light. We were thanked for informing the police of our observation. They said they were happy to check that all was in order.

One Saturday morning found me in the doctor's surgery. I had a pain on the left side of my chest and it was really painful to use my left arm. After an extensive examination he said 'I know what you have done, but I have never seen it before. You have pulled the muscle off the left breastplate. The only way that you could do that is holding onto a rope and jumping off a cliff.'

Would abseiling down a sixteen foot load of straw do it?' I asked.

'It's possible.'

'What happens next?'

'I'll bandage you up and you get a couple of weeks off.'

I thought about this as I left the surgery. Sick pay is not really enough to live on with a wife and two kids. I went and talked with Jeff Binding and he suggested he could use a week of his holiday and he would drive my lorry while I navigated. So that is what we did.

Our first journey out we parked in Dudley Port overnight and the next morning we went to the trading estate to unload. He drove through the entrance but didn't notice the white tips on the grass. At the end of the bottom of the estate there was a left turn. Jeff started to turn the wheel but the lorry went straight on. Black ice on the road. He was going slow so we just went onto the grass for a foot or so.

'Black ice. You didn't notice that the tops of the grass were white?' I asked.

'I was concentrating at where I had to go to unload,' said Jeff.

Another lesson learnt.

The week went well, me navigating and Jeff driving and bandaging me every night. It did cost me a few pints on the Saturday night.

He was getting better training than many who learnt on empty lorries. Going up and down the Ho Chi Minh, Jeff new exactly what gear he had to be in to go up the many hills.

A few weeks later Jeff put in for his test a lot more confident than he was a few months before. He went with me for three days just to refresh his memory. He had only been driving around South Molton weekends as we shunted trailers.

The week of his test saw us go to London and then another load of reinforcing bar for Newton Abbott. This was a regular return load and paid a reasonable rate. His test being the following day we stopped at Graham's were I was going to try and get him a lift back to South Molton.

As we pulled into Graham's, Steve Tapp was there with Gregory and Son's new Mercedes 1632. Steve noticed the L plates and asked what was going on. I told him that Jeff had driven a few trips while I sat in the passenger seat navigating. He looked at Jeff and said 'Put they L plates on the Mercedes while I get the teas in. I'm going to have some of that.'

Jeff had been told that he would be driving a Volvo on his test but that day he was told that the Volvo was off the road and that he would have to take Humphrey, the Scammell Crusader.

I told him that the Crusader was ok but the gear box was worn and so for first gear push the lever toward the left front corner of the cab and he would be ok. Reversing would not be a problem as he'd done a lot of reversing trailers at the chipboard factory.

He did well and despite all, he passed his test. Shortly after he got a job with a straw merchant. Who wouldn't take on a young man with experience of driving lorries in London, Birmingham and Manchester.

It was 1979 that the large Homebase and other DIY stores started to open in large numbers. B&Q, named after Richard Block and David Quale opened their first store at Southampton in an old cinema.

I delivered a load of chipboard to a shop in Fleetwood, Lancashire. I was there 8.00am when they opened. It was a full load of around twenty tons and there was no forklift, so the load had to be hand-balled off. There were a few lads unloading but they were young and carrying a few boards each. I decided to help so I picked up a full pack, about twenty five boards. When I got into the shop I discovered that I still had my chest fully bandaged and couldn't bend to put the boards down gently. I had no choice, I bent over a bit and dropped the boards which shot all over the shop floor.

The manager saw I was in pain and came over and asked me if I was alright. I told him about the chest muscle and showed him the bandage. I also told him that I couldn't wait all day for the boards to be unloaded. He told me that the fork lift hadn't been delivered yet. He pointed down the street, to a café and told me to go and get something to eat and he would make sure the boards were unloaded quickly and they would be put on to the shelves after I had gone.

While I enjoyed a nice breakfast I thought to myself I might wear this bandage for a few more weeks. I was supposed to wear it for a month minimum and NOT work. With a mortgage to pay, I put up with the pain and kept working.

When you drive a lorry you are expected to fix it - calling someone out to repair it is time consuming and expensive. I used to carry a box of bits, a spare length of electric cable and some electrical tape. Large rubber bands made out of inner tubes. These were used to hold the trailer number plate on if the fixing was broken. Electrical fuses and other bits and pieces. In the world of transport you learn to do what ever is necessary to get the job done. 'Adapt and fix' were the words: if you haven't got the right thing then use something else and adapt it for your needs.

Late one sunny afternoon Francis Pidler and myself were parked on the grass verge outside the Massey Ferguson tractor plant, Banner Lane, Coventry. That's were we spent the night as we were to load first thing in the morning.

As it was nice weather we decided to heat some water and have a wash outside in the sun. The slight problem was that neither of us had a bowl. No problem I said as I removed the innards of my safety helmet. I balanced it on the diesel tank and put the hot water in it and after removing my shirt had a good wash.

I then washed out the helmet with clean water and let Francis have a wash.

'This is a proper job,' said Francis as he splashed water everywhere.

'Yes,' I replied. 'A safety helmet is useful - I use it as a toilet, if I'm stuck in the middle of a city.'

Francis lifted his head, spitting water everywhere. 'I hope you washed it out after.'

A new DIY store was being built in Watford on the outskirts of London and when I arrived there was chaos in the store. Bits and pieces all over the floor. As soon as a shelf went up something was stacked on it. It was obvious that they had not prepared for twenty-ton of chipboard to arrive. The forklift would take one stack of chipboard off my trailer and then unload a pallet from another vehicle while the first stack of chipboard was put on a shelf. Then he would take another stack off my trailer. After about three hours I'd enough, went into the store, pushed the security guard out of the way and walked into the office. There were a few people sat around in the office and, speaking to no one in particular, I said, 'As my lorry is taking so long to get unloaded I'm going to lose my return load worth over two hundred pounds. Do I bill *this* store for that loss or do I send the bill to Head Office?'

One of the men got up, came over and asked what the problem was. I told him that it was expected to unload a lorry in one hour and not the four hours it has taken so far. If the lorry is not unloaded in the next twenty` minutes I lose my return load and I want to know who is going to pay it.

He got the fork lift driver to just put the rest of the load on the floor and sort it out later.

I left Watford at 4.00pm and had to get to Purfleet in Essex by 5 o'clock to get my loading tickets for the docks or I would have to wait until the morning. I rang DJV Forwarding who were in charge of the load and they said as long as I was there by five and got the loading tickets I could load at Purfleet Deep wharf. When I told them I was in Watford they said, 'We'll see you in the morning.'

'Get the tickets on the desk. I'm on my way.'

I decided the quickest route would be to take the A110 and head for Enfield and then drive South East and pick up the A13 to DJV's office near Purfleet. With liberal use of the police siren I got to the A13 and it was two minutes to five as I got opposite the office on the other side of the dual carriageway. Traffic was light and there was no other choice but to turn right across the central reservation and arrive at the office just as they were closing.

When I entered the office they said, 'We just saw what you did.'

'Needs must,' I replied.

'Were you really in Watford?'

'Yeah, at the new B&Q store.'

'We couldn't get here in an hour in a car.'

I went to Enfield and then cut down to the A13. I reckoned that would be the quickest way'.

'Wouldn't have thought of doing that,' was the reply.

Friday we were in the office looking forward to an extra day off as it was August bank holiday so I wouldn't go up the road again until Bank holiday Monday. 'I need a volunteer,' said Rodger. 'There's a new DIY store being built in Luton and they want their chipboard Sunday as they're looking to open on the Bank Holiday Monday.'

'I'll go,' I said.

The others left and Roger asked if I was sure. The return load was straw from a farm near Luton.

I realised I would have to load the straw Tuesday. 'That's fine, Christine is with me next week so we will go and see my brother in London Monday and have a bit of sightseeing.'

We left early Sunday morning and unusually I was unloaded very quickly. I suppose it was because they were waiting to get it on the shelves.

When we got to the farm there was a company trailer all ready loaded with straw. It was not normal for a trailer to be left on a farm to be loaded. Not one to miss an opportunity I dropped my trailer and took the loaded one.

We drove to a lay-by at Denham, dropped the trailer and drove the tractor unit a few miles to Northolt air base were my brother, David, was stationed in the RAF.

On the Monday, David, Val his wife, the two children, Christine and I spent a pleasant Bank Holiday in London. Tuesday, after a lovely breakfast, we drove to Denham, picked up the trailer and delivered the straw to Devon. When I got back to the yard Reg Gregory was not happy. He believed that as I had picked up a loaded trailer I should have returned on the Monday. I pointed out that I had made an agreement with Rodger that if I worked the Sunday I would get the Monday off. Also who ever picked up the trailer that I dropped would also be picking up a loaded trailer as it would be loaded by the time that driver got to the farm. End of story as far as I was concerned.

Another thing that annoyed me was that Reg knew that the trailer was parked at Denham without me telling him.

The rule of the road is 'you don't know nothing and you don't see nothing'. With a bonus scheme there is always someone who continuously complains they were always getting the worst-paying loads. These were usually the same people who drive illegally.

I pulled into Graham's Café at Bridgwater one evening. I was loaded with slab wood and heading back to the chipboard factory. One of Gregory and Son's lorries was already there.

'What's up?' I asked the driver.

'My driving hours are up; so I've parked up. Anyway there's not much happening,' he replied.

I said 'There's a load for London waiting for me at the chipboard factory, as I'm the only one that's going to be back home tonight.'

I went into the café and when I came out the lorry and driver had gone. When I got to South Molton. he was coming out of the town, and heading back up the Ho Chi Minh trail, illegally, with the load that I was supposed to have. So much for camaraderie. I learnt then not to tell anyone anything. That particular driver became known as the 'Two Faces' on what was to become the CB radio phenomenon.

Going around the North circular road, in London one day, I was passed by a money convoy. Three armoured Artic lorries carrying money from the Royal Mint, with police motor cycles as escorts. The lorries were painted white and so was my Volvo, which also had a red horizontal stripe horizontally around the cab. As the convoy passed I turned on my headlights and put on the siren. The two police riders at the rear of the convoy thought it was so amusing that they dropped back and included me in the convoy. Straight through red traffic lights, this was great but after a while the convoy indicated that they were turning right and going into the city. As I was going straight on I turned off the siren and headlights and slowed down to the correct speed limit. I waved to the police riders who waved back as they went through another set of red traffic lights. There were a lot of vehicles behind me trying to work out why a lorry from Devon had been given such preferential treatment.

Along with our new Mercedes came a Scania 110 or 111. Clifford Cockram was employed to drive it. Maurice Williams left the company and I was given the F88 Volvo F88, registration number PUN903S. I was happy with that as it also had double bunks. John Williams and Paul Bennett also left the firm at this time and the two Ford lorries were sold.

Two new Northern Ireland trailers were purchased. These were great as they had orange indicator lights along the side. Great for reversing. A new law was brought in while I worked for Gregory and Son. All lorries and trailers had to be fitted with side bars to stop cyclists and others falling under the wheels of the vehicle. They were also a great help for climbing on and off the back of the vehicle.

At around the same time as the driver change-around Jeff Binding came into the yard one Saturday morning, driving a battered Volvo F88. The Gregory drivers were all there washing their lorries.

'Bleddy wars!' exclaimed Reg Gregory, 'What have you got there?'

'This belongs to the hay and straw firm that I work for. It may have had a hard life but at least it is a driving job. They're hard to get when you are under twenty five years of age. 'Take it back and come and work for me. I can't have you driving that rubbish.' Jeff shot out the yard with the old F88 and a week later he started for Gregory and Son.

Jeff got to drive 'HNX' which had recently been fitted with a new back axle and the maximum speed was now sixty five miles per hour - the standard speed for a Volvo F88.

In 1981 citizen band radios (CBs) were made legal and lorry drivers across the UK were fitting these radios in their cabs. Many used an illegal American band-wave as the band Britain allocated was different to other countries and not very powerful.

I paid a lot of money for a pair of Johnson and Johnson radios. They were small, but impressive fitted with a power mike and a decent aerial. The range was great but often used to interfere with other people's conversations. I used to keep the power mike turned down. For a couple of minutes I used to turn the mike to maximum on the Ho Chi Minh trail, just to tell Christine that I was on my way home and to start cooking dinner. It was then turned down for a conversation to more local people.

Over the years drivers copied the American truck drivers who use their own language on the radio and every one has their own 'handle' (nickname). Mine was Smurf.

Most CB radios had 40 channels although most lorry drivers used Channel 19. Other channels were used for more quiet conversation, although anyone could listen in.

If you were in a strange town there was always someone who would give you directions to your destination.

There were people who you would talk to on a regular basis. Many of these will come and pick you up and take you back to their home for a bite to eat. One such person 'Lady Caroline' and her husband 'Logman' - also a lorry driver - became good friends over the years. They were members of the South West Truckers Club and lived between Shillingford and Waterrow on the Ho Chi Minh trail. One evening I parked near Waterrow and tried to get Caroline on the radio but no answer.

Then a male, who I did not know, came on the radio and asked where I was parked. I told him that I was just outside Waterrow and he told me that he was crippled and had just moved to Waterrow with his wife. He said his wife would drive and pick me up and I was invited to their house for supper. This wasn't the last time that I visited them. As he was house-bound he loved to hear of the places I delivered to. It wasn't long before all the truckers were talking to him and giving him a wave as they passed by. CB radio was a connection to the rest of the world for him.

Drivers would talk to each other as they drove along the roads and road conditions and weather reports were given. There was a lady in Chiswick, London, who went by the handle of Peppermint, was always giving road reports. Very useful when trying to find the best route to the M4.

In winter, road information was essential to be able to safely travel along the Ho Chi Minh trail and many other roads.

There were a couple of ladies on the CB in Tewkesbury: Puzzler and Gemini, who often chatted with the lorry drivers on the M5. I was parked in Tewkesbury one night and Puzzler told me to walk down a little lane where she picked me up with her car. We collected Gemini and went to Puzzler's house where we had something to eat and played Trivial Pursuits - the game was all the rage at the time. Puzzler's husband was also a lorry driver. Again we became good friends over the years and even talked about swapping houses for a week's holiday. Unfortunately the idea never came to fruition as Puzzler and her husband moved away.

On another occasion I had a load for Tewkesbury and I drove into the industrial estate. I could not find where I had to unload so I went into the nearest factory and asked if they knew where my place of delivery was. The secretary gave me directions and I was about leave when a man's voice from the next office asked me to come and see him. I went into the office and there was a well-dressed man seated behind a large desk.

'Where do you come from?' he asked

'South Molton'

'I come from Oakford. Do you know where that is?'

'I do, my family lived in Oakford before they moved to South Molton.'

'What is their name?'

'Lester and Ivy Lock - they used to live in the Old Bakery.'

'I remember them well, had lots of children.'

He told me that his family had been Lords of the Manor for years.

When I got home and told mum that I had talked to the Lord of the Manor of Oakford she was amazed. She told me that actor Jon Pertwee, the original Wurzel Gummidge, had also lived in a big house in Oakford. As a lad Jon used to come and play with my older sisters and brothers, apparently he liked jam sandwiches. But then who doesn't?

Christine was riding shot-gun again, one day, as the children were with the mother-in-law-. Today's trip was to Dudley Port with a load of 8ft by 6ft chipboard and on the way I decided to stop at Hill Common - just the other side of Wiveliscombe on the Ho Chi Minh Trail - for breakfast. Hill Common was one of four cafés between Barnstaple and Taunton, the others being Bay View, Red Deer and Petton Cross. Now there are none. We went into the café and I introduced Christine to Bob, the owner.

'You can't be his wife,' he said. 'The one he brought in here last week was blonde.'

'That was me wearing a wig,' replied Christine.

Christine one, Bob nil.

On the way to Birmingham we wondered whether the return load would be steel from Round Oak or slab wood from one of the sawmills in Shropshire. On the way up we both had a chat on the CB radio with Puzzler. While unloading I rang the office and Roger told me that I had to go to Burghclere sawmills near Newbury in Berkshire.

'I'm in Birmingham.'

'I know but the chipboard factory is desperate for timber and nowhere else has any.'

So off we went to the village of Burghclere.

It was a sunny day so I was wearing my Italian wooden clogs with leather tops, ideal for a hot day as I could slide them off and drive in bare feet.

The slab wood was in large, round bundles and being eight foot wide was loaded across the trailer instead of length-ways down the trailer. All went well until about the fifth bundle. As the loader driver dropped it the bundle went to the right, hit the fourth bundle and it bounced back just as I walked forward to push it tight to the previous bundle. It was still in the air as it hit me, at the same time I stopped and jumped backwards. I landed in bare feet, the heavy bundle trapping my clogs. That had been a close thing; I could have broken both legs but all I had was a couple of scratches. The bundle was lifted up so that I could recover my clogs. If they had been safety boots my legs would have been trapped under the wood. That must be number three of my nine lives. Only six left. We finished loading with no further problem, although Christine was concerned about my legs I assured her I was ok. I went and collected the paper work. The boss gave me a nice gold pen to sign with.

'Nice pen,' I said as I signed for the load. When I went to give the boss his pen back he said, 'Please keep it. Our phone number is on it and you might need it when you come back for another load.

That night we parked in Newbury. Newbury was the same as Hitchin in Hertfordshire: lorries were parked in the middle of the street and the toilets were at the end.

As I came out of the toilets another driver told me there was someone carrying a clip board and walking around my lorry. I walked quietly up to the lorry and there was the man.

'What do you think you are doing?' I asked.

'I knocked on the cab but no one answered.' he said. 'I'm building a model F88 and I need some measurements for the air tanks.'

He finished measuring, I showed him around the cab and then he was gone. You meet all sorts on the road.

The cab of a Volvo F88 is seventy-six inches wide, sixty-six inches long and floor to cab roof is 50 inches. One hundred and thirty seven and a half cubic inches.

The bed is seventy two inches by twenty one inches. I lived in this box, sometimes for six days. The main people that I talked to, until CB radios came along, were forklift drivers.

This is why it was essential to get out when parked-up and go for a walk. To get some exercise, sometimes in search of food and sometimes to go for a drink. When parked at Corby steel works it was a three mile walk to the pub and back. On a nice summers evening it was quite enjoyable. I had a set amount of money that I took with me and when it was gone that was it. Some days it would be cereal for breakfast, lunch was a sandwich and an evening meal I cooked in the lorry. The next day it might be a pint and fish and chips, especially on the Isle of Sheppey, Kent, where you can find the best fish and chips in the world. A mile there and a mile back from the lorry park, the fish was so big you would still be eating it by the time you were back at the lorry.

Roger's concrete, at Faringdon, was another place near Newbury where we used to collect slab wood from. Faringdon is between Swindon and Oxford and close to the main road.

One afternoon I arrived at Roger's Concrete about four thirty in the afternoon. The fork lift driver said he would load me in the morning. Not what I wanted to hear, but any way, I walked to the office and asked if I could park in the yard for the night as the forky wasn't going to load me until the morning. The boss said I was welcome to stay the night, but asked why he won't load me that night.

'He's playing in a darts match tonight and he wants to get some practice in, so he wants to leave on time.'

'What does he think this place is, British Leyland?' replied the boss and stormed out of the office.

I was loaded that night but as my maximum driving hours were nearly up I decide to park at the concrete works anyway - at least I could leave early the next morning. I cooked a meal and then, as it was a nice evening, I walked to the pub in the village. I brought the fork lift driver a pint and had a couple of games of darts with him. Eventually the opposing dart team arrived and I walked back to the lorry for an early night. Diplomatic relationship with the forky had been restored and I took the opportunity to phone Christine and tell her where I was to. There were no mobile phones in those days so I did not phone her every night, although I always tried to find a phone. That often meant walking to the nearest pub.

A modern expression is 'a bad day at the office' and this day was going to be a bad one. I was getting ready to unload at a yard in the Tottenham area of London. While removing one of the sheets off the lorry, I ignored the golden rule: Do not pull on a rope, because it might break. Instead grab a hand-full of the sheet and pull. This day I pulled a corner rope and it broke. I went backwards at warp speed and smacked my head on the concrete. The lights went out. When I came-around, the first thing I noticed was that the trailer was partially unloaded. I don't know for how long I was knocked but it must have been at least ten minutes. I can't remember if anyone was with me when I came around. I felt the back of my head and discovered a large bump, otherwise I seemed to be ok. There had been a small bump on the back of my head since the accident at Lanivet all those years ago it is still there now.

Later in the same day I was at Roger's concrete, Faringdon to load slab wood. The top yard was level with the main road but to get to the bottom yard there was a gentle slope just pass the office and that yard was about fifteen feet below the level of the office. This meant that the people in the office had an excellent view of the bottom yard.

I was around half-loaded and standing on the trailer, when I caught my foot on something and fell head first off of the trailer. As I hit the ground I did a forward roll, something I'd perfected when I had a motorbike, which I fell off numerous times. As I lay on the ground I slowly checked my body. First slowly moving the fingers of each hand, then the arms, then toes and legs. The adrenaline had stopped being pumped into my body so I did a quick check: no pain anywhere so all seems well. So many people have some sort of accident and immediately jump up only to find when the adrenaline stops that they have serious damage to their body. Don't do that; check yourself first.

The forklift came along with the next bundle of slab wood while I was lying on the floor. He backed up beside me and asked what I was doing.

'I just fell off the trailer.'

'Are you hurt?'

'No, I don't think so.'

Why are you still lying down then?'

I told him that I had knocked myself out in the morning and now I had fallen off the trailer, 'I think the best thing to do is stay here. The woodchips that I am lying on are soft and warm from the sun, and while I am down here nothing else can happen to me.'

'That's ok but you're stopping me loading this bundle. Could you go and lie somewhere else?

I got up very slowly and did another check. Everything seemed to be fine so I went and got some straps and started to strap the load.

When I finished I went to get the delivery tickets form the office. One of the girls had seen me fall off the lorry and the people in the office were very concerned about me. I told them what had happened in London and now I felt fine.

'The woodchips are very soft and the sun is really hot. I was very comfortable lying there,' I told them.

'You are the first person that we have ever had sunbathing down there in the yard,' said the boss. He sounded very relieved.

'You are off to see the Queen,' said Roger Gregory one day. Go to the Crown Sawmill at Windsor Great Park and pick up a load of round timber for Aaronsons. I got to the sawmill and was surprised to see that the whole area was concreted. Every other sawmill I had been to was compressed earth. There was a six-wheeled vehicle the size of a small lorry. It was obviously designed to transport timber.

'Follow me,' said the driver and he took off along a road which appeared to be a miniature of the Ho Chi Minh trail. It went up and down and round and round, past the polo ground, and through some woods. We came to a large, cleared area and stopped. I'll load you here said the driver and off he drove into the woods. About ten minutes later he returned with a load of wood which he transferred on to my trailer using his onboard crane. After about an hour I was loaded and strapped down.

'Where do I turn around?' I asked.

If you carry on along the road a couple of hundred yards you will come to a main road. Turn right for the M4. That was the only time that I went to that sawmill. I still reckon I should have had a crest on the door as I had worked for the Queen.

We used to take paper pulp from Tilbury docks to various paper mills and this day it was a load of pulp to Thatcham. After unloading I went into Newbury to park up for the night. As it was a nice evening, it was time for a stroll. Fish and chips consumed I decided to wash it down with a pint of ale.

I had washed and changed so I went into the nearest pub. On the way to the bar you always have a quick look around and in this bar the walls were covered in yachting and golf trophies. At the bar, nearest the door was a young woman about twenty years old. A little further on was a group of men some in suits and some in Arab dress. I headed for the gap in the middle and got myself a pint. I had a thought, why was this lady in here, on her own, with all these men. She was too well dressed for a lady of the night (they normally frequent pubs near lorry parks) and this pub was nowhere near the lorry park.

Naturally I engaged in conversation with her as my Arabic is pretty none existent. It turned out that she was the personal assistant for one of the Arabs.

At some stage during the evening he came over and spoke to the young lady and she introduced him to me. When he asked me what I did for a living I told him that I was in road transport. After a few minutes more chat he went back and joined his friends.

I can't remember if the young lady said he was a Sheik or a Prince.

That's lorry driving, meeting princes and paupers and all in between.

I did four loads to the North of England and took loaded timber back from Canonbie just North East of Gretna Green. I ended up with this run because my lorry had two diesel tanks. One extra large one fitted on the side of the chassis and a belly tank. This was flat and fitted across the chassis behind the cab and doubled as a walkway when connecting the air pipes and the electric susie coils to the trailer.

Canonbie sawmill was a driver's dream. If I was going to be late they would wait until I got there and then load me without complaining. As I had previously telephoned, the load of milled timber would be ready and waiting for me. The loads used to be delivered to a sawmill at Calverleigh, near Tiverton.

Another Bank Holiday Monday saw me heading to Hartlepool with Christine riding shotgun. We arrived in the early evening and found the shop where we were to deliver. It was closed, so we drove around looking for somewhere to park. There was an area of waste ground opposite the brewery which was ideal for a night's sleep.

There was a pub either side of the brewery so after eating dinner we decided to sample the local brew and went into the pub on the right.

The telly was on and Christine was looking forward to watching the film until the barman said, 'Sorry no women allowed in the bar, you will have to go into the lounge.' Of course he said this after he had served me so off we went into the lounge where the juke box was making more noise than a Foden lorry going up hill. Just what we didn't want after eight hours of sitting next to a Volvo 290 horse power engine all day. We had a quick game of who can drink their drink first, decided the result was a draw, and left.

We decided to try the pub on the left of the brewery. This pub was quiet and comfortable so we stayed there for a while before taking a walk around the town.

After unloading the chipboard the next morning, it was a drive across England to Canonbie and load wood for Calverleigh.

Wednesday we took a load of chipboard to the North of England and again went to Canonbie sawmill and loaded wood for Calverleigh.

We stopped the night at the Truck Inn, Carlisle.

The Truck Inn was a purpose-built complex with a large lorry park. There was a large café with an adjoining bar and a dance hall with music every night. There was a serving hatch between the bar and the café for those who would like a beer with their meal. There were some rooms that could be rented for those drivers who didn't want to sleep in their cab.

There was a very large lady, I used to refer to her as big Bertha, in the bar every night. Usually by closing time she would be well in-drink. One night I went into the café for a tea and Big Bertha was lying on the floor. There were four men trying to lift her up, in the end they gave up. People coming in the café treated her as a roundabout. She was still there when I left the bar, went to the lorry park and my bed.

Another evening I came out of the café and noticed a lot of blue lights flashing in the lorry park. Along with a few others I walked over to see what was going on. There was a fire engine, police and an ambulance next to a Ford lorry fitted with a day cab (no sleeping area).

The firemen removed the windscreen from the Ford and then put two ladders against the front of the cab. Then we found out what had happened. The driver had got Big Bertha into his cab and she had passed out. Now the fire brigade were rolling her down the ladders where the paramedics took over.

The conversation now changed to what the driver was going to tell his boss about the missing windscreen. It might have been interesting to be a fly on the wall.

When Christine and I went into the Truck Inn, I wondered what the night would bring. It wasn't what I expected!

We ate dinner and then went into the dance hall and it was packed. We managed to find two seats next to a couple of inebriated Scotsmen who invited us to join them. I sat opposite Christine.

The night progressed and we tried to understand what our companions, with their broad Scot accent, were saying. Suddenly a blonde lady walk up to me and sat on my lap. The look in Christine's face was not very welcoming.

'Hello, how are you? she said. 'I've not seen you for a long time.'

I have to say I did not recognise her and her accent was more Mancunian than Scots.

'I am well,' I said.

I pointed to Christine and said, 'This is my wife.'

She looked Christine and said 'Oh, hello. Well I must be get on, nice to meet you.'

She turned to me and said, 'Nice to see you again.' She got off my lap and walked away.

'And who was that?' asked Christine.

'I have no idea. She sounded like she came from Manchester. If so, then she may be one of the girls that frequent the café next to Everest transport.'

'Who are Everest Transport?'

'They're in Trafford park and we get lots of return loads from them. We often park there for the night and obviously use the adjacent café.'

Christine knew we went to Manchester occasionally as I sometimes returned with products from Proctor and Gamble that I had brought from their shop while waiting to load.

This incident had, or so I thought for twenty years, been forgotten. The occasion was my fiftieth birthday and we had hired a room with a bar and everyone was very happy. Then Barry, a Morris Dancing friend of mine, stopped the proceedings. It was time for him to do an Eamonn Andrews impression and host a This your Life episode. And I was to be the victim.

It all went well, and we got to the end. Or so I thought. Instead Barry made another announcement: 'Stephen, you've made many friends and met many interesting people as you travelled up and down the roads of Great Britain. We have searched all corners of the Empire to find her. You haven't seen her for twenty years. But tonight she is here. Come in Blondie!'

I was still trying to work out how they'd found someone I didn't even know when the door opened and a tall Morris Man in a long dress and wearing a blonde wig rushed across the room and jumped onto my lap. I didn't know whether to laugh or cry. I looked to Christine and she was laughing her head off.

As I said before, we used to deliver to a factory at Edmonton, North London. If I parked there overnight the foreman would tap a coin on the window about 6.45am.

'Come on driver let's get you unloaded!' he would shout.

By the time I was pulling into the unloading area, the foreman and another man would be undoing the straps. After the straps, all three of us undid the sheet ropes and as 'Boxer' as the foreman was known, and myself folded the sheets, the other guy would unload the 8ft x 6ft sheets of chipboard. Then, while Boxer made us all tea, I would ring someone and try to get a return load. This day I hit the Jackpot: load of Coca Cola to Exeter. Even better, the collection point was less than a mile away.

Just after 8.00am I was parked outside the Coca Cola factory. As I was being loaded I asked if there was a factory shop but was told there wasn't. However, a couple of people kindly found me a two litre bottle each.

It took forty five minutes to get from Coca Cola to Heston services, on the Eastern end of the M4 during the day, or up to an hour and a half, if I left after four thirty. From Heston it was a three hour drive to Exeter.

The load was delivered to Cantrille and Cochrane on Marsh Barton trading estate, Exeter. This was an excellent place to deliver, as soon as you arrived they unloaded you. When my ticket was signed the ticket the supervisor always say, 'You must already have got plenty of Coca Cola would you like some Corona instead? After asking me what flavour, he would then go off and bring out five or six bottles.

It was an hour back to South Molton and hopefully pick up another trailer for London, which was pretty easy as ninety percent of drivers didn't like driving in London. After four weeks of doing this run I had enough soft drink to open a shop. The girls in Graham's were given some, kids would come down our house to play and go home with a bottle of Coke or a bottle of Corona. For one reason or another these loads started to drop off. This was a shame as I liked Edmonton. The lay-by to park, unloading at the factory - the cafés still remained and we continued with the occasional delivery there. It may be because my mum was a Londoner but I loved the Cart Overthrown pub at Edmonton. At five minutes to eight in the evening someone would go and open the double doors and the barman would put two drinks on a table just inside near the doors. Someone else would move one chair a little bit away from the table. All this was done without anyone speaking and it was not always the same people that did it. At eight o'clock an old gentleman would wheel-in a wheel-chair with his wife sitting in it. Before they had got to the table both outside doors were shut and someone stood by the table in case the man or lady needed any assistance.

I played pool with a man about the same age as me. He was disabled, a legacy of polio that was rife in London in the 1950s. We never played for money or beer; we just paid our way and enjoyed the game.

One night two men came in, one was about my age, the other was maybe a few years younger. They sounded like they were of London/Italian descent. They asked if we wanted a game of doubles and we could play for two pounds. I said I was happy to do so but my friend didn't want to as he was on short wages.

In the 1970s there problems with strikes and electric cuts were frequent. Factories were only allowed electric for some days of the week and my friend, Peter, worked at a factory.

I told Peter that I would pay if we lost, it would come out of my night-out allowance. Just push the balls to the pocket. If they don't go in they will be there for next time. The first game went according to plan. The young lad got a bit enthusiastic and hit the white ball to hard. It went around the table and illegally knocked the black ball into a pocket. An illegal shot. Two pounds please. We were paid and then the older one said, 'Do you want another game for four pounds?'

'No we'll play again for two pounds.'

I said to Peter, 'We have nothing to lose, stick to the same plan.'

I noticed that the barman was also taking an interest in the play. We won the next game. Another two pounds. It was getting late and the older one asked, 'One more game for a fiver? As I declined the barman walked over and said, That's it, lads, no more games of pool.'

The men left with the older one having a go at the younger man about his poor performance. The barman stood beside us until the door closed. He turned to me and said, 'Mother says there is no need for you to hurry home. Would you like another pint while you play pool?'

Normally when I go to a pub I always leave just before closing time so that the locals can have a drink on their own, after hours, if allowed. 'Mother' is the usual name given to the lady owner who usually drank in the lounge bar.

After that night, just before closing time, I was always asked, 'Would you like another pint?' It turned out it was because I had offered to pay for Peter if we lost. Londoners like that attitude.

I was sent to load-up at a sawmill just west of Kidderminster. I remember that I went down a steep hill, at the bottom of which was an hotel. The sawmill was just past the hotel, on the top of the next hill.

I arrived around 6.00pm and the sawmill was closed. Opposite the hotel, across the road, was a large car park half of which had a tarmacadam surface while the other half was just hardcore.

I parked on the hardcore bit then went into the hotel. I explained that I was due to load at the sawmill in the morning and asked for permission park the lorry on their car park. Permission was granted as long as I did not park on the tarmac.

After a bit of a kip I decided to eat in the hotel having perused the menu when I was in there earlier. I had trout caught in the local river and after played pool with the locals, one of whom was the forklift driver from the sawmill.

As time went on the pub seemed to get busier. In fact there suddenly seemed to be a very large amount of customers arriving. Another pint and some more games of pool and I was introduced to the landlord. I have to admit I was starting to get a bit sleepy and I asked the landlord what time it was. I can't remember the exact time but it was a lot closer to one in the morning than midnight. This was in the days when pubs officially closed at 11.00pm.

'Where have all these people come from?' I asked the landlord.

'When the pubs kick out in Kidderminster they all come out here.'

''What do the police think of this?'

'Go and ask him. He's sitting over there at the corner table,' replied the landlord.

Work started to drop off so I was allowed to do my favourite job: 'tramping'. I would deliver a load to London, Birmingham, Manchester, Leeds or practically anywhere. While I was being unloaded I would telephone a nearby firm and get a load to anywhere that I wanted to go.

Lorry drivers had their own trade magazine called 'The Headlight'. Not only did it have excellent articles on new laws and changes to rules, it had a section on transport cafés and lists of companies that supplied return loads.

The best idea was to get a load to London and then another load to hopefully to Manchester where I could always get a load back to London. These loads usually paid better than slab wood. If timed right I could deliver to London, having driven up on a Sunday, load to Manchester. I could deliver to Manchester and load back for London in one day. The following day, with an early start, I could do the exactly the same trip.

Convoys Wharf dealt with paper, including paper for newsprint and had a large area and quay at Deptford. The wharf was closed down and for sale in the year 2020 and, I understand, undergoing a planning application to build residential units. In the 1970s the area was so large that I used to drive along one street to the wharf. After loading, one would leave along another street.

I often loaded paper reels for the West Country or South Wales at the wharf. As each roll was loaded, a wooden wedge was put behind the reel to stop it rolling backwards. Most reels were about four feet wide and were loaded two across the trailer. A 'scotch' was used to hold the last rolls on the trailer. A 'scotch' is a triangular piece of timber, just under eight feet long, with rope attached at each end. The 'scotch' is put against the end rolls and then tied to the trailer. After sheeting down the load, the rear rolls were crossed either with a strap or two ropes. Normal reels were around fourteen feet high when loaded but newsprint could be over fifteen foot and normally delivered in London. Once I picked up a load of newsprint for the Daily Mirror in Manchester. Newsprint was not normally delivered outside of London and it was the only load of newsprint that I ever delivered. Apart from keeping my eye on the height of bridges and going carefully around roundabouts there was no problem with the delivery.

I used to love going to Convoys Wharf. The canteen was the best in London; you could even get 'devilled' kidneys for breakfast and any paper you wanted, for free. The newspaper lorries went to Fleet Street early and always brought back a bundle of newspapers. The loading times were quite quick compared with other docks and wharfs.

There are some incidents that remain in my mind. One day I was in a narrow street in Bethnal Green. I was folding a lorry sheet on the ground when a police car came racing along with its blue lights on. The car drove straight across the sheet, around the corner at the bottom of the street and was gone. Thankfully I got out of the way quick enough to avoid being run over. Still it wasn't all that bad. I had eaten in a lovely café at the end of the street and after I had unloaded I was given a ten bob note by the warehouse supervisor for a cup of tea on the way home. This was a tradition in the old days in London.

One firm that I used to do work for was Bolton Roadways, Bolton. My first load for them was from Corona soft drinks in South East London. On arrival at the works I was told that they are not supposed to load a lorry that does not have Bolton Roadways written on it. I told them that a lorry had broken down and they had hired me. After a couple of phone calls I was allowed to load for Aintree, Liverpool.

After unloading at Aintree it was back to Bolton Roadways yard to pick up one of their own trailers loaded with toiletries for a warehouse in Maidenhead. Then it was back to South East London for another load of Corona to Aintree.

Come Friday it was back to Bolton Roadways yard to pick up my own trailer which had been loaded, usually with products from Proctor and Gamble, for the West country.

This job went on for a while, and although the M1 and M6 were quite busy, it was a job that I enjoyed doing.

One run that sticks in my mind was one to ABC Birmingham. The delivery to ABC went well and I was given the usual coffee and toast when I arrived. Whilst I was being unloaded I telephoned a company for a return load, 'Will you do a load of bagged cement to Plymouth?' I was asked.

'Of course,' said I.

'Here is the address of a storage company just down the road from where you are. The cement company are storing their cement and distributing from there, as their own drivers are on strike so don't tell anyone what you are loading.'

Off I went to the address given. When I arrived I was told to park in the corner of the yard and tell no-one what I was doing. A little later a cement company Artic arrived and started to unload. The driver came into the rest room and made himself a cup of tea.

He looked at me and said, 'A funny thing about this strike; we are taking cement to storage facilities all over Birmingham.'

'If you are on strike, why are you delivering cement at all?'

He shrugged, 'The union says we can take it to storage, but not to customers. What are you up to?' he asked.

'I am waiting for a load of steel to be cleared. They're never too quick at the steel companies.'

He looked out of the window and saw that his lorry was almost unloaded. 'I'll see you,' he said as he walked out the door.

As soon as he was gone, I backed into the shed and loaded the cement that he'd just delivered. That evening I parked at Graham'o Café in North Petherton. I had to be on a trading estate in Plymouth at 9.30am the next day to tranship the load onto smaller vehicles for delivery around the city. That night I went down to the Compass Inn with Jeffrey Binding who was also parked at the Café.

When we came back there was a young lady I recognised, parked beside the fuel pumps talking to one or two drivers. She was often there, having recently split up with her husband. She used to come and talk to drivers. I gave Jeffrey the keys to my lorry while I went over to say hello. Soon after I went and put the kettle on and, while I made the tea, Jeffery went to say hello. Tea-drunk we went to bed in our separate lorries.

After breakfast the next morning I asked Jeffrey for my keys.

'I don't have them,' he said.

So we searched the cab. No sign of the keys.

We tried his keys and they partially fitted my lorry so at least I could get to Plymouth albeit without any lights working.

I decide to drive to Stuart's, the Volvo lorry dealers, at Rockbeare, near Exeter, using hand signals, on an Artic!

'We don't stock keys just blanks,' said the storeman. 'I wonder if the one from my old lorry will fit,' he said. And went off to find it.

While he was gone I decided to have a look at Stuart's new Volvo breakdown lorry and as I was looking in the cab Mr Stuart came along.

'What do you think of the new Volvo?' he asked, sounding very proud of his new acquisition.

'It's not very good,' I said. 'There's no steering wheel.'

He immediately shouted, 'Shut the gates! Don't let anyone off the site!'

The foreman came running up and asked, 'What's the matter boss?'

He pointed to the new Volvo, 'Some bugger's stolen the steering wheel from the new wrecker!'

'No, boss it's on the other side of the cab. It's left-hand drive.'

I beat a hasty retreat back to the stores where the storeman had found a key. We tried it in the door lock. It worked perfect so we tried it in the ignition and again perfect. My life was saved!

'How much is it?' I asked.

'Nothing, it's a spare. I'll just get another cut.'

I expressed my gratitude and managed to get to Plymouth more or less on time.

The original keys? They were found in the car of a young lady from North Petherton, down beside the handbrake, having fallen out of someone's pocket. At least I got a spare key out of it, which was tied under the radiator cover of the lorry.

Accidents are a hazard faced by every driver and in the summer caravanners have more than their fair share. I have seen a caravan start to wobble and then lift up the towing vehicle, on a motorway, and spin round and face it in the opposite direction. It happens in a couple of seconds leaving the driver very little time to act. This is why I always give caravans plenty of room.

On one particular day it was about six in the evening and I was running South trying to get to Graham's before my hours ran out. I was in the middle lane going up the hill from Gordano Services at Bristol, following a car and caravan. It was going pretty fast, maybe too fast. He passed a few vehicles including an ambulance that was ambling along. We got near the top of the hill at the split level section and the caravan twitched a little so I slowed down. The back of the caravan went left and immediately went right as the driver over -corrected. I hit the hazard warning switch and started to brake, I knew what was coming. The car and caravan went across the left hand lane and hard shoulder and onto the grass verge. Instead of using the grass verge to slow down, the driver turned hard right back across the motorway. He was now heading for a twenty foot drop so he carried on turning right into oncoming traffic. Fortunately, as he was braking hard, the caravan pushed the back of the car into the crash barrier. As the car bounced off the barrier the caravan hit it then slid into the barrier and brought the whole thing to a halt.

By the time the car and caravan had come to a halt I had stopped half way past the accident scene. Although the car in the fast lane must have seen my hazard warning lights come on, he could not have seen what was happening, but he wisely stopped as well. On the left hand side, the ambulance that the car and caravan had pulled across in front of had also stopped. It was extraordinary that only one vehicle was involved. With all vehicles on the motorway now stopped I jumped out of the cab and ran across to the stricken car assessing the situation as I went, I noticed with relief that the ambulance had moved onto the hard shoulder, its blue light flashing. There was a lad about ten years old in the back of the car. I opened the door and asked him if he was hurt. He was pretty shook up, but he said the he was ok. I said, 'This lady will help you.' I looked at the paramedic, pointed to the boy and gave a thumbs up sign, indicating that he looked alright and left the door open for her to check him out.

By this time the driver and female front seat passenger had both got out of the car. As I got next to the male driver to give him a quick check -over the lady passenger shouted across the bonnet, 'I knew we should have gone by train.'

His reply was, 'There, there dear, we are insured.'

That'll bleddy cheer her up, I thought.

The ambulance driver then helped the woman away from the drop to the next carriage way below. The paramedic confirmed that the lad was ok and it was safer for him to stay in the car at that moment. The police quickly arrived and I told them what had happened, at the same time giving them my contact details. It decided it was time for me to move as the cars in the left-hand lane were already moving. I moved off slowly with my hazard warning lights still on until I got the lorry up to speed I then pulled into the left-hand lane and headed for North Petherton, wondering when will be the next accident that I come across. The family were lucky to have survived that accident uninjured, perhaps next time they *should* take the train.

One rainy day, slowing as I approached the toll booth on the M4, and as it was busy, I put the lorry into second gear. The long tyre lever that I kept next to the door had slid along and was now touching the accelerator. As I was going slow I decided to lean down and pick it up before it caused any problems. I tried but there wasn't quite enough room so I decided to open the door and give it another try. That was a bad idea. Two seconds later I was lying on a wet motorway as the lorry headed for the nearest chicken coop [toll booth[. Thankfully I wasn't hurt and with a quick sprint and a jump I was back in the cab, with my foot on the brake, being stared at by every passing car. I was a bit wet but with the heater on full I soon dried out.

Jeffery Binding, Clifford Cockram and myself, one day all had loads to the Midlands. We agreed to meet that night at ABC Birmingham and could run home together early Saturday morning.

I got to ABC before five and so went in and had a cup of coffee and a chat with the lads, 'Coming down the pub? they asked.

Why not I thought, the other two will work out where I am. It was Five-thirty we all went down to the Tyburn House for a quick pint of Ansell's finest.

We ended up playing pool for beer and as I had won a few games by the time Clifford and Jeff arrived I was under full sail. I blamed it on the fact that I hadn't had anything to eat. They had a pint each and then decided we should go to another pub; one I had never been before.

We went into the pub and Jeff asked me what I wanted to drink.

'A pint of Ansell's,' I tried to say, but it didn't sound like that - it was more like 'Ash puunt eff ensshaalls pliish.'

'I'm not serving him. He's had enough,' said the landlord.

'No, no - he's not drunk,' said Jeff. 'He lives on Exmoor and they all talk like that. It's rumoured they still eat their young up there.'

'I'm not happy - he can have a half,' replied the Landlord.

Beer consumed it was off to the chip shop, with me going in last. I ordered fish and chips and discovered that I didn't have enough change so I asked Jeff for the odd pence. They both decided to pretend that they didn't know me. After a minute or so of winding me up Clifford said, 'Give the poor old chap a couple of pence, Jeff.'

Eventually he gave it to me and I paid for my meal. We walked back to the lorries eating our chips and after a few minutes we arrived outside ABC. We had a bit of a chat and then decided it was time for bed. I went to put the key in the door and the lorry moved slightly, knocking the keys out of my hand. You know, just like when you come home after a good night out and as you put the key in the front door, the house moves slightly.

The mudguards of a Volvo F88 stick out a couple of inches and the keys must have hit the mudguard and bounced into the darkness. There was a street light a few yards away which gave some light.

I got on my hands and knees, looked all around, and under the lorry. No keys. Clifford and Jeff didn't seem to be helping much.

There was a drain next to the front wheel of the lorry.

'Perhaps they went down the drain,' suggested Jeffrey.

I couldn't see anything so I tried to lift the drain cover.

'You won't lift it,' said Jeffrey. 'The front wheel is on top of it. You'll need to move the lorry forward a bit.'

'I can't move the lorry. I've lost the keys!' I said in a loud stage whisper.

'Alright,' said Jeffrey. 'Don't shout at me, I'm only trying to help.'

'What's this over here?' asked Clifford as he bent down.

'Here they are!' he said, and handed me the keys. He denied that he was standing on them all the time.

The next morning we drove back home without incident but with me not talking to them very much.

I told the story of the missing keys to Clifford's wife, in the presence of Clifford, thirty-five years later.

'How do you remember that? It was years ago and you were well inebriated,' he said.

'I never forget,' I replied.

In August 1981 Gregory and Son closed down. I had worked for them for two and a half years and enjoyed most of it. The job had changed, with sleeper cabs; tachographs instead of log books; side bars on lorries and trailers; and ratchet straps for the loads.

I remember Reg Gregory came down on a Sunday morning and gave me a cheque for my wages and redundancy. He had taken no deductions and apologised for the situation. I had no problem with it, after all, he gave me a job when I needed one.

9

The Three Week Sabbatical

Now I needed a job. With another driver named Terry I went down to Gregory Transport, North Tawton [no relation to Gregory and Son, South Molton] who were advertising for drivers.

Terry went in first and then me. I was asked about experience and then he called Terry back in.

'You've got the job,' he told Terry. 'You start next Monday, driving long distance. He told me that I had also got a job but they couldn't take me on for three weeks - and that I would be driving a bulk tanker, doing farm feed deliveries for a while.

On the way home Terry seemed happy enough, but I wasn't. I understood the job I applied for was long distance. Instead I would be driving to North Tawton and back every day - it was just not feasible.

The next day it was off to Smythe's Transport, Barnstaple, along with Jeffery Binding. This time I went in first and then Jeff. We were both given jobs but had to wait a month before we could start as they were awaiting delivery of two new lorries. We would both be driving Volvo F88s.

In the meantime North Devon Transport phoned me and asked if I would do some loads of straw for them. I declined but gave them Jeff's number. I told them I wanted some time off with the family as it was unlikely I would be having another holiday for some time.

The following week Gregory Transport were trying to get hold of me. They left messages in all the pubs in South Molton. They had given Terry an Atkinson Borderer tractor unit and sent him to Erith, North Kent. The Atkinson was prehistoric compared with the foreign lorries pouring into the UK. The cab was wooden-framed and covered in metal, the same type of build as lorries in the 1930s. It was also under-powered with a 180 horse power engine, noisy and uncomfortable.

Terry left the trailer in Erith, Kent and drove the tractor unit back to South Molton. He told Gregory's where the trailer was and said when they had sent him a day's pay he would tell them where the tractor unit is.

I never did return Gregory's phone calls. I felt they had misled me by letting me think I was applying for a long distance lorry-driving job and then offering me the position of driving a bulk tanker, locally. In addition, I certainly didn't want to drive an Atkinson when I had a Volvo lined up with A D Smythe.

A couple of weeks later Bill Hockin phoned me and asked me to do some work for him. I had enjoyed three weeks' holiday on the dole and now decided I would be happy doing a week's work for Bill.

It started off mainly shunting trailers around North Devon. Thursday I had to change trailers with Melvyn at Graham's. A nice little run and a good breakfast. When I got back it was to take a couple of trailers to a tyre company and check the air pressures in the tyres and then take one of them to Shapland and Petter, door manufacturers, in Barnstaple. Later in the day it was back to Shapland and Petter and pick up the loaded trailer. One door was to be delivered to a building site in Swindon and the rest around London. My Swindon drop was supposed to happen at ten that evening. I told Bill that I had to go home and have eight hours break first, therefore I would be at Swindon around two in the morning.

The door was delivered to Swindon without a problem and then I drove on to West London. As I got to London I had to drive on side-lights as the batteries didn't seem to be charging. I parked on-site where it looked like they were turning an old hospital into flats. Half of the load was unloaded there. I remember thinking it was lucky the weather was dry as the doors were on a standard flat trailer. Shapland and Petter used box van trailers for their fleet. The next drop was Wembley and a block of flats. The builder came out picked up a door and said to me to bring a door and follow him. We went into the building, into a lift to a floor near the top of the building, along a corridor and then put the doors outside a room. As we went back to the lorry I said I will have to stack them next to the lorry as I haven't got time to carry the doors for him. He was worried that someone would steal them, I told him that they were fire doors and weighed a ton (around 1 hundredweight each, actually). They were not ones with cardboard centres, and nobody was going to walk off with them. In the end he stacked them inside the building and I left.

The next drop was three doors for a Gentleman's Club in Chelsea, unfortunately the address on the delivery ticket was incorrect. I decided to park the lorry and go in search of the Club on foot. I found it and walked in through the front door. The gentleman receptionist told me I would have to use the tradesman's entrance. I told him that I had a delivery of doors for him and if he would be so kind as to inform the builders, I was outside I would fetch my lorry from down the street.

With that consignment unloaded I headed for Oxford Street. When I got there I could find no access to the street from the end that I was. I decided to go to another delivery address in Albermarle Street, deliver there, and then try to get to Oxford Street from a different direction. As I started to drive down Park Lane two Police motor bikes came up beside me, blue lights flashing, one gestured for me to go faster while the other went ahead and stopped the traffic at the next junction. I looked in my mirror and saw a convoy of six Rolls Royce cars coming along, surrounded by Police cars and motor bikes. I changed down and slammed the accelerator to the floor. The trailer didn't have much weight on it by now, but I was driving a Fiat and not a Volvo. I got that Fiat up to fifty but the Rollers behind were gaining on me; two more junctions and I was going to turn off anyway. I got past one and then the Police waved me over to let the convoy pass. Well I slowed down to below thirty and the convoy roared past, six limousines full of gentlemen in Arab dress.

Albermarle Street is just off Piccadilly, less than half a mile away and is a one way system, I had to double park but there was reasonable room for cars to pass until someone came up in a great big yank car. The builders made a few comments about buying a mini and whether the driver had a licence or had passed a test. He did scrape by eventually and I was soon unloaded. I now had only two drops left but time was going on. I got to the T-junction at the end of Albermarle Street and found I couldn't turn left or right because of illegally parked cars. Nothing for it but to blow the airs horns. People started to come out of the shops to see what the noise was about. Then from the direction of Old Bond Street came two Traffic Wardens, one quite young and one aged about fifty. The young one had his pen out and was writing tickets as quick as he could as people were running back into the shops to get their car keys. The older one booked a couple of cars and as the street started to clear he walked over to me and explained that there was a running battle between wardens and shopkeepers and now the wardens had a legitimate reason to book them.

The road was eventually cleared and I turned right toward Old Bond Street - because of the one way street system I had to go back down to Piccadilly. There were a few roads that I attempted to go along to get to Oxford Street but all without success. I was going around Piccadilly Circus for the fourth time when a driver of a local lorry waved me down, so I stopped, blocking off the Circus.

'Where are you trying to get to, driver? he asked.

'Oxford Street,' I told him.

'You have no chance of getting that thing there on a Friday.'

'I am beginning to realise that.'

'I would give up and come back another day. Do you have anywhere else to go?'

'Cheapside.'

'You may get to there,' he laughed.

I gave up on the idea of delivering in Oxford Street and set off to Holborn and then along the A40 to Cheapside and the State Bank of India in King Street. King Street is not too wide and so I had to go around the wrong side of the Keep Left signs to enter the street. With headlights and hazard warning lights on I proceeded slowly into King Street to be met by a lady coming the other way in a car. She stopped so I got out and walked up to the car. She wound down the driver's door window.

'Do you know that you've got your headlights turned on?' she asked.

'Yes,' I replied, '*and* the hazard warning lights, to indicate that I am doing an unusual manoeuvre. I have to drive on the wrong side of the road to get past the Keep Left signs and get into this street.'

'Oh, I wondered why you were on the wrong side of the road. If you can go the other side of the road I will guide you out into the main road and then I will be able to carry on.'

This she did and I proceeded along King Street, to the State Bank of India.

I asked where the builders were and the concierge, resplendent in National dress, told me that the builders, from Birmingham, did not work on Fridays. These were the same builders that were at the Oxford street address that I could not get to.

After I told him that there were three fire doors to be delivered, he helped me unload them and stack them in the area of the bank where the alterations were taking place. I then rang Bill Hockin and his wife answered, saying that Bill was up North and she would try to get hold of him. I told her that I could not deliver at one site as I could not get to it and also that the builders were probably not there anyway. A little while later she rang back and said go back to the site where I had delivered in the West End and leave the doors there. So I drove back to Albermarle Street and talked to the builders there. They said it was nothing to do with them. So I telephoned Mrs Hockin again. While I was waiting they made me a cup of tea, which was very welcome.

A few minutes later Mrs Hockin rang back.

'There is a big Securicor Depot somewhere in Battersea, take the doors to there.'

'I've seen it from the train a couple of times but I do not know where it is exactly. If I pass it on the way home I will drop them off; if not I will bring them back to Barnstaple.' [there was no return load booked for me]

As I left the site I could here an engine ticking over. That's funny I thought to myself, I'm sure I had turned off the Fiat engine, although at some of the drops, I had left it running to try and charge the battery a little bit.

When I arrived at the lorry I discovered that I *had* turned off the engine and that parked behind the lorry was a coach whose engine was running. He must have been there a while, patiently waiting. I walked past him and down to Piccadilly; the traffic was stopped in every direction because I'd blocked the road. It was five to five on an Autumn Friday evening, in London.

I jumped into the Fiat and started off, getting as far as the end of the road before coming to a halt. Illegally parked cars were everywhere, so, again, I pulled on the air horns. People came running out of the shops, the two traffic wardens appeared as if by magic. The younger of the wardens rapidly filling out tickets as fast as he could and the older one walked over to me.

'You've made his day.' He nodded to his younger colleague. 'Can you come back tomorrow?'

'No, I've had enough of London for one week - I'm heading as fast as I can for the West country.'

With that I turned right and headed to Piccadilly and the road home, hoping the traffic jam I'd created had now cleared.

I got as far as Graham's at North Petherton and that was it - no driving time left. I had stopped at Membury Services and had something to eat so I wasn't hungry. There was a friend at Graham's called Arthur Colwill, who drove a Leyland Marathon, pulling a fridge trailer, for Greenaway's of Stratton, near Bude.

As I pulled into to Graham's Arthur was just getting out of his cab. He walked over to the Fiat, 'Hello Locky, coming for a drink?' he asked.

'I'm a bit knackered, but I'll come down for one. The fresh air will do me good.'

So we walked the few hundred yards to the Compass Inn.

'What are you doing driving for Billy?' he asked.

I explained that I was doing a bit of casual work and that next week I start work for A.D. Smythe. I told him what I had done the last couple of days and that I could do with a good night's sleep.

'It sounds as if Hockin likes to get his pound of flesh.'

'He certainly does; but in all fairness he pays for every minute you work and never quibbles.'

Friday nights were usually busy but we found a couple of empty stools at the bar. I'd drank about half a pint before I fell asleep on the bar.

'Come on Locky, time to go home,' a voice said in my ear. I woke up drank the other half of my beer, apologised to Norah and Ed for using their pub as a dormitory and walked back to the lorries with Arthur.

'I think it's a good job that you are going to work for Tony Smythe,' said Arthur as we got back to the lorry park. You don't seem to be able to stick the pace on Hockin's.'

He laughed and continued, 'Still you'm cheap to take out for a drink.'

Cornish humour!

'Good night Arthur.'

'Good night Locky, I'll see you again.' He was still laughing as he climbed into his Marathon.

As soon as my head hit the pillow I was asleep. No alarm clock, I would wake up in the morning, when I was ready. All I had to do was get back to Shapland and Petter and unload half a dozen doors. Just enough weight to stop the trailer bouncing around too much going down the Ho Chi Minh.

When I awoke in the morning Arthur was long gone, along with everybody else. I treated myself to a good breakfast and then, at nine, I started the final leg of my journey. By eleven the trailer was empty at Shapland and Petter and I was finished. I telephoned Billy and he asked where I'd been.

'What do you mean?' I asked.

'I spoke to you last night and told you that I wanted you empty at nine because the Girl Guides want the trailer to decorate for Barnstaple Carnival.'

'I can't remember seeing you last night.'

'It was about midnight, I was with Melvyn, another of Bill Hockin's drivers. Anyway get the trailer around to this address and leave the sheets at Shapland and Petters.'

He gave me an address and unusually it was somewhere with easy access.

I apologised to the Guides for being late, dropped the trailer exactly where they wanted it and took the Fiat back to the yard. I gave him my time sheet for the week which, as usual, he paid immediately.'

There are no phone call charges for London yesterday?'

'No, I used the customer's phone, even the long distance call from the Bank of India.'

I'm not sure that he got the joke but instead said, 'Thank you for the work you've done - I'll see you again.'

'Sooner than you think,' I said. 'You'll have to take me home to South Molton. It's pissing down with rain out there and I am not hitch hiking in this weather.'

Reluctantly Bill drove me home in his jag and he was still back in the pub in Barnstaple with his other drivers before one o'clock.

This week's work turned out better then I thought. A week later the dole office wrote to me and said that I had not claimed my money. I wrote back and told them that I had been working. The following week they sent me a cheque anyway.

10

A.D. Smythe Transport, Barnstaple

At eight o'clock on a Monday morning Jeffrey Binding and I arrived at Smythe's Transport, Castle Park Road, Whiddon Valley, Barnstaple.

It was a fairly new depot built on a new trading estate. There was a downhill slope into the yard. On the left was a two-story office block, then a large shed containing the workshop and a large storage area. At the end of the store was the wash area and diesel pump. On the right the parking area for lorries and trailers was marked out with angled bays.

Smythe had about twenty-four lorries, all Artic tractor units. An ERF B series, fitted with a day cab and an old column change MAN, registration WOD which was used for shunting. The rest of the units were pretty evenly split between MANs and Volvo F10s and F12s and two Volvo F88s.

Jeff and I were allocated the two F88s. Most of the tractor units were two-axle but there were some three axle Volvo F12s.

All vehicles were known by their registration plates, mine was WFJ 701S or woof-ah-ju, as in 'just'. There was also a Ford Transit pick up and a Ford transit Van fitted with double rear wheels, that had once been clocked at a hundred and twelve mile per hour. The trailers were a mixture of two and three axle.

The chipliners had curtain sides with extra straps fitted to them, about twenty five to thirty. Normal tautliners had under twenty straps. The roof was steel with a walk-way all the way around, about a foot wide. The centre was open, fitted with reinforcing bars and covered with a plastic canopy held down with 'bungee' bands. There was a ladder fitted on one of the back doors. This ladder folded flat to the door when not in use. There was a smaller ladder that hinged on the bed of the trailer and stowed under the bed of the trailer when not in use. For loading bulk wood chips the plastic canopy was rolled back and the wood chips tipped in the hole using a big bucket fitted to a forward-loading tractor. To unload, the side curtains were pulled back and the chips were pushed off using a forward-loading tractor.

It is said that Tony Smythe helped design the chipliners with Boalloy Trailers of Congleton.

The early chipliners had a steel pole fitted at either end of the curtain. The front pole slotted in behind the headboard of the trailer and the rear pole dropped into a ratchet system at the back of the trailer. The ratchet system was used to tighten up the curtain and then the side strap were used to tighten the curtain down. When full of wood chips the chipliner curtains used to bulge a bit making them look like they were a bit pregnant.

The problem with one ratchet was if there was a small amount of load at the front of the trailer one still had to undo all the trailer straps to open the curtain. Later models had ratchets at both ends of the trailers. This made them better for multi-drop work.

The interesting thing with Smythe's is that you got paid a set sum for the week. No overtime and no bonus; so it was nights out that one went for.

The lorries were washed every Saturday by the yard men Colin 'Ginger' Paul and Colin Vanstone, each one taking around ten minutes. The third yard man, Bill Taylor, was always busy sorting trailers.

Loaded trailers were taken from the chipboard factory back to the yard, many drivers not securing loads. I always strapped the load and in the end I used to wash my lorry Thursday or Friday and was never asked to go back to the yard on Saturday.

If you got up to the factory early Saturday you would go home early. If you got there late then you would start late Monday morning. Sometimes you helped loading trailers before you 'went up the road'.

During the week if you were up at the factory you would end up shunting trailers for a few hours. You never got away early to get to your destination unless there was a chance that you would get unloaded the same day

Shunting trailers was ok. There was always four or five people to help sheet down flat loads so they always got loaded first. With tautliners you just had to close the curtains.

Multi-shop deliveries took a long time to load as each board had to be packed individually. Usually two trailers were dropped at the end of the factory and the tractor units used to move other trailers.

Breakfast - and even lunch - was eaten at the factory before the Ho Chi Minh was travelled but one could still be parked up in London by seven in the evening.

Loads to shops and ABC stores were done by Smythe's, Torridge Transport, Bill Hockin, and one or two owner drivers.

Loads of eight feet by six feet chipboard were delivered to large furniture factories in the Derbyshire area, London, Manchester, Banbury and Warrington, as well as many other, smaller companies.

Warrington was the favourite delivery as the very large forklift there could lift three packs at a time which meant around ten minutes to unload.

Loads back for the Chipliners were woodchips from Wigan, Birkenhead, and sawmills from around South Wales.

From up North there would also be loads of paint from Leyland to Swansea and cardboard tubes from Billington tubes, Bolton, to the steel works at Port Talbot and a carpet manufacturer up in one of the Welsh valleys or Frome in Somerset.

The cardboard tubes were the preferred load as they were light, just enough weight to stop the trailer bouncing too much. The tubes could also be loaded at night while the driver was on a rest period. I also used their rest room to cook my meal and watch television.

At Port Talbot one had to reverse through the steel mills to the end where the three foot cardboard rolls were thrown off the back of the trailer. This was fine as long as they were not pouring molten steel. At the first sign of bright light I stopped and covered my eyes.

Molten steel is as bright as the sun. If you did look at it all you could see for a long tim was bright orange glow. If you didn't look then the steel would soon cool and go to a maroon colour. Then you could carry on.

The carpet factory meant driving through the factory watching the height of the doorways, Whereas the paint was a twenty-ton load and therefore it took a bit longer to get to Swansea, over the Welsh hills.

From Swansea it was usually back to Caerphilly and load wood chips for South Molton. The nice thing with Caerphilly was that any meal in the canteen was 50p. That usually meant the biggest breakfast of the week.

I remember one trip with paint. We had already loaded up North; I was running with Adrian Richards and by Friday night we could only get as far South as Cannock. We stopped in the town rather than the nearby, well known, transport café. Deciding that it would probably be quieter and we would get a better sleep. While I was eating my evening meal two of Evan's Transport from Bideford pulled into the lorry park.

I finished my meal and the decision was made to go down the pub, and, just to be social, I went along. The others ate in the pub and then decided to go along to a club.

I had one pint in the club and then went back to the lorry. I was saving my money for food the following day.

The next morning I was up at five-thirty. I ate some cornflakes and made tea for myself and Adrian (I always had two mugs in the lorry). I opened the door of Adrian's lorry and put the tea on the floor. Adrian did seem a bit reluctant to get out of bed so I drank my tea and left Cannock heading South for Swansea, on my own.

Paint unloaded I drove to Caerphilly, loaded chips, then back to South Molton and unloaded so that the trailer could be loaded over the weekend. Then it was straight home - I would fill up with diesel Monday morning.

Adrian never caught me up that day so I have no idea what time he got home.

On normal Monday mornings Jeff Binding and myself would often leave just after six. We both lived in the same street.

We would usually run together, mostly to the same delivery point. We would take the straps, ropes and sheets off one load and while that was being unloaded we would get the other trailer ready for unloading.

If it were chipliners, as soon as one curtain was pulled back and the rear straps were taken off, unloading started. With both trailers empty it was time to go and get loaded.

Flat trailers were usually sent to London and loaded back from the docks at Purfleet, Essex or Rochester, North Kent. Occasionally we would go to Tilbury docks, also in Essex. The normal loads from these docks were timber for builders' merchants and a few times a year, reels of paper.

Reels of heavy paper were loaded at the Hythe, Colchester. This paper was delivered to Barnstaple and was used for magazines.

Rochester docks was at the end of a long curved road. A couple of hundred yards before the actual dock gates the road doubled in width and on the left trailers and other stuff were parked.

Late one afternoon around four I was heading toward the dock gate when I met Neil Russell coming the other way.

Neil was one of Smythe's nicest drivers, a real rough diamond, he called everyone boy and always seemed to be smiling.

As he stopped he said, 'Drive on in, quick. I'll park up and come and help you.' I did as instructed, went into the office to get my paperwork, and when I got back to the lorry Neil was on the trailer spreading out the dunnage ready for the packs of timber. Dunnage is four inch square timbers, four feet or eight feet long. The latter was preferred as it spanned both packs of timber and made the load firmer. One piece of dunnage was put close to each end of a pack of timber and then another one on top, at each end, above the one below.

The docks were not busy at the time and I was quickly loaded sheeted and strapped. I drove up to the end of the wide bit of road and parked behind Neil.

We had something to eat and then headed for a pub where there was football on that evening and Neil was a real fan.

I didn't really know, at the time, just how *much* of a fan. He was very vocal but, as everybody else seemed to be the same, there was no aggravation.

The next day we left Rochester early, but so did everyone else. There was a rail strike and the whole of Kent, in cars, seemed to be heading North West into London. Oh, for an orbital motorway but that was way into the future.

Driving through London Neil was out of sight around a corner and the traffic was at a stand still. All the cars in front were indicating to turn right but were using both lanes. I took to the pavement and passed them, as I did I got on the CB radio and said to Neil, 'I've had enough of this I'm using the pavement.'

Neil replied, 'I've been doing that for the last ten minutes.'

One evening, around six, I pulled into the railway yard at Portishead to discover Neil Russell already parked there. Pleasantries exchanged, we settled down to eat a meal and catch up with the week's news.

Suddenly there was a knock on the cab door. There was a man standing there.

'I wonder if you can help me?' he asked. 'I'm from the rugby club the other side of the lane. We had a trailer dropped off earlier ready for the carnival on Saturday. The thing is, it's in the wrong place and we need it moved. Just back a little and perhaps the angle altered slightly. What do you think? Could one of you do that please?

We finished our tea and went to take a look.

The trailer was designed to be coupled to a smaller Artic unit than a standard thirty-two tonner. We couldn't couple up to it but we believed we could move it to where he wanted it.

As I was the last in we decided to use My F10 to move the trailer. After dropping my trailer I drove across the lane and reversed under the little trailer just far enough to lift the landing legs off the ground. If it slipped off the fifth wheel it would come to no harm. We connected the airlines to the trailer and pushed it gently backward and with a spin of the steering wheel we pushed the trailer back to where it was required - much to the delight of the club members.

'Will you come into the club house and join us for a drink?' they asked.

We told them we would go back, reconnect my trailer and then we will return.

About five minutes later we were all sat in the club house, glass in hand. It turned out to be an interesting evening, given that we went into the club house well before eight o'clock. As we enjoyed the hospitality of our new friends we were often distracted by scantily clad ladies, young and old, as they tried on their carnival costumes ready for the following evening.

As their guests, we were not allowed to pay for our drinks although I'm sure we tried to - once or twice anyway. As the night went on a friendly challenge was raised that the Devonians could not drink as hearty as people from Somerset. I cannot remember who won but we did have an enjoyable evening.

The next morning being Saturday we did not leave too early and we stopped at Hillcommon for breakfast; then back to the yard where we took great delight in telling everyone about our night of free beer and scantily clad women.

Neil was one of the best drivers that I have ever met. Always happy and always willing to give anybody a hand. He was what my old cockney mum would call a Diamond Geezer.

Dougie Braunton - CB handle Dougal - was another of Smythe's drivers. He was a fairly big man but most of the time as gentle as a lamb; another driver who was usually in a happy mood and seemed to really enjoy life. However he was responsible for knocking me out one day.

We both had flat trailers loaded with chipboard for delivery to Nailsea near Bristol. It was very close to end of work time when we arrived at the factory and we expected to unload the next day.

We were surprised when the fork lift driver came over to us and told us that if we quickly pulled into the shed he would unload us straight away. We did as told and the straps and rope were quickly undone and thrown to one side; the sheets untied and pulled of the load. Before unloading could begin we had to fold the sheets up, so Dougie took hold of one end and me the other. We folded in both sides and then took hold of an end each, to fold them into the middle and then it would be rolled up and put to one side. Tightly holding my end, head down, I ran to the middle of the sheet and Dougie did the same.

The next thing that I remember was waking up leaning against a wall. Apparently we ran straight into each other, clashed heads and I was knocked out. Dougie had picked me up and sat me against the wall, the forky had moved the sheet and unloading had continued.

I soon came around and, appearing not to suffer any real damage, we got the other trailer ready to unload. We soon left Nailsea and decided to go to nearby Portishead and call it a day. I'm happy to say that I did not suffer any long term effects for the head butt.

Early one evening Dougie and me were running North together and decided to stop at Gordano services near Bristol for a quick cup of tea. After coming out of the café we noticed there were a lot of suited people around the petrol kiosk; so we decided to walk over and take a look.

We learnt that they were all from a petrol company marketing their new gift promotion. The idea was that drivers were given vouchers when purchasing diesel and when a certain number was achieved they could be traded for a set of soup bowls.

Dougie told one of the suits it was a waste of time as he had the required number of vouchers but there were no bowls available anywhere. The man in the suit said to another man go and get a set from the car, and Douggie shouted, 'Get two 'cause my mate has the same problem!' The man came back with two boxed sets of bowls and gave one to each of us. We thanked him and went back to the lorries.

I never did find out whether Dougie had enough vouchers for a set, I certainly didn't, but now that I had a set of soup bowls I gave my vouchers to another driver. I still have some of those soup bowls nearly 40 years later.

Usually Mondays meant 'going up the road' and returning Tuesday, or Wednesday if the load was for superstores and shops. Very often the return loads were taken to the yard, and the trailer dropped, to be delivered to the customer by one of the shunters. An exception was woodchips which were usually unloaded by the driver who had loaded it at the sawmill. Empty trailers were usually left at the chipboard factory for loading.

There would be at least one shunter and two or three drivers loading at the factory. Shop deliveries took between one and two hours to load but eight by six loads took about twenty minutes.

Flat trailers had two large 'half' sheets and one full length fly sheet about fifty feet long, Ten feet longer than the trailer. When I left the firm there was also a slightly shorter fly sheet, coloured blue.

This sheet was to go under the green fly sheet and on top of the 2 half sheets. The blue sheet must never be roped or strapped over, this was so it did not get damaged.

When a flat trailer was being sheeted there were usually so many people helping that by the time the driver had rolled out the sheets and climbed down, sheeting the load was completed.

Drivers were allowed to leave the factory to go up the Ho Chi Minh trail when there was just about enough time to get to their delivery point. Mr Smythe made sure that they did a day's work.

On Saturdays, drivers were expected to go down to the yard, in Barnstaple, to wash their tractor unit and to fill up with diesel ready to go up the road on Monday.

If you were at the chipboard factory and your empty trailer was not required at the yard you were allocated a loaded trailer to take down to the yard. Many drivers used to take theses trailers the twelve miles to Barnstaple without securing the load, risking prosecution if the load fell off. Personally I was not willing to take the risk and always made sure that the load was strapped. Strapping a load and checking the lights and tyres took around half an hour but, inevitably, someone wanted the trailer in a hurry. so after a few months I was not asked to take loaded trailers back.

Then I started to wash my unit during the week instead of joining the queue Saturdays when the lorries were normally washed. It took about ten minutes to wash a unit, with around twenty units to wash, well you can do the maths.

I used to go down to the yard, fill up with diesel and then back to the factory and do some shunting, strap and rope my load ready for Monday, and be home indoors by midday.

I think it was early in January 1983 when I parked up in Northolt and stayed the night with my brother David and his wife Val. After the obligatory visit to the Sergeants' Mess RAF Northolt on Thursday evening, on Friday morning David and I had breakfast together just before seven. There was no hurry as I had a load of timber for Barnstaple, so I should easily be there by midday.

What a shock. When we looked outside we realised it had snowed during the night. Snowed a lot.

As the trailer was parked in the station yard I got a move on; coupled up the trailer and left the station yard before the commuters were rushing to park. There were not quite so many commuters as normal as the snow was deep - no problem for a lorry but a challenge for many cars.

I got close to the motorway before everything came to a halt. There must have been an accident somewhere because the traffic was stationary for nearly an hour; time for me to have a quick kip.

Eventually I got to the motorway and surprise, surprise there was very little traffic and no sign of any gritting truck. I think everyone had decided to stay home and I didn't blame them.

I also wanted to get home but what I didn't know was this was going to be one of the worst journey that I would ever make. The motorway was littered with abandoned vehicles, parked all over the motorway. My saviour was a van driver about a half a mile in front of me. Using the CB radio he constantly informed me of parked vehicles in front of me and which lane I needed to be in to avoid any problem.

Speed was between thirty and forty miles per hour, approaching any services the lane to be in was either the middle or the fast lane as there were parked cars queueing to get into the packed services, blocking the hard shoulder and the slow lane.

As we headed further West the weather deteriorated. The M4 into Wales was closed and impassible. I just hoped we could get to Bristol.

Somewhere in the area of Leigh Delamere services is a steep hill that you go down if you are heading West. As we approached the top of this hill my pilot told me to slow down as 'smokey' - CB slang for 'police' - had stopped West-bound traffic. As I was in the middle lane I pulled slightly to the right into the fast lane and put on my hazard warning lights and started to slow down.

The few vehicles behind me behaved very well and as I kept flashing my brake lights we slowly lost speed. In front the police were sending East-bound traffic across the motor and back toward Wales.

I was at the front of the queue and a police man came over to me and told me that there were so many accidents on the East-bound carriageway that they were closing the motorway. They were advising people to park in the next services until the snow could be cleared.

While this conversation was going on there was a cloud of snow coming from the hard shoulder as a Welsh lorry went careering past the stationery traffic and coming close to colliding with the diverted traffic. Whether the driver had gone to sleep or was driving way above the safe speed for the conditions, I do not know.

I do know he was in serious trouble for 'failing to stop when signalled by police'. Possibly 'dangerous driving' or at least 'due care and attention'. He was on the edge of losing his HGV licence.

While the policeman went over to talk to the driver, the snow had stopped and another policeman let us proceed. However a lot of the snow was turning into thick ice and soon it was starting to snow again.

Turning South onto the M5 brought no relief as I was still faced with snow-covered, slippery motorway although the hill down to Avonmouth wasn't quite as bad. The blinding white of the snow was affecting my eyes and the constant concentration was giving me a headache. I decide that if I could get past Gordano services I would stop at Graham's Café at North Petherton. I had been snacking on biscuits and chocolate wafers and had milk to drink, so I wasn't hungry - I needed to close my eyes for a while.

I eventually arrived at Grahams, nearly four and a half hours after leaving London - normally a two and a half hour journey. I took off my boots and lay on the bunk. After a nice sleep I went into the café, which was fairly crowded, each table hosting drivers from different areas. After getting a tea and ordering some food I joined the North

Devon party. The discussion was whether to stay at the café or chance the Ho Chi Minh trail in some of the worst conditions most of us had ever driven in. Someone telephoned the Police at Wiveliscombe for a road report [you could do that years ago]. The message came back that Wiveliscombe hill was passable. However when the driver told the police that we were driving lorries he was told we should stay where we were. Our choice was to spend Friday night at the Compass Inn bar and drown our sorrows or drive the worst road in the worst conditions possible - at night.

Just west of Bampton, on the Ho Chi Minh trail, was the highest point on the road with the wind blowing from Exmoor, right across the road. This could cause large snow drifts, up to ten foot high.

Seven of us decided to head for home, so off we went in convoy.

From North Petherton to Wiveliscombe is fairly flat with a couple of small hills or 'hop ups' as they call them in Australia. They are fine in the dry but on snow they could be deadly, so 'slow and sure' was the order of the day. There was an M&D tractor unit, pulling an empty fridge trailer who took the 'front door' as we CBers say, and the rest of us followed keeping plenty of distance between the lorry in front. We managed the steep 'hop up' at Preston Bowyer but the snow was getting deeper as we headed West.

At the bottom of the hop up is a roundabout and a snow plough was clearing the road. The plough stopped and let us through - he had sense enough not to stop us coming down a hill.

We carried on through the virgin snow which has better grip than snow that has been driven on.

At the next hop up M&D, myself and Jeffrey Binding managed to get up the hill but the fourth lorry spun out and blocked the road behind us.

We three drove on to the bottom of Wiveliscombe hill which was covered in snow. We knew if we could get up this one we would probably get home. The hill gets steeper and steeper as it goes up, then after a few hundred yards it flattens out a fair bit and then goes around a right hand bend with a steep drop on the left. A lorry has to use the right hand side of the road here, well away from the wooden fence which shields the steep drop. Then the road hairpins left and steepens to about eight percent; after a couple hundred yards the road turns right and starts to get less steep and after another few hundred yards drops down the other side.

The real danger is, after the hairpin bend, if a vehicle slides back down here there is a real danger of crashing off the side of the hill.

M&D went up first and we waited at the bottom. After a couple of minutes he radioed back that he had reached the top and was a little way down the other side and was deliberately blocking the road.

Jeffrey and I were both loaded with timber and it was decided that Jeffrey went next as his lorry had a diff lock. This will help him grip if his wheels starts spinning.

A couple of minutes later he radioed back the he was also at the top: time for me.

I selected a low gear and decided to stay in the same gear all the way up. Unfortunately my diff lock was not working so I just hoped there would be no problem.

The trick is, if your wheels start to spin, to put that wheel on the bottom of the hedge and hopefully you will find a bit of grip in all the rubbish.

I got mostly around the hair pin following the wheel tracks of the ones in front when the offside wheel started to spin a little. I drove right across the road and got the driving wheel onto the bottom of the hedge and it found some grip.

Gently I coaxed the lorry up the hill and, avoiding the wheel tracks of the others, I managed to get to the top and slowly started to descend the other side.

Suddenly there was a voice on the CB radio, it came as a surprise as the radio waves had been unusually quiet that night. No normal chit-chat, with drivers only speaking when there was something to report about the road conditions.

The new voice was 'Highwayman' from Cambridge, someone I knew quite well. He drove for Ceiba-Geigy and delivered glue to the Chipboard Factory at South Molton among other places. We were coming to an S bend which then went into a long left-hand bend. Halfway around the bend one of two tankers had slid into the offside hedge and 'Highwayman' had pulled in behind him so as not to block the road.

We stopped, and went past them one at a time letting the lorry in front get well away before the next one went. The road at this point was quite narrow and we were careful not to get stuck or hit the parked lorries.

Safely through, I advised them that if they did get moving, just to drive up and park in the lay-by a couple of hundred yards up the road and carry on in daylight the next day.

The rest of the trip was uneventful and we got to South Molton in one piece. Jeffrey drove into the back entrance to the lorry park and I followed and parked beside him.

I decided my lorry was not quite 'parallel' to Jeffrey's and professional pride made me drive forward onto the road with the intention of reversing back in a straighter line.

I stopped, selected reverse and the lorry just sat there with its wheels spinning. I was tired and hungry, a four hour drive had taken eleven hours and my eyes were aching after looking at snow for so long. I got out, locked the cab, and arranged with Jeffrey to come back in the morning and try to move it.

The next morning we got to the lorries to find some council workers there, so we borrowed a couple of their shovels, cleared the snow away from the wheels and parked the lorry correctly.

On the late night news it had said that Wales and the South of England had experienced a horrendous snow storm with the M4, M5 and many other local roads blocked with snow.

We had Saturday, Sunday and Monday off as many roads were still unpassable. On the Monday afternoon Tony Smythe phoned Jeffrey and I and asked If we would go to Caerphilly, Wales, the next day. We were told to meet Bob Lovelace (another of our drivers) at the chipboard factory at seven-thirty the next morning. We had to take three empty chipliners to Western Softwood at Caerphilly and bring back three loads of wood chips.

Seven forty five the next morning we joined another convoy, this time heading East toward the M5. I took the front door this time, with Bob Lovelace behind me, Jeffrey Binding and then, another addition, 'Scrumpy' driving a Bill Hockin lorry, and also some others who I cannot remember. It didn't take long to realise not a lot of snow clearing had gone on. The Ho Chi Minh was still white, no sign of tarmac anywhere. My thought was that if neither sunshine nor Somerset council had cleared Wiveliscombe Hill, we wouldn't be going very far.

Mechanical diggers had widened the road through some of snow drifts and I was now amazed that we had travelled this road on the Friday and got through.

We climbed from Bish Mill up the hill to Combe's Land Cross and up the small 'hop up'. As I went around the long left-hand corner I saw a BMW car approaching us and he wasn't hanging about.

I grabbed the microphone and shouted, 'Speeding car! The BMW shot past me barely missing the lorry; the others behind me gave him as much room as they could. He got past Bob and Jeffrey but Scrumpy was coming around another left hand-bend and the inevitable happened. The BMW hit the front wheel of Scrumpy's lorry, bounced off it and shot through the low hedge into a field.

The force of the impact turned the front wheel of the lorry causing it to follow the car partly through the hedge, leaving the road completely blocked.

Jeffrey stopped his lorry and ran back to see if any one was injured. After about ten minutes he returned.

While waiting for Jeffrey I had moved forward a little and parked across the road - one accident was enough. I tried to get someone on the CB as we needed the emergency services to close the road. Scrumpy's lorry could go nowhere until the emergency services and a tow truck arrived. No one answered on the CB; perhaps they had all decided to stay in bed, and I wouldn't have blamed them.

Bob Lovelace eventually radioed me, when Jeffrey had got back to the car. Scrumpy was shaken-up but uninjured and happy to wait for a tow truck. The driver of the BMW, however, said that he was trapped, so Jeffrey had carried on through the deep snow to the farmhouse and alerted the emergency services. He then returned to the car and found that the driver had somehow released himself. After some discussion concerning the man's driving Jeffrey got back into his lorry and we carried on to Wales.

It was bitterly cold with traffic on the motorway reasonably light - though some of the snow had melted. Spray from other vehicles constantly landed on our windscreens. As our washers were frozen it meant getting the driver in front to drive through one of the large puddles so that a serious amount of water could clean my windscreen. In my case this meant Bob moving up to the front, finding me some water, before returning to his former position.

As we travelled across Wales I noticed that the exit roads had not been cleared of snow and there was usually a six inch step of snow to climb over to leave the motorway.

When we got to the turn-off for Caerphilly we slowed right down so as not to cause any damage to our suspension - as there was very little traffic this did not hinder anyone else.

The return run was uneventful and the road had, by that time, been cleared of Scrumpy's lorry. We got back to the chipboard factory and unloaded still in daylight.

The next day it was back to normal for everyone. Although the Ho Chi Minh trail had plenty of snow still on it, we had proved that it was passable by lorries.

Another snowy day found Jeff Binding and myself at a chemical plant at Queensferry, just west of Chester.

We were loaded, there, with two hundred gallon containers of silage-additive for Mole Valley Farmers, South Molton. The containers were on pallets that had been left out in the snow and the plastic retaining straps weren't exactly tight. The loads were sheeted and strapped and we headed South, managing to get to Portishead before our time ran out.

It was getting near closing time when we got to the White Lion pub - a quick couple of pints and then across the road for a Chinese supper was the plan.

Inside the pub we found several Torridge Transport drivers having an impromptu Christmas party. At closing time there were a few drinks that were not going to be consumed by the inebriated drivers and of course Jeff and I were only to happy to help them out.

Hagar, one of Torridge Transport's drivers, was the first to pass me a pint and then came one or two shorts. Needless to say we slept well and had a late start the next day 'because of hours regulations'. It was down to Hill-common for breakfast and then to Mole Valley farmers.

Jeff was in front and parked to unload, we took off his ropes and sheets and found that the snow on the pallets had turned to ice and a couple of drums had moved on their pallets.

The manager came out and said that one load was for the South Molton branch but the other should have gone to Holsworthy. I volunteered to go to Holsworthy and as Jeff gently moved forward to let me out of the yard the strap broke on one of the containers. It slid off its pallet and fell to the ground. Two hundred gallons of mild acid went everywhere. There was nothing I could do so I decided to head for Holsworthy.

Nine miles from South Molton I stopped in a large lay-by and checked the load, all was fine. I had just gone through Hatherleigh when a car behind me started to flash his lights. I pulled over on a straight bit of road and walked back to the car. The driver told me that there was liquid coming from the back of my trailer. I told him that it was mild acid and he should go and wash his car and if there was any problem later with the paint work he should get in touch with Smythe Transport.

After he had driven off I reversed the trailer so that the liquid would run onto the grass verge and not down the water course. There was a farm a few yards away so I knocked on the door and asked if I could use the telephone. I asked for the fire brigade and when I was put through I informed them that I had a chemical spillage. The line was not very good and they thought that I was reporting the spillage in South Molton. I told them that mine was a separate incident. Because I was outside the farm I was able to give them my exact location.

After I put the phone down and the farmer's wife asked what happens now, I told her that sooner or later the fire brigade would turn up and also the police. Her son was only about four years old so I made sure I shut the gate on the way out. As I looked back, both mum and son where beside the gate waiting for the action to start.

It was only a few minutes before the first police car arrived, the driver, a sergeant, used to be stationed at South Molton. About ten minutes later the fire brigade arrived. The fire officer walked up to me and I handed him the paperwork that contained the 'Hazchem' code. This code gives the fire officer all the information needed to deal with that chemical. He asked me if I knew where the spillage was coming from and I told him that it wasn't running very fast but, because of the nature of the liquid, I had not been near it.

While this was happening a tall fireman lay on the grass while his comrades pulled a white chemical suit on to him. Once fully dressed he approached the trailer while the others got ready with a hose. A few minutes later the tall fireman returned to the group. He was hosed down, and then the trailer.

As to the cause of the leak, ice had forced a tapered valve to open. The cure was to turn it off. All of the other valves were also checked. I was allowed to proceed. I told the fire officer that the load was for Mole Valley Farmers at Holsworthy. As it was market day in Holsworthy it was decided to escort me to my destination in case of another incident.

As we were about to get into our vehicles two-tone sirens were heard and a red and white chequered chemical unit came into sight. It stopped beside us and the crew all piled out - the driver looking decidedly flushed. The unit had been scrambled from Barnstaple as the Exeter unit had gone to South Molton. They were not too happy to find the situation had been dealt with - they really wanted to put their training into practice. They had been told it was a two thousand gallon tanker. I told them the telephone line wasn't very good.

Disappointed they turned around and headed back to Barnstaple. With a toot on the air horns of the F88 and a wave to mum and son, we headed to Holsworthy.

As I drove into Mole Valley Farmers there was a bit of a panic when they spotted the fire engine behind with its blue lights flashing. I wound down the window and shouted, 'They are with me!'

I think that just made it worse.

Finally unloaded, the fireman gave my sheets, ropes and trailer another wash and then went home with something different to talk about in the pub. Thankfully we never did another load from that chemical factory.

Scrumpy had a girl friend called Elaine who was a hairdresser in the Bridgwater area. She had an American Trans Am car. One evening she came into the Compass wearing a new fur coat.

'Have you got another one of those?' I asked

'Why'

'I could do with a couple of new seat covers for the lorry,' I replied.

The other drivers thought it was funny but Elaine did not and didn't speak to me for the rest of the night.

As time went on the two Volvo F88s were sold and I received a Volvo F10, registration number TUO 800T, and Jeffrey a Volvo F12. The F10 and F12 had a full width cab unlike the F88s which were not quite so wide. The F12 had a slightly bigger engine than the F10.

It was a Friday morning and the man at Everest transport, Manchester said, 'Sorry mate, no loads for the South West - the nearest is to Oxford.'

Mr Smythe could find nothing but I knew there were always timber panels from Timbmet, Stamford in the Vale near Oxford.

I'll take the Oxford load,' I said and off I went to Kellogg's to load cornflakes - a nice light load.

Five minutes later I was behind a long queue of lorries, all loading for Oxford. Loading was quick and I got to Oxford around lunch time only to find another long queue. This queue was not moving quite so quickly. By three o' clock there were still several lorries in front of me so off I went to see the manager. As soon as I spoke he asked me where I came from.

'South Molton, near Barnstaple,' I told him.

'I'm from Barnstaple. Now what can I do for you?'

'I have to collect a load from Timbmet to deliver back home, but I will lose the load if I am not there by four'

'No problem,' he said and told me to drive around the back of the warehouse.'

Half an hour later I was unloaded and on my way to Timbmet and from there to spend the night in the Compass Inn at North Petherton.

It wasn't often that we were asked to find our own load but sometimes the normal places let you down. One day this happened in London and, at the time, return loads were scarce. I was getting desperate as it was late-afternoon when a company asked if I could deliver to Plymouth at 8.00am the following day. They told me it was a complete hotel kitchen and weighed about three tons and pays a twenty-ton rate. I told him if I can park overnight, where I load, I would do it.

The next morning at three I left London, no traffic and just enough weight on the trailer it was great. The F10 was designed for forty-four tonnes so with this much weight it was like a Range Rover carrying a suitcase.

A quick stop on the way for tea and at seven thirty I was climbing the hill outside of Plymouth. As I passed a mobile crane a sudden thought came into my head. Would they hire a mobile crane from Honiton to unload the kitchen, when a site fork lift would do?

I found the hotel right in the middle of Plymouth and the size of my lorry, when I parked, caused chaos. The size of the problem became apparent. Waiting there was the hotel manager, the brewery area manager and a few others; soon the mobile crane from Honiton turned up. It seems they had no idea where to put the new kitchen as the old one was still in place. The crane driver and myself were told to go and get some breakfast and come back in half an hour.

By the time we returned it had been decided to unload the kitchen by hand and store it in an empty hotel room. The trailer was eventually unloaded and the restaurant bar was open so we all went inside. The brewery manager told the barmaid to give us what we liked so the crane driver and myself ordered a steak and a drink. I had no load back from Plymouth so it was up onto Dartmoor for a quick nap in the sun, then across country to the yard. There was just enough time to diesel-up and get my trailer ready for the morning. I was home at three in the afternoon.

I was most insistent that I did not drive over my hours or overload - after all it is the driver that pays the fine and loses his or her's licence.

Many sawmills did not have a weighbridge and so the weight of a load was guess work; of course there was the option of finding a public weighbridge but most of the time it was guess work and the load wasn't weighed until we got to the chipboard factory.

I used to put on a little less woodchips than some drivers and occasionally the load would be underweight.

The laws were changing, vehicles of five axles would be able to run at thirty-eight tonnes gross weight. Until this became law the maximum weight was thirty two tons. Sometimes the weight would be over for certain combinations. If this happened to me, usually on loads of 8ft x 6ft boards, then I made sure that the offending amount was taken off.

One day Mr Smythe called me into his office and told me that because I did not put as much wood chips on the chipliners as some other drivers I would only be pulling flat trailers from now on - these were not his exact words but the meaning was implied. This did not bother me for two reasons: One, wood chips could contain a lot of sawdust and it blows everywhere when loading and unloading. Two, one usually did three trips a week and getting three nights out. Flat trailers meant shop deliveries usually taking two days per trip, therefore four nights out per week and therefore more money. Also with flat trailers you could see if the load was moving around.

Looking at my last diary in Smythe's employment I was taking chipliners up the road and then on the return journey changing trailers at Bristol. Turning around and going back up the road and on the last trip of the week having a flat trailer; possibly loading back from Avonmouth docks or with fertilizer from Fisons or ICI Avonmouth.

This meant four or even five nights out. Who needs chipliners?

A few weeks after my meeting with Mr Smythe I was sent to Braunton with a flat trailer to load, what can be described as, 'ladies cotton products.'

The load was about fifteen foot high and so I crossed the front and back with rope, twice, as I usually did with higher loads. I came back and dropped the trailer in the yard. A few minutes later Tony Smythe came into the yard while I was talking to Ginger, one of the yard men.

'Who roped that load?' he asked Ginger.

'What's up with it?' I asked

'Nothing,' replied Tony Smythe. 'It's practically perfect.'

'I loaded it,' I said. 'I suppose I am never going to get back onto chipliners now.'

'Probably not,' he said as he walked away.

Trailer five was a flat trailer and the wooden bed was coated in glass fibre. This trailer was always the one used for transporting sheep fleeces. They were loaded in Sanders yard, Pilton - now a car park.

As the fleeces were loaded they were covered in salt to preserve them and the fibre glass was to preserve the trailer from the salt.

Fleeces travelled pretty well but I did have one load that started to slip so I put two ratchet straps on the bulge and the straps straightened the load. Ropes were normally used to finally tie the load.

Most of these loads went to a company in Yarm, North Yorkshire. I had to back down a narrow lane in the middle of the town. Needless to say this often caused a little traffic chaos.

One winter's day I had delivered a load and as I was shovelling the excess salt off the trailer using the company's shovel one of the yard men asked me if I had my own shovel as heavy snow was forecast for that night. When I replied 'no' he said to keep the shovel that I was using. I washed the shovel very thoroughly before I put it in the lorry as there is always a fear of spreading animal diseases - especially anthrax.

I still have the shovel although it has been fitted with a new handle.

Jeffrey Binding and myself were in the yard one afternoon and we were told by Bob Lovelace, now the transport manager, that there were three loads of chipboard to take to Edmonton, North London, the next day. Billy, one of the shunters, was to take the third load. Billy came from

Essex and occasionally he would take a load to London and then go on to visit relatives in Essex.

'You won't see me tomorrow,' said Billy. 'By the time you two get there I will be long gone.'

We left a 6 am and drove to Strensham Services where we decided to have tea and get a paper. When we got there Billy was parked up having a kip and when we left he was still there. He arrived at Edmonton just as we were leaving. We did make some comments about old men needing their sleep. Billy was about fifteen years older than me.

Cox's Pharmaceuticals had a factory on the same industrial estate as Smythe's Transport and we often took large cardboard barrels of powder to Essex. On this particular day I was told to put some on top of a load for Edmonton; so I put them on a pallet. I parked at Edmonton that night and the next morning drove into the yard to unload.

'What's that on the front?' Boxer asked.

'Drums for Essex,' I replied as I pulled off the fly sheet.

'Well you can take them to Essex first and then come back and I'll unload you. Neil was here last week and I told him that we are to paid to trans-ship Smythe's loads.'

Then he noticed that the drums were on a pallet.

'I'll take 'em off this time but not again. I'm going to phone Smythe and tell him. What's the phone number? he asked.

'It's on the cab door,' I said.

So while the fork lift driver unloaded, Boxer went and tried to telephone Smythe.

He quickly returned and told me he could get no answer.

'They probably don't open the office until eight o'clock,' I told him.

He noticed that the carpets on the floor of my cab were quite clean.

'What do you clean the carpet with?' asked Boxer.

'Some green powder that is mixed with water. Why?'

I spilt some oil on the carpet at home, do you think it would clean that?'

'Probably. I'll bring you some next time I come'.

Diplomatic relations restored, I brought him a coffee jar full of the cleaner on the next trip.

ABC at Leeds, another distribution point for the chipboard factory was a regular delivery for Smythe's and there was always the question of the quickest route. From Birmingham, the M6 to Manchester and then the M62 to Leeds or the A38, M1 and M62.

Jeff Roberts, driving a Scania favoured the latter, while I fancied the M6. Jeff Was loaded for ABC and my load was for a new company, nearer the city centre.

The result was basically a draw. Jeff radioing on the CB that he had just arrived at ABC as I pulled into the new customer's yard. It might take a little longer in winter to use the M6, M32 route as it crosses the Pennines - not always a good place to be in the winter.

One winter's day I was unloading at ABC Leeds and it was snowing hard. Room had been made for me to unload inside the shed (my one and only time). It was not long before the city stopped running buses and other traffic was quickly disappearing off the road.

After unloading I telephoned the yard and Bob Lovelace gave me an address of a town a few miles away.

'There's a load of animal feed for Barnstaple waiting to be picked up.'

I told him that it was snowing hard and traffic was going along very slowly.

'Take it easy,' he said. 'Give us a ring in the morning, when you've loaded,' and he put the phone down.

Take it easy? Had he forgotten the trip to Wales in the snow?

There was an A road to where I had to load and as I got closer to the town I came to a steep hill going down. It was completely covered in snow and no other traffic around. I managed to negotiate the hill and eventually got to the feed mill. There was a large lorry park, also covered in snow and as I drove around the back of the already parked lorries one of my front wheels dropped into a hidden hole. An hour or so of digging and a pull from another lorry and I escaped from the hole. Time for a meal in a nice warm pub. By the next morning the snow had mostly disappeared.

I thought that driving for Smythe's Transport I would have finished hauling straw but I was wrong. One summer's evening found Jeff Binding and me parked in a field at the back of a village near Doncaster - a place not known as the straw capital of England. I had eaten but Jeff hadn't so it was agreed that we would go to the pub.

So about seven thirty we were seated at the bar of the local hostelry. The other side of the bar was a barmaid of about twenty and a landlady of about fifty. Jeff ordered his meal and then the barmaid said she was going upstairs to have a bath. Jeff did offer to scrub her back but she declined. The landlady then said she wondered where her husband was, having left to go to a nearby village at lunch time and not yet returned.

'I bet he is in another pub spending his money,' she declared, 'instead of spending it in his own pub. What I need is a new husband.' She was quite good-looking so I said, 'If you are looking for a new husband I would like to put my name forward. I can cook and I am good in bed.'

'Who told you that?' laughed Jeff.

'Your wife, for one,' I replied.

Whereupon Jeff seemed to lose his sense of humour for a while. His dinner was consumed in relative silence and we returned to our lorries for an early night.

The next morning at around seven, my lorry door was opened and a voice said, 'Come on the let's get you loaded!' And the voice walked away leaving the door open. I jumped out of the bunk, got dressed and had a quick swig of milk. I walked over to the farm hand and said 'What's the idea of leaving my door open?'

'It was your mate's idea. He reckoned it was your turn to load first and suggested I leave the door open. That way, he told me, you would get out of bed - even it were only to shut the door.'

As we were talking I noticed Jeff heading toward the village to get the papers and his fags, with a grin on his face. Normal service had resumed. It is the small victories in life that count.

Another interesting job that I had from Doncaster was a load of railway sleepers for the Dart Valley Railway in Devon. Loaded on a Friday I arrived at the railway Saturday morning to be told that I could not be unloaded until Monday. I phoned the office and was told that Adrian had a similar problem in Plymouth and was bob-tailing it home and he would pick me up and take me back Monday.

All went according to plan and I was taken back Monday by Adrian. When I got to the railway I was told that they had a gang of men to unload the sleepers and that I could have a look around the station and workshops. The railway was closed at the time so I had access to practically everything.

Hull was a place we often visited. Tractors were delivered to the docks, some already built and some in knocked-down form and had to be put together prior to delivery. Today's load, however was a consignment of two potato harvesters. Like a high-sided trailer with a pick up at the front, the harvester had a conveyor belt to lift the potatoes into the back. When loaded on my lorry these harvesters were over fifteen feet high. They were bound for South Wales - an easy job one would think.

The instructions were to head for Pembroke docks, turn left at a certain junction; carry on until the sign for the church is seen, turn left for the church take the next left and the farm is a few hundred yards along the road.

I stopped near St Clears for the night and parked next to a lorry with a container on the trailer. The driver and I had a chat. It seemed there were two roads West from St Clear, both had low bridges and we were too high to pass under these bridges.

I took the right-hand road out of the town and asked at an agricultural firm if there was a way to avoid the bridges. They showed me a route where there was a level crossing and so avoided the bridge. It worked perfectly and soon I was nearing Pembroke dock

So I turned left up the hill, left again at the sign for the church and I soon came to a T junction on a little back road. 'Turn Left' said the instruction so I did. The lane was very narrow and overgrown. The CB aerial attached to my wing mirror was bent over by tree branches, I had no idea what was happening to the harvesters. It soon became apparent that this was not the correct road.

I came to a Y junction and managed to jack knife the lorry around and head back the way that I had just come. At the junction where I had turned left I took the other road. I soon came to another junction where I turned left and eventually came to the farm.

When I questioned the lady about the instructions she said, 'Nobody uses that road so we don't count it.'

There was no answer to such logic.

'Turn around and head for Castle Martin,' she said. 'You will soon catch the boys. One is pulling the demonstrator harvester for you to take away and the other tractor is to bring back the other harvester. If you carry on down the road a little there is the village green you can turn on that.'

So I drove down the road a little and there was the village green - no bigger then a postage stamp.

No chance of turning there. At this point I should have tried to reverse back to the cross road but it was a very narrow road. So I decided to carry on down a hill - after all it couldn't get any worse, could it?

The hill was about one in twelve and as I went down I met a car pulling a caravan going up. The car stopped and the old driver exited his car and started to unhitch the caravan. By the time I'd got out he had completed the manoeuvre but the brakes weren't holding the caravan and it was slowly going back down the hill. I managed to help him turn it into a hedge. Next, he turned his car around, coupled-up the caravan and proceeded to drive back down the hill.

I followed at a distance and at the bottom of the hill was a bridge. The sort with vertical iron railings, but the bridge was narrow and on a slight curve. The unit went across ok but the trailer-wheels road along the railing and tilted them out slightly. At the other side of the bridge was a very full car park and on the right side, straight in front, was a sandy lane to the beach.

I had no choice but to back down the lane. I was getting a bit peed-off so I decided that if the trailer sank then I will pull the pin, drive the tractor-unit back to Devon, and resign. As it was the trailer didn't sink and I was able to re-cross the bridge and go in search of the tractors. Things seemed to be getting better - little did I know, but the worst was yet to come.

It was but a few minutes before I caught up the tractors and was told that we were to go to the tank training ground at Castle Martin and use the tank loading ramps to unload the harvesters.

As we drove along on my left I could see tanks of the West German Army driving parallel with us and firing their guns!

A little further and the tractors stopped beside a gate. One of the tractor drivers got off, unlocked a big gate, opened it and proceeded to drive across the firing ground with me following at a distance.

As I suspected all hell broke loose. Within a few minutes an Army Land Rover caught up with our little convoy, by which time we had now reached the unloading ramp.

I sat and waited while the farmer had a discussion with the army.

The Army Officer asked, 'What are you doing?'

The Farmer answered, 'Unloading some potato harvesters. I was given a key to the gate and permission to use the ramp.' He then pointed to the ramp.

The Army Officer said slowly, 'You are supposed to ring-in and ask if it is safe to do so before you enter the area. You have just interrupted a live firing exercise for the West German Army and they are not happy. You may have caused a very awkward international incident.'

The farmer muttered some sort of apology and we were allowed to unload the new harvesters and load up the demonstrator model.

I have to say I was glad to get back on to the road again. I made my way back to St Clears using the same railway crossing and went back to the same lorry park. In the café was my friend who had been hauling the container. Over a meal we discussed the day. He had taken a different route to me and had got his trailer grounded on a hump-back bridge and was stuck until a tractor pulled him off. We both agreed that South West Wales was not our favourite place.

The demonstrator harvester was delivered to a Welsh agricultural dealer with no further problems or bullet holes.

Monday 11th June 1984 I delivered chipboard to DNS Leeds and loaded fertilizer from L&K Fertilisers-Kemire Ltd, Saxilby, for Mr Mennel at The Barton, Lydford, Devon who had ten tons and the other ten tons went to Thomas Oke, Holsworthy.

Mr Mennel was a regular customer of Thomas Oke and I delivered to the farm a few times. The lane to the farm was straight and mostly level with an S bend just before you get to the farm yard. From the S bend the lane gently sloped up to the yard. A pretty easy place to get an Artic to. In addition there was a pretty young milkmaid who worked there and always gave me tea with scones and cream.

One damp day I arrived at the farm and the slope to the yard was a bit slippery. I went and found Farmer Mennel and asked if there was anyone else on the farm as I needed to back down the lane a bit, speed through the S bend and try to roll up the slope. The farmer said there was only him and the maid and they would not be going down the lane. So I backed up a couple of hundred yards and proceeded forward. I went though the first bend and eased off the accelerator. Suddenly a red car appeared from the direction of the yard and, on seeing me, went straight on through an open gate and into a field.

I rolled into the farm yard as farmer Mennel came out of a barn. I told him that there was a red car that just came from the yard and disappeared into a field.

'Oh my God!' he exclaimed. 'I forgot about the milk recorder.'

When she (the milk recorder) drove back into the yard the farmer apologised and I commented on her quick reactions. If she hadn't acted in the way she did it could have ended very different.

The road from the West to Saxilby, on the A57, had a fifty pence toll bridge just a few miles from the village and a roadside mobile café where two ladies did excellent food.

Jeffrey Binding and I were being loaded at Saxilby one Friday afternoon when another of Smythe's lorries drove into the yard. When we were all loaded we decided to park up for the night and leave around five in the morning. We hoped to get through Leicester before too much traffic built up. There was one problem, the other driver, Derek Monk, had no trailer side lights as they kept blowing fuses. At the trailer electrical socket we disconnected the side light wire and connected the brake light wire to the empty connector. At the light end we swapped the brake light connectors with the side light connectors. Hey presto the side lights were on but no trailer brake lights. The next morning we left early got through Leicester without mishap and when daylight came we swapped the wires back. We all got safely back home.

I was loaded at Saxilby one evening and went to the toilets to have a wash. I came back got into the cab and made a cup of tea. I was moving my towel when it caught the tea pot and tipped the scalding liquid over my feet. I quickly got my left sock off but by the time I got my right sock off, my ankle down to my toes were scalded. I knew this was serious so I wrapped the cold wet towel around my foot climbed out of the cab and went in search of help. Thankfully the firm worked a night shift. The fertilizer plant was alongside a canal with a wide area between the canal and the building. The lorry park was to the west of the building next to a B road. I walked beside the canal toward a group of men next to some wide doors about halfway along the building.

I was waving my arms but, they told me later, because of the sun behind me they could not clearly see me. In the end the pain was too much and I fell to the ground to get their attention. They realised that something was wrong and they ran down to me.

It was decided that I needed hospital care and after moving jobs around one of the men was free to take me to the nearby Lincoln Hospital. Although my foot was seriously hurting there were some patients worse than me. There was one young lad who had used four inch nails to climb a tree, slipped, and slid back down the nails.

It was gone nine o'clock, nearly three hours after the incident. There were lots of people going past obviously dressed for a party and I said to the man who had kindly taken me to the hospital that if I don't get seen soon then I am going to that party, I could do with a drink. About ten o'clock a nurse looked at my foot, now very swollen but because of the wet towel quite clean. She told me that the skin was dead and could cause problems with the wound. She got a big pair of tweezers and ripped the skin from the wound. Then removed any little bits left. I wouldn't believe that it could be any more painful but it bleddy was!

She put a burn dressing on my foot and bandaged it up. She told me to visit my doctor and get the wound re-dressed. It was imperative that the wound was kept clean and regularly dressed.

We left the hospital and we made our way back to the lorry.

The next morning, a Friday, I started for home. When I stopped for breakfast I phoned the yard and told them what had happened and I would be there after lunch. My right foot I wrapped in a plastic carrier bag to keep it clean and I wore a sandal so that I could use the brake although I made good use of the exhaust brake.

I told Bob Lovelace I was ok to work but not on the Saturday as I had to see the doctor. I was allocated a load for London and Bob told me to ring him if there was any change.

Saturday morning I went to the doctors and a nurse re-dressed my foot. When she finished she told me to come back Monday and she would do the same again. I told her that I couldn't come back Monday as I would be delivering a load to London. I told her that I couldn't afford to stay home.

She gave me a load of burn dressings and stressed that the wound must be thoroughly cleaned before it was dressed.

Christine was worried about me carrying on working; she knew I was in a lot of pain. I told her I will try one trip and promised that I would ring Monday evening.

When I wasn't driving I used a new fertilizer sack over my sandal to keep my bandage clean. When I parked-up I used a bowl of warm water to clean the wound and then I let it dry in the evening sun. It was a good job it was summer.

One evening I was at Graham's Café and I went into the shop at the petrol pumps. I asked the man behind the counter if he could let me have some warm water to clean my wound, as it was a lot easier than boiling a kettle. He found me a chair and told me to sit in the shop and he would bring it out.

So there I was sitting in the shop moving my foot around and around the bowl. A women came up to me and asked what I was doing. I told her and she asked to see my foot. It looked like raw meat, but I showed her. The next thing that I knew she had fainted. By the time I got assistance she was coming around. I decided that I wouldn't show it to anyone else.

A couple of days later I was in the old railway yard at Portishead, watching telly, with my foot out of the window drying in the sun, when Dougie Braunton pulled in behind me. As he walked up to my lorry he had a good look at my foot. It was starting to heal around the edges but still looked pretty raw.

He told me that I shouldn't be driving but I said it wasn't that bad. The next day I was called into the office, Dougie was so concerned he had told Tony Smythe that I shouldn't be driving. Tony Smythe asked me if I felt that I was safe to drive, I told him I was and that was the end of it.

Eventually it did heal up pretty good although two toes are a little scarred.

J&S Marine was a company in Barnstaple that serviced munitions. During the Falklands war I returned to the yard one afternoon and was given a trailer with two Exocet missiles bound for a frigate at Plymouth docks. They were in two long wooden crates and on the side of the crates was written EXOCET MISSILE. Everyone had heard of these missiles as one had sunk HMS Sheffield in May 1982. I decided not to sheet down the load.

I was given two hours to get to Plymouth as the docks closed at five. The missiles were a comparatively light load so it was straight across Dartmoor via Okehampton and arriving at Plymouth with rush hour starting. The idea of the unsheeted load worked; I pulled away from a set of traffic lights and all the cars stayed where they were. They weren't going anywhere near something that could sink a ship.

I arrived at the dock at 4.45 pm. I found the ship and went on board to sort out unloading. As soon as I got on board a siren sounded.

'What's that?' I asked

'A fire alarm,' replied the naval officer as he put a rope across the gangway. 'No-one allowed off-ship.'

He was now uncoiling a rope.

'What's that for?' I asked.

'The fire party will take one end of this rope to the fire and if the smoke gets too thick they can follow the rope back to the gangway.'

Then I heard someone shouting from the dock. It was a docker sent to unload the missiles and it was nearly 5.00 pm.

'Permission to leave ship,' I said to the naval officer and before he could answer I had jumped over the rope and was going down the gangway. He was probably better off without a civilian on deck - whether it was a practice fire or a real one.

The missiles were on the dockside by five minutes past five. Amazing how quick dockers work when there is a war on.

Around the same time Mr Smythe told me to take an empty trailer and be in Portland Naval base at 8.00 am. I left at four in the morning and was on the dock well before eight, parked next to HMS Brecon.

Dead on eight o'clock a party of sailors appeared on deck and raised the Union Jack. Then one of the sailors came across to me and said, 'We're going to have breakfast - you can join us if you want.'

A free breakfast? I was out of that cab quicker than you can say antidisestablishmentarianism.

'This boat doesn't make any noise as we walk on it,' I said.

'This boat is a minesweeper. It's plastic-hulled to avoid being blown up by magnetic mines. We are off to the Falklands so we are lightening the ship. That is why you are here.'

So much for the Official Secrets Act.

When breakfast was over it was back to the dock. There were about ten large wooden cases next to the lorry.

'There's your load,' said the sailor pointing to the crates. 'A couple of tons of sonar equipment, surplus to requirement.'

In a few minutes the crates were loaded. I was then sent to Southampton to load ten tons of steel. After loading at the steel works I phoned Smythe and told him that the alternator on my lorry wasn't working very well. Come back to the yard and we will fit a new alternator tomorrow. So off I set, I didn't get far when the silencer developed a hole in it. I stopped and telephoned Smythe who said bring it home and we'll fix it tomorrow with the alternator.

A few miles along the Ringwood bypass and the heat from the leaking exhaust gasses melted some plastic brake pipes and I came to a halt. I telephoned Smythe and he said that they would send out a fitter from Volvo, Southampton with a new silencer and some brake pipes.

The fitter eventually arrived, fitted the new silencer but he had brought the wrong brake pipes and said he would have to go somewhere else to get them.

'Bring back an alternator as well because by the time you get back it will be dark and I do not have enough power to work the headlights. It was dark by the time he got back and fitted the parts, it was around nine o'clock at night. I was well over my time but one law saved me: In time of war and when working for the MOD the driving rules were relaxed. So I drove back to Barnstaple, arriving around two in the morning. Twenty-two hours, but only around eight hours actual driving and I had plenty of rest and sleep while waiting around. I wrote across the tachograph card working for the MOD. As I had signed the Official Secrets Act in 1968 there was no way I could tell anyone what I was doing, and therefore I was immune to prosecution. Neat eh? Know the rules - that's what I say.

The next day I got out of bed about ten and went down to the lorry park in South Molton with Christine where a brand new Mobile Job Centre Vehicle was parked. Christine went in and got a job working at the local hospital. She still holds the record for the first person to get a job at this Mobile Job Centre Vehicle.

At eleven o'clock I rang Smythe and he said come down to the yard in an hour or so. He said he appreciated that I had done a good job the day before.

Just after mid-day I went down to the yard and he sent me up to the chipboard factory to do some shunting. at three o'clock I was told to go home. The next day, Friday, I washed my lorry, and did some shunting up at the chipboard factory before getting my load ready for Monday. I finished at around five.

We did have a little row following this: the sonar equipment was bound for Rosyth in Scotland and Smythe said that Neil Russell was delivering it. I said that, as I had loaded it, I should take it.

In the end neither of Neil nor myself took it. As the company could not get anything else to go on the lorry with it, Harris and Miners from Bovey Tracey took it. Unlike Smythe's transport they had regular runs to Scotland.

On another trip I was sent Vosper Thornycroft in Portsmouth and after unloading I decided to go and have a look at the 'Victory' which is in another part of the dock. I used to do a fair bit of sight-seeing with a lorry, but this time I was told that it was a pedestrian-only area and I would not be welcome - and they were right. I did get turned around so I parked the lorry and walked down.

A full load of pharmaceuticals was regularly delivered to Revlon situated in an old army camp at Eastbourne. I seemed to get more than my share, but it was a good run. The downside was that the fork lift driver would take off one pallet, then disappear into a shed for five minutes before returning and doing the same with the next.

One day I was being unloaded and a man came along and started measuring the lorry. I asked him what he was doing and he told me that a new factory was to be built and he was drawing-up the plans for it. I told him the measurements of an Artic and also the maximum measurements of a wagon and drag.

We also discussed what a lorry driver would like. As the company wanted to keep the floor level I said a canopy is needed sixteen feet high where a lorry could be unloaded onto the floor and the delivery put away after the lorry had gone.

A couple of years later this is what was built. The canopy was about thirty feet wide and ideal for its purpose. This must have been one of the rare occasions that a lorry driver had been consulted about building a new loading area.

And yet they still had the same forklift driver and still the same method of unloading. Apart from once: I arrived at the factory but after removing the sheets an aerial torpedo, on a trolley, was revealed at the front of the trailer.

'What's that?' asked the forky.

'That,' I said, 'is an aerial torpedo. Don't catch any of those little flags sticking out when you move it.'

'What would happen if I did?'

'There would be a big bang and this factory and half of Eastbourne would have to be rebuilt.'

I didn't have the heart to tell him that the torpedo was not armed. But on this one occasion I was unloaded quickly, the pallets were put on the floor beside the lorry and in half an hour I was gone.

Parked in Worcester one night I didn't start until eight in the morning. As I headed for the motorway I noticed that there were a lot of people on foot all around, all heading in the same direction. Then I was going along roads with crowd barriers either side and lots of people, who were waving to me and I waved back. Some worried-looking policemen but no other traffic. Unusually, all the traffic lights were green. I got to the motorway in a very quick time. That evening the situation was clarified. That day the Queen had visited Worcester and the road she travelled into the city was the one that I had used to get out. I must have missed her by minutes.

A regular but challenging job was to take plate steel from railway trucks at Barnstaple, to Appledore ship yard. The steel was loaded on the railway trucks on a frame which kept it eight foot wide but on the trailer it was loaded flat making it nine or ten feet wide. The challenge with this load, at that time, was to get it across the old Bideford bridge. I used to drive down the middle of the bridge to avoid decapitating pedestrians. With headlights and hazard warning lights on I hoped that any car and caravan coming the other way would stop. It worked about forty percent of the time. At the shipyard the lorry was parked under a very large gantry crane to be unloaded. I would go for a walk along the river for an hour while unloading took place.

An old MAN lorry, registration number WOD, was one of the shunters and kept on local work. One day Tony Smythe said to me there was a load for Manchester and I would have to take the Scania 141 as my Volvo was off the road. I told him that I would not drive the Scania as the last time I did I pressed the exhaust brake button and the air horns came on. Not a lot of good for braking but a least people knew I was approaching.

He said, 'OK. You can take the Scania or WOD.'

I said 'I will take WOD.'

I gave WOD a good clean inside and out, hot-wired my CB radio, chucked the rest of my gear on the bunk and off I went. WOD was a column gear change but that was no problem as North Devon Farmers Bedford pick-up truck was a column gear change and also a couple of cars that I had driven. The cars and pick-up truck were four speed boxes and the MAN was twelve, but hey, that's only four times three and I had driven it around North Devon a bit.

So off we went. As I was going North bound through Birmingham on the M5 I saw Dougie Braunton heading South. The CB came alive as Dougie said to another driver, 'I've just seen WOD heading North-bound.'

'No way!' said the other driver.

I keyed the mike and said 'Way.'

'What's going on Smurf?' asked Dougie.

I told him that I was asked to take Geoff Robert's Scania and explained about the exhaust brake and telling Smythe that I would sooner take WOD.

'Is she running OK?' asked Dougie.

'Sweet as a nut since I got her up to sixty miles an hour and cleared the dust off her.'

'I can't remember the last time she was on a motorway,' said Dougie. 'Anyway before I lose you, you're clean and green all the way. You should get there easy enough.'

'You got the green light South-bound and I'll catch you on the flip flop - ten ten,' I said.

'You keep the shiny-side up - ten ten,' said Dougie.

I think WOD enjoyed herself on a nice easy run up North instead of working hard going up and down the hills around Barnstaple and it sure put egg on the face of Tony Smythe who I guess didn't think I really would take the MAN.

One of the worst loads to have was lime from ICI near Buxton. The lime was put in hundred weight paper sacks and loaded by hand. Which meant unloading four hundred heavy, dusty white bags by hand at the destination - a dirty dusty job, ideal for a driver with a flat trailer. I'll give you one guess as to who did the majority of those loads and delivered them. Most of the lime went to water companies to put into your drinking water. I think it was to soften the water.

Loading could take up to four hours with the loaders regularly stopping for a drink. After loading there a few times I used to get invited to join them for a brew (cup of tea). Maybe it was because I never complained about the time it took to load. I had four hours to eat and then have a little nap.

'A nice load for you Stephen,' said Bob Lovelace one day. 'A load of doors from Shapland and Petter for a new hospital in Dumfries and three doors for a brewery at Port Dundas, Glasgow.'

Scotland? We didn't normally get to go that far and there were a few drivers annoyed that I was doing the job.

Going up the motorway, carrying around twelve tons of doors was brilliant. I was flying up every hill and made really good time until I got to Dumfries. There was a low railway bridge just before the hospital. I literally scraped under it with the rope twanging against the rivets on the underside of the bridge. Thankfully a passer-by helped guide me through.

Unloading was reasonably quick and on to Glasgow and the brewery. I phoned Bob Lovelace who was happy with my progress and told me to go to a new chemical plant North West of Glasgow. There was a building company from Bideford working there and I had to bring back a load of excess materials, tools and plant. I arrived at the plant to be told that the various bits and pieces had not been sorted yet as I was not supposed to be there until Friday and this was Thursday.

I dropped the trailer at the plant and bob-tailed to the nearest village. I found a little car park opposite a pub, parked up and went in.

'Is it ok if I park my tractor unit in the car park opposite?' I asked the barmaid.

'I'm nay bothered. It's the council's car park,' she replied.

I had a meal and a pint and watched the telly until a load of teenagers came in at half past seven to watch 'Top of the Pops'. Time for an early night. I had been told not to arrive the next morning until nine o'clock so I had plenty of sleep that night as it was going to be a long drive home the next day - or so I thought.

Loading the next day took some time as the bits and pieces were all over the site. Eventually I left with half a trailer load, weighing about six ton. Bob Lovelace told me to head South and ring him when I got nearer to Manchester. He was obviously trying to get some thing else to fill up the trailer.

Nearer to Manchester I was told to ring back in an hour; and then in another hour. Time was going on by now and around four o'clock he told me to go to ICI at Buxton - to be honest I was not a happy man. By the time I got loaded I wouldn't have time to get much further South. It was going to be a long run-home in the morning. From Buxton it usually took six hours' driving time as it was across the Pennines.

By the time I left ICI it was late and I decided to park in Buxton and leave about six in the morning.

I woke up on time to find it had snowed - a lot. All roads out of Buxton were closed. This was serious. Buxton lies in a deep valley on the edge of the high peaks and every road out starts with going up a steep hill. I ate some breakfast and as daylight came a local driver walked into the car park.

'How do I get to the M6 from here?' I asked him.

'You don't, not when there's snow on the ground. Your best bet is to stay put and leave when the snow is melted. You can take the A515 South East to Derby and then the A38 to Birmingham. But the A515 is not the best road in the world.'

I decided to give it a try. With hardly any traffic on the road I did have plenty of room to manoeuvre. It took a while to cover the thirty three miles to Derby and the A38 dual carriageway. The rest of the way home the road was clear, even the Ho Chi Minh trail. I got home late Saturday afternoon - so much for a nice easy run to Scotland.

Sometimes it works the other way. A Scots driver and myself loaded reinforcing bars from River Road, Barking and arrived at the delivery point in Newton Abbot only to be told that one of the loads should have gone to Manchester. We phoned Bob who said the company would pay for one of us to drive to Manchester so we must sort it out between us. 'Jimmy' said he wanted to be home that night so I went to Manchester. By the time I arrived at Manchester it was too late to unload and I would have to wait until the morning. A nice easy day for a change.

Bert Griffiths ran a company just off the East India Dock Road in the East end of London. He specialised in expensive wood veneers. The company was in a dead end street and at the end of the street was a footbridge over railway tracks. Bert's little factory was on the left side of the street as you looked down it - on the right was a yard and premises of a dairy. There was enough room to park an Artic beside Bert's without blocking the gates to the dairy if one went right back to the end.

Bert owned a large Jaguar car, one of his associates a large Ford and the third one also had some sort of limousine. To load, one parked in the main road and went to the factory and told them you had arrived and, as usual, the one pallet of veneers was not quite ready. Although there was double yellow lines on the main road there seemed no problem with the traffic wardens.

As a regular driver it was always the same greeting.

'Hello Steve, you alright?'

'Fine thanks and you?'

'Yeah, good thanks. Do us a favour and make a cup of tea, we're gasping here.'

'We'll be done in five [ten to fifteen] minutes,' he added.

I would go into the kitchen and make a pot of tea. Four bone china cups and saucers, four tea spoons, a covered silver sugar bowl, a small milk jug and a large pot of tea, all put on a silver tray and delivered to the workers. Bert was a man of class and it showed.

'Right that's finished. Let's have that tea. Thanks for making it Steve, you got one for yourself haven't you?'

'Yes Mr Griffiths. Thank you,' I answered.

I did discover the other drivers were never offered tea; maybe it was because I didn't moan that the load wasn't ready or maybe it was because I make great tea.

Tea consumed, the cars were moved out of the street giving me room the reverse in and load. After loading I was given the delivery tickets and ten bob (50p in new money). It was a tradition in London to give the driver ten shillings (now fifty pence) for a cup of tea on the way home. The timber merchants, Silverman's in Bethnal Green, was one of the few that I experienced carrying on the tradition when I was driving lorries.

I often parked outside Bert's overnight, it was close to the main A13 road and there was no charge.

One night I was parked there and decided to walk to a pub and ring Christine, tell her what I was up to, and when I may be home. I turned right and went a little way and there was a pub - so in I went.

Having telephoned Christine I was enjoying my pint and contemplating an early start in the morning. 5am was the usual time, which would see me on the M4 long before the traffic started building up.

There were a group of lads discussing football teams and one turned to me and asked me which football team I supported.

' I don't support any. I'm not that interested in football,' I replied

'What are you some sort of pansy? Don't like football?' said a rather rude man.

'To be honest I don't know much about football. I prefer motor racing. I used to support Wolverhampton Wanderers when I was younger.

'Wolverhampton Wanderers?' he gasped. 'You really *don't* know much about football, do yah?'

We all had a laugh at that and the ice was broken. I was included into their midst for the rest of the evening.

Another evening I was parked outside of Bert's and this time I turned left and went to a different pub. I went in and ordered a pint and asked if I could use the phone.

'It's through that door, in the hall,' said the landlady. 'Leave ten pence beside the phone for the call.'

'I'm calling Devon. Will ten pence be ok'

'Yeah, that'll be fine' she said.

I finished speaking to Christine and went back into the bar. On my right was a man sitting down and next to him were two or three others standing. The one sitting down asked if I was from Devon and I told him yes. Then he asked if I was parked up next to the dairy and I told him I was.

Then he said, 'So you're the one that keeps blocking the dairy gate.'

I told him I was not blocking anything.

'You're always blocking our gate and it's costing us money.' This man had obviously had plenty to drink and now he was starting to get on my nerves.

'If you keep on mate you're gonna get a smack,' I said.

'What's going on here?' asked a voice from behind me.

I turned around and there was a big bloke, all of six foot tall and quite thick set.

'This fellow here keeps on about me blocking the gate to the dairy. I've told him that I am not but he still keeps on and now he's starting to get on my wick.'

The big man said, 'We're all milkmen and if the lorry delivering the milk cannot get in the gate he just turns around and takes it back. This means we do not have any milk to deliver and therefore make no money.'

I told him I was not obstructing anyone and that when I go back to the yard I will ask the other drivers to do the same.

'Tiny' as he was called, made the other man apologise. I shook his hand and he bought me drink. Later we left the pub, walked past my lorry and over the footbridge to a lovely pub. That night was the first time that I had ever crossed the bridge. I decided, in future, I should be more adventurous.

I used to load paper rolls form the Hythe, Colchester. There was some sort of docks there. I used to load rolls of paper from a shed right at the entrance so I never went into the docks. The lorry was backed up a slight slope to the loading bay and the paper rolls were rolled on to the trailer using gravity. The rolls were heavy paper, for magazines, and were about four feet high and the same wide. Two rolls, side by side, would fit perfectly on the trailer. Stacked one high they came to about eighteen tons in weight and travelled perfectly on the trailer.

There was a sawmill in Ascot where we used to load timber. It was cut across the trunk and was all wriggly around the edge and therefore a bit of a challenge to secure to the trailer. This was not a load that I relished.

One dull weekend I decided to wind up Jeff Binding. Sunday I was in the New Inn with Jeff and a few other drivers, and as usual, they knew where everyone else was delivering the next day.

'Jeff you're supposed to be loading back from Afro Timber, Ascot, tomorrow but I talked to Tony Smythe yesterday and he's changed the return loads around,' I said.

'In what way?'

'I want to be back home tomorrow night so I am doing the Afro Timber and you're doing the paper rolls from Colchester.'

'I am not doing any paper. I don't have any chocks and I've never done paper rolls before,' said Jeff.

'You can borrow mine and the back scotch. You'll be fine.'

'I'm doing the timber and that's it.' said Jeff.

'I'll tell you what I'll do: the first one to unload at ABC has to do the Afro Timber.'

'OK,' said Jeff knowing his F12 is about five miles an hour faster than my F10.

Monday morning we left one behind the other and when we got to the motorway Jeff took the lead and made sure he stayed there. When we got to London, however, I managed to get past him and then took off. Once I was out of sight he asked on the CB which bridge I was using to cross the Thames. As I didn't want him to see me across the river I told him 'Chelsea' and would be around a bend before he caught me up.

In fact I just went straight on to Westminster and then, ignoring the three ton limit, carried on along Victoria Embankment. I gave him a running commentary and of course I gave an answer that put me about two hundred feet in front of him. I eventually got to ABC at Bow about twenty minutes in front of him.

As soon as I stopped I told the fork lift driver to tell Jeff that the first lorry to unload has to go immediately to Ascot and load timber as the customer is waiting for it.

When Jeff arrived he said to me, 'You never crossed the river at Chelsea, did you?' I just smiled.

Then the forklift driver did his bit and Jeff walked into the office and telephoned Smythe. I had followed him into the office and I heard Jeff say that I had gone through a three ton limit. I took the phone from Jeff and heard Smythe say, 'I didn't think he could read.' Then I gave the phone back to Jeff and went back outside.

Jeff came outside and said 'I'm doing the Ascot load and you're doing the paper.'

'I know. Whatever made you think it was any different?' Jeff was then very rude to me but I still helped him get his straps and sheets off.

While he was unloading, I phoned Smythe and asked if I was still doing the paper.

'Yes,' he replied. 'What's going on with you two today?'

'Don't worry - he just lost a bet, that's all.'

'I don't want to know,' he replied .

Jeff and I went our separate ways and I loaded my paper and headed back into London to park up for the night.

The next morning I met Jeff on the A361 between South Molton and Barnstaple.

'What have you done with the rest of the paper?' he asked.

'This is it - eighteen tons of heavy paper for magazines.'

'If that is all it is I could have handled that.'

Maybe I shouldn't have told him. I didn't want to lose that particular job.

I delivered the paper to the printers in Barnstaple and always got a copy of every magazine they printed. They kept me in reading material for a few days.

I used to like the run to the paper store at the Hythe. Opposite the store was a pub, ideal if you are parked there overnight and it opened at seven in the morning for breakfast.

I was parked outside the pub one morning when Jock, from Evans Transport, Barnstaple arrived. He got out of his lorry and asked me where somewhere was. I told him I didn't know but there were a lot of dockers in the pub having breakfast, they would be sure to help out. I was just going in for breakfast and he told me he hadn't had his yet.

'Let's go in then - I am sure there's room for one more.'

I had booked in the night before. Jock said that it was the earliest he had ever been into a pub. When you're on the road it pays to know were you can get food, which leads me to another story.

Henry Miller, one of Smythe's drivers, had been stopped by the police in London and was not allowed to continue until his load was chained. The problem was the chains were in Liverpool.

I was given a load to ABC in Bow, in the Eastend of London. A chap from Liverpool, that I had never met, was bringing the chains to me at Bow, so I could take them to Henry.

Apparently the Liverpool driver had never been to London before. He arrived about ten o'clock in the morning having left Liverpool very early. He definitely did not go in a straight line to me through London.

We put the chains in my cab.

'Have you had breakfast?' I asked

'No, I ate a sandwich on the way but I could do with something now.'

'Follow me,' I said and started to walk down the road. We were on an old trading estate and there were three roads in front of us. I pointed to the one on the left and said, 'There's a café down there, but we are going in here.' I pushed open a wooden door in the fence on our left which took us into a timber yard. We walked into the canteen and ordered two breakfasts and two teas. When we got our teas we went and sat at a table.

'Are we allowed in here?' he asked.

'Yeah, we deliver timber to here sometimes and the canteen is run separate to the yard. Also the food is cheaper than the café down the road.

The Liverpool driver was picking up a load of timber from Rochester docks in Kent. It was easy to pick up the A2 from Bow, back to the roundabout on the main road, turn left at the roundabout and follow the A2 road straight to Rochester. He was very happy to have such an easy way out of London. I think he had forgotten that he would have to come back through London to get back to Liverpool. Me, I went off to find Henry and gave him his chains.

There was another Smythe's driver, we will call him 'Captain'. In the yard he always seemed to be rushing around in circles and continuously calling everybody 'mate'. Captain and myself were shunting at the chipboard factory and I was told to take a load back to the yard. I strapped down the load, checked the wheel nuts, tyres, lights and brakes as per rule. Eventually I got back to the yard and was told to take a trailer to High Wycombe. When I found the trailer it was loaded with a curved wooden bridge about thirty six feet long and seven feet wide, made by Laminated Wood at Bideford. This load was going to be a doddle, I thought to myself, I will be able to fly up the Ho Chi Minh with this one. I got to Graham's at North Petherton and there was Captain's MAN parked there. I went inside ordered a meal and sat beside Captain. I couldn't help myself!

'You're a bright one. You've got the wrong trailer,' I said. (This *has* happened in the past with other drivers - but not me).

'Oh no mate! what I am I going to do mate? Should I ring the office? Or should I take it back. Do you think they'll sack me mate? I don't want to lose my job. Was Bob very angry mate?'

He was getting really upset so I said. 'Sorry, I'm only winding you up - every thing is fine. You loaded the trailer yourself so it has to be right.'

'You bugger. You had me going there, mate.'

We finished our meal and I checked his tickets and showed him on the map where he had to go, and off he went.

About a month later I was in Rochester docks loading hardboard and Captain turned up. As soon as I moved out of the way he put his lorry in my place, ready to load. As I was sheeting my load I heard lots of shouting and looked across to Captain's lorry where he was shouting at the loader. As I walked across I immediately saw the problem. Hardboard came in two sizes eight by two and eight by three and Captain hadn't realised it. He had told the loader to put three eight by three packs of hardboard across the trailer which was eight foot wide. Of course as soon as the loader pushed one pack level with the side of the trailer the other side there was an overhang by a foot, so Captain got the loader to push that side level and obviously the other side then stuck out a foot. Also he had thrown his sheets off the back of the lorry onto the floor which meant the loader had to drive around them.

I told the loader that Captain wasn't all there in the head and he hadn't realised that the boards came in two different sizes. I asked the loader to take off the three feet pack that he had just put on, drive to the back of the trailer and I would throw the sheets on the packs, they were stacked two high. That was done and he then loaded the pack on the opposite side of the trailer. I went and told Captain that there were two different size packs and to just let the dockers load them - they knew their job. After he was loaded Captain did apologise to the dockers but he had questioned their skill and knowledge and that was unforgivable.

While he was strapping down his load I went and phoned the office to tell them that we were loaded. Tony Smythe answered and told me that I had to go to Bert Griffiths for a pallet of veneers.

I told him that I had been away for two nights and Captain can go there as he had only been out for one night. It must have been on a Friday - darts night.

I went and told Captain he had to go to London and pick up a pallet of veneers and when he asked me what was the name of the firm it had gone right out of my head, no matter how I tried I couldn't remember it.

'Ah, you're trying to wind me up again,' said Captain. 'You're not going to catch me again.' Try as I might the name wouldn't come.

'Go and ring the office and they will confirm what I said. I'm going to the canteen.'

He came in the canteen five minutes later and confirmed that he had to go to Bert Griffiths.

'How do I get there?' he asked.

'Go up the A2 until you get to the A13, turn left and go to the first set of traffic lights and turn right, Bert's place is the second road on the right.' I then told him the procedure about parking.

Then he asked if he could borrow ten pounds.

'You only left home yesterday,' I said with surprise.

'I know, but I bought a few drinks last night.'

I lent him the ten pounds even though I took a limited amount of money with me.

As we left the canteen the dockers cheered. 'Don't come back again,' was heard from one.

Saturday morning I had left the yard and was going along the road when a red car passed me at speed and stopped at an angle in front of me half-parked on the pavement. It was Captain. He had the ten pounds in his hand. 'Thank you for the loan,' he said, abruptly. He handed me the money - got in his car and sped off.

I discovered a few days later that he had been sacked. The Friday he had gone to Bert Griffiths he had sat in his lorry for about ten minutes then decided there was room to squeeze the lorry past the cars and in, so doing, he hit all three. Apparently Bert Griffiths was not best pleased. I was the one Captain blamed because I was the one who should have gone and loaded the veneers and not him.

There were a lot of wooden beams we delivered for Laminated Wood and most were a pain in the backside. I took one to a school at Heathfield, Devon. Try as I might I could not find the school, the only time that I failed to deliver. As I had to load and deliver fertilizer from Exmouth dock the rest of the day, the beam went with me. I wrapped it in a blue secondary fly sheet that had now been put on all flat trailers. After moving it from trailer to trailer during the day. I finally ended up leaving a trailer at Exeter Services and bob-tailing home - of course the beam had to go with me. It weighed about one and a half hundred weight (seventy Kilos) and I got it off the trailer and tied it to the cat walk behind the cab. The office found the school was in Heathfield, Kent!

Another beam was for a house in Essex. I left the main road and drove into the village only to be told that the house was on the main road. I drove through the village, and back onto the main road.

I knocked on the door of the house and the lady answered in a dressing gown. The builders were not due until 11am so I was a bit early. They did arrive about an hour later.

One day I arrived at Rochester docks and found that Mike Fallon was there, loading. 'I've got a wooden beam for Pall Mall - you know London, do you want to take it?' he asked.

'No thanks,' I said, 'but it's easy to find. Follow the A2 go back into the city but do not go across Southwark bridge, keep on the North side of the river. Go past Cleopatra's Needle, under the railway bridge, turn right along Northumberland Avenue until you see a sailor at the top of a tall column (Nelson). Go out the top left-hand side of the square, that is Pall Mall and where you want is the brown door about ten houses down on the left.'

'How do you know the door is brown? Nobody knows London that well.'

'I do,' I said. 'I delivered there last week.'

I was at a Homebase store in North East London and I had climbed on to the top of the load to slide the top packs of chipboard to the outside of a pallet. The store's forklift had short blades and if it picked the boards up without pushing them across, then they would have fallen off the forks.

I caught hold of one of the plastic bands holding the boards together and pulled. The boards moved a little way but then the band broke. I went backwards off the load and managed to twist in mid-air, landing on my gloved hands. Then my face hit the floor followed closely by my knees. I somehow bounced and came to a stop with my head jammed under a trailer wheel. As I lay there I heard someone shout, 'Get an ambulance!'

Not registering that it was for me, I checked to see if my hands and legs worked. All seemed ok apart from both knees were pretty painful and my head was still jammed. I knew there was only one way it was coming out so I jerked my head back and was free. There was a lot of skin left on the ground. I sat up and realised that the inside of my mouth was hurting and bleeding quite a lot. By this time there were four or five staff who had come to my aid and someone got a chair for me to sit on, from where I was able to access my injuries a bit better. First I rolled up my trouser legs and checked my knees. They were starting to swell up with what felt like some sort of fluid but the knee caps felt ok. Running my tongue around I felt a long cut on the inside of my bottom lip which was bleeding. Lastly I touched the right side of my face which was all raw. Then the manger asked me if I felt ok. I replied, 'I don't think I've broken any bones - the worse thing seems to be a cut on the inside of my lip.' Then the ambulance arrived.

I was checked over and the ambulance man said I ought to go to the hospital at Romford.

I said, 'I feel fine.'

He took me over to the ambulance and told me to look in the mirror. The whole of one side of my face, from my eye to my chin was raw.

'You need to get that look at and some stitches in your lip so we need to run you down to Romford hospital.'

'How far is it?' I asked

'About seven miles'

'I'll drop the trailer and follow you down with the unit, so I can get back.'

'I don't think that's a good idea,' said the ambulance driver

'We'll pick you up with a car,' offered the manger. 'I'll write down our telephone number and you can ring us when you're sorted.'

So off I went in the ambulance.

I rang Bob Lovelace from the hospital and I told him I had fallen off the load and that I would ring him later when I knew the extent of my injuries.

Then I sat in casualty for seven hours with blood dripping on the floor, which no-one seemed to worry about. Eventually I was given seven stitches on the inside of my bottom lip and the side of my face was sprayed with a plastic solution which sealed it from the atmosphere. Although it didn't look too nice it worked well. First I rang Homebase for my lift, and then I rang Christine to tell her I was a bit knocked about and was going to park up and see how I felt in the morning.

Homebase had sheeted the load down. I put a couple of straps across the back and I was back on the road. It was only a few miles to Noakes café, next to DJV, near Purfleet. The café owner had his back to me when I went into the café.

'What can I do for you?' he asked without turning around.

'A tea and a bowl of rice crispies,' I mumbled through my swollen lips.

It was then that he turned around, 'Go and sit down and I'll bring it over to you.'

I was pleased that he had cereals, as I didn't fancy chewing anything. I sipped the tea when it cooled down. After eating I went to bed and despite the pain, eventually dropped off to sleep.

The next morning it felt like I had done ten rounds in a kick-boxing fight. I managed to crawl out of the bunk and dress. I went into the café, had the same meal as the night before, and climbed back into the cab. I turned the key and the lorry wouldn't start. I have to say I was completely fed up by this point and just wanted to be at home in my bed. I don't think I had ever been so low in my driving career. Then I thought, I am a driver - so sort it.

I managed to get going with the help of a couple of other drivers. Two drops left. Urgent air freight and B&Q. The B&Q store was the nearest so I went there first and then delivered the air freight. I walked into the office, still feeling cheesed-off. The guy at the desk was writing so I put down the delivery tickets beside him. He looked up at me and said, 'What happened to you?' By now I was also getting fed up with this question so I said, 'Some bloke accused me of cheating at pool last night - he's still in hospital. Now how long is it going to take before you unload me?'

'We'll do it straight away,' he said.

I rang Bob Lovelace and told him I could manage to load at Purfleet docks (it's my job) but I was going to need the next week off.

I got home Friday and that was it for a week. My knees and face were really swollen, my mouth hurt, my arms hurt and my legs hurt where they had been jarred on impact. No marks on my hands as I was wearing leather gloves. My calculations, based on travelling downward at thirty foot per second per second, meant I had hit the concrete yard at sixty miles per hour.

On the Saturday morning Jeff Binding came down to see how I was.

'Why didn't you ring in Thursday night? I had the transit van home and was ready to come up and change over with you.'

I told him that the last time I changed over with someone there were so many drops on the way home that it would have been quicker to keep the trailer I had. Anyway I got another night-out pay from it.

Eventually all of the DIY stores fitted their fork lifts with Standard Four Foot Forks.

I was lucky compared with some. Colin Vanstone crashed while driving a MAN to work one morning. I am not sure of the facts but the lorry ended up in a field at the bottom of a hill and Colin was seriously injured. He remained in a hospice for the rest of his life. The MAN was written off.

Richard 'Hank' Thornley of Torridge Transport, died after falling off a load in Plymouth.

There were a few of us sitting in the drivers' rest room one day and Mr Smythe walked in, 'I need a volunteer to do some three o'clock starts for the next couple of weeks,' he said. 'If anyone is interested, come up and see me.'

Nobody moved and I was thinking why would anyone have to start at 3.00am with normal loads. This could be interesting. Maybe a same-day delivery to Scotland. All drivers like a nice long drive, so I went up to the office. Get in first I thought.

The job was to go to Newton Aycliffe, in County Durham, with a load of chipboard and then twelve miles to Darlington and load second-hand steel girders and bring them back to the yard. I had to be in Darlington by 1.00pm because the girders had to be sorted while they were being loaded. Much to his surprise I told Tony Smythe I would have a go at it. But there had to be a bit of flexibility with it. He agreed.

This is what happened: Friday night the lorry and load were parked in South Molton lorry park away from other lorries.

Monday morning I got up around 2.15am and at 3.00pm I drove out of the lorry park. The Ho Chi Minh was practically empty at that time of the morning. Just before seven I stopped at the Oakamoor café, between Walsall and Burton on Trent, for breakfast. I allowed for the traffic to get busy by the time I left the café but from there to Newton Aycliffe it was all dual carriage way and motorway.

The factory where I had to deliver the chipboard was right beside the main road and I knew that they stopped an hour for lunch hence the early start. I arrived there around 11.30am, was unloaded and I was at the steel stock-holders just before one o' clock. The trailer was reversed into the building and then dropped and I parked the unit outside while the trailer was loaded. Technically I was finished for the day. Around five I reversed into the shed and coupled up the trailer. There were two men that helped me chain down the load before I drove outside and parked-up for the night. There was a pub at the end of the estate where I went and had dinner before an early night.

Tuesday I started about 7.00am and drove back to South Molton and parked-up.

Wednesday I started at 7.30am and took the trailer down to Barn-staple. I washed the lorry, went up to the chipboard factory and loaded my trailer ready for Newton Aycliffe the next day. I helped load a few other trailers and then went home at 3.00pm.

Thursday was the same as Monday. Friday was the same as Tuesday but I took the trailer, loaded with steel, straight back to Barnstaple.

Then I took an empty trailer back to the chipboard factory. I connected up to the trailer for Newton Aycliffe, strapped it down and then parked in South Molton lorry park. Not even five o'clock and I was finished for the week.

Over the weekend Jeff Binding asked me why I was doing these early starts.

'I'll tell you when the contract is finished,' was all I would say.

After three weeks it was over and on the Saturday morning Jeff asked 'What's it all about then?'

'How many hours have you worked this week?' I asked.

'Probably sixty.'

'I have worked exactly forty-one hours and I have got the same pay as you. Also Tuesday and Wednesday I only worked seven hours each day.'

'I knew there was something in it for you to get out of bed that early but why did Smythe agree to let you do those hours.'

'Simple - no one else volunteered for the job.'

I won't say what Jeff's reply was but it was similar to the rest of the drivers' comments when they found out.

At ABC Nottingham the fork lift driver was the most obnoxious person I have ever met. Apparently he was a part-time football referee where his parentage was often questioned. Smythe's often delivered to ABC and very often there were bolts of cloth to be delivered to some other place, in Nottingham, on the way.

On one occasion I arrived at ABC Nottingham about ten minutes past twelve.

'You're late. We don't unload after mid-day - you will have to wait until tomorrow morning,'said the fork lift driver.

I pointed out that there were no special delivery instructions on the delivery tickets so he has to unload me. He turned around and walked into the office and returned after about a minute.

'Your boss is on the phone and wants to speak to you,' he said.

Tony Smythe asked me what was going on and, when I told him, we agreed that matey was talking rubbish and that he didn't make the rules.

'I'll phone the chipboard factory and get them to sort it out.' said Tony.

'Give me a couple of minutes,' I said. 'If I haven't phoned you back in an hour then ring the factory.'

I walked back to the lorry and said to the 'dictator', 'I hope you're happy - you've got me the sack. My boss said I should have known about unloading times and it is my fault that I have to wait until tomorrow.

'If Mr Smythe thinks I'm waiting here until tomorrow morning he is mistaken. He's sacked me and I'm going home. I'll find a lay-by, drop the trailer there, and take the unit home. I might even pull someone else's trailer down to Devon and make myself a few quid. Then I'll put the unit on a friend's farm and ring Smythe at the end of the week. When he pays me what he owes me I'll tell him where the unit and the trailer is. You'll get your chipboard next Tuesday or Wednesday.'

'You can't do that!'

'You watch me mate.' I got into the cab and started the engine.

The forky stood in front of the lorry with his arms outstretched, 'Hold it, Hold it!' I will unload you now.'

I stopped the engine and climbed out of the cab.

'Don't be long about it. Enough time has been wasted already.'

An hour later I phoned Smythe and asked where I was going next.

It is not only dockers and forklift drivers that can make a driver's life a misery - there are the other motorists. Going north on the M5, when it was two lanes, I was catching up to another Artic so I indicated that I was going to overtake and pulled out into the next lane. The driver of a Volvo estate racing-up to me wasn't prepared to slow down for a lorry. He went up the hard shoulder, then across the two lanes to get in front of me. He slowed down slightly until I got close to him and then he stood on his brakes, forcing me to stop in the fast lane. Luckily there was little traffic about. As the Volvo accelerated away I wrote down his registration number. Five minutes later I was in the police station, on the Services, making a complaint.

The sergeant told me if the driver was prosecuted it would be costly to me to attend court in Birmingham. He suggested, instead, that he put out a message to stop the Volvo and check it over, also breathalyse the driver. The driver was probably a salesman and the police would visit him at his place of work and talk to him in front of his boss.

I agreed with that idea and was about to leave when the policeman said, 'Next time don't brake. It will be another twat off the road.' His words not mine.

Somewhere in Derby I drove into a small trading estate. It had been snowing and nobody had cleared the snow from the outside of their unit. The area was on a slope and as I tried to go back up the slope the wheels of the lorry just spun. The person that owned the unit was complaining to me about blocking his entrance. I pointed out that if they had cleared the snow earlier then I would not be where I was.

He got a few people to clean the area but it took a couple of hours and time was going on.

I rang the office to confirm that the return load was still on.

'It's too late now, they're closed for Christmas and you're sacked. Leave the trailer up there and come home with the unit,' said Mr Smythe.

The place where I had to load was only a couple of miles away and, no, they had not closed so they loaded me. I rang Smythe and told him that I was loaded and did he still want me to leave the trailer where it was until after Christmas. He told me that if it was loaded I might as well bring it home with me. It is beyond words and not the first time he had sacked me.

As you have already noticed a good day can quickly turn into a bad day as happened one Friday. Having tipped in London I was in Purfleet dock at 11.00am waiting to load - I waited and I waited, and I waited. At four in the afternoon I was told that I wouldn't be loaded until the morning. I was seriously annoyed with this as I could have got a load somewhere else if I had known earlier. Behind me in the queue was a driver from Plymouth who was doing a favour for a friend. He had no gear at all for sleeping-out so I lent him a blanket.

The next morning we were ready to be loaded at 7.30am. At nine thirty I was told that my load was at a different wharf nearer London. By the time I reached the wharf the dockers had stopped for breakfast. Eventually I was loaded and headed for Bridgwater where I was to change trailers. Around twelve thirty I was going through Vauxhall, West London and the clutch went on the Volvo. Nothing for it but to drive to Bridgwater without it: pretty easy once I was out of London. At Bridgwater lived a Smythe's driver and to be honest he was a bit of a prat. When I got to the lorry park I found the trailer was on its knees (the landing legs had not been wound down when he dropped the trailer). Also the ropes were all loose. It takes about ten minutes to wind the trailer legs in low gear to get the trailer high enough to couple it up. Worse still was coupling up with no clutch. Then another half-an-hour to tighten the ropes. As my ropes were in a lot better condition than his I didn't bother to leave my ropes but took them with me. Let Mr Bridgewater sort out some way to secure the load Monday morning; I wasn't very polite to him the next time I saw him. Because of his laziness it was nearly 7.00pm when I got home.

Never go on holiday when you drive a lorry, I did and this is what happened. I arrived at the yard at eight o'clock. There was my tractor unit parked outside the store shed. 'You're driving that MAN over there,' said Tony Smythe.

'What's the matter with the Volvo?' I asked

'Go and look,' he said.

So I wondered across to the lorry. The offside looked fine but the nearside had suffered a lot of damage. Tony Smythe was stood behind me and said, 'The new driver turned it over going down 'Black Cat.'

I wasn't impressed but these things happen and it was going to be rebuilt. The MAN was the only spare unit so it was drive that or have a couple of weeks more holiday, unpaid. So, no choice there then.

Off to London again. This MAN was the older model with column change but no problems for me. On the return journey I joined the M4 at junction three and started to climb a hill to the motorway. I changed up a gear and the clutch pedal did not return, it just stayed on the floor. I quickly steered to lorry onto the hard shoulder and it rolled to a halt. I climbed out of the cab, stood on the bottom step, leaned over and pulled the clutch pedal back up. As I did I felt that the lorry was moving backwards down the hard shoulder. I looked up at the mirror on the door and I was indeed going backwards. I put my hand on the footbrake and stretched up and put the lorry in gear. Then I quickly climbed into the cab. I must have knocked off the handbrake with my shoulder. The handbrake lever was L shaped on the end and one just pulled it to put it on. Turning the L bit to the side put the brake off and that is what I must have done. I tried the clutch again and it stuck again. I drove in low gear along the hard shoulder until I got to a flat bit where I could pick up speed and then change up.

I got the lorry back home only to be told that it would be three weeks before they got the new part. There was nothing for it but to drive it without a clutch until the fitters got the part or fixed my Volvo. So that is what I did.

Like most drivers I was eventually asked to drive in a carnival, to which I agreed. The carnival was at Barnstaple and I was told to take Jeff Bindings F12, six-wheel unit, as my unit was being repaired. I went to Barbican Road and found that the trailer that I was to pull was a low loader with small 'scrambler' motorbikes tied on the back with some small bushes and other stuff for effect and decoration. It was the Barnstaple Junior Scramble Club. During the carnival the young lads sat on the bikes, which were secured to the trailer.

The towing pin on the trailer was well back from the front of the trailer and the sliding fifth wheel had to be secured as far back as it would go so that the trailer landing legs would clear the back of the unit. With the tandem axle of the trailer fitted at the end of trailer this made a slightly over legal-length lorry and a pig to manoeuvre.

The carnival started off and I was somewhere in the centre. As we got to the junction of Victoria Road with Newport Road, where I needed to turn right, I realised that this over-length vehicle was not going to get around the corner if I went left of the keep-left sign. I decided to get the trailer as close to the kerb on the left hand side and then cut across to the right of the keep-left sign and cut across the corner of the junction. The only problem is people walking along either side of the trailer. If they got caught between the trailer and the curb the low side of the trailer would cut their legs off. I had to stop, get out of the lorry and clear the people away from the trailer and then inch around the junction. By the time I had done this the carnival parade in front had gone out of site around a corner. I was slightly worried about this as I had no map of the route. The lady in the cab with me, something to do with the club, had earlier been drinking from a bottle of white wine and appeared to be a little tipsy. I asked her if she had a route map - she didn't. When I got to the square there was just a mass of people and as I got closer they parted to let me through. That route took me into Boutport Street and up the High Street. I had a thought: what happens if the front of the parade had gone along the Strand and were coming along the High Street from the other end. I didn't dare to dwell on it. As I had small kids sat on motor bikes, I had to drive very slowly and I never caught up with the rest of the parade until it ended.

I took the trailer back to the yard to be sorted out in the morning. I picked up my own unit and then went to the Fair, parking the unit among the fair lorries. My unit had never been to a fair. After the fair I took him back home ready for Monday. Altogether quite a nice day.

Of all the docks that I loaded from I would say that East African terminal at Tilbury, Essex was the worst. Jeff Binding and I arrived there one afternoon only to find there was a union meeting going on in the canteen. So no food until they finished, which was about six o'-clock. All the other lorries including Jeff had loaded and then it was my turn. It was now past eight and it was obvious that the forklift driver wanted to get home. He was just dropping timber any old way onto the trailer and after being ignored by him I threw an eight foot piece of timber at him, nearly hitting the checker. After that he decided to square up the load to my satisfaction, which I did thank him for. After loading you have to leave the large dock complex because most docks did not allow sleeping overnight so the nearest place to park was Grays, twenty minutes away

Between the dock and the loading yard was a large shed. Forklifts could drive direct from the dock through the shed and into the yard or store products in the shed. Lorries could enter the shed at the left hand end and drive out of the right hand side. They could be loaded from the shed or from the dock, making it a shorter journey for the forklifts.

I parked in the shed and four packs of timber were put on the front of the trailer. 'That's it,' said the loader.

'Where is the rest?' I asked.

'On the boat,' he says.

I looked at the empty dock. 'Where's the boat?'

'It's sailed with the rest of your timber on it.'

Unbelievable. I strapped the four packs of loaded timber and drove slowly out of the shed. It would be impossible to drive a load like this very far. The lorry would turn over on the first bend. I walked the couple hundred yards to the office and was told that there was nothing else for the West country so it was the four packs of timber or nothing. As it was Friday, Bob said go with the four packs of timber. So it was back into the shed to get the top two packs taken off and put on the rear of the trailer. When I asked the docker to move the timber he told me that the timber had been loaded and that was the end of it. I told him that the load was unsafe and as I was a shop steward I was not moving the lorry until I was satisfied that the load was made safe. I turned the tachograph to break and went to the canteen for lunch leaving the lorry in the middle of the shed blocking all four directions.

After about twenty minutes the forklift driver came into the canteen and told me had now levelled the load and asked me to move the lorry. I told him I was on a break and it could not be moved for another forty minutes, and it wasn't.

I was in the King's Arms pub in South Molton one Friday night when two strangers walked in and after a while we got talking. They both lived at Tilbury and also had a cottage next to the pub in Church Street, South Molton. They left work at 4.00pm Friday afternoons and drove straight to South Molton for the week end. They both worked at 44 Berth, at Tilbury Docks.

44 Berth dealt with paper pulp, large bales of waste paper that were delivered to Wiggins Teape at Stowford Mills, Ivybridge or Hele, near Cullompton as well as other paper mills. It was a regular return load for West Country hauliers. The biggest problem was the long wait to load, which could be hours on a bad day. When I commented about the long wait they told me that one was a forklift driver and the other was a checker. The checker said next time you get there, get your delivery tickets and come and find us - we'll sort you out. Pints were purchased and the newcomers were welcomed into the King's Arms crowd.

A couple of weeks later on a Friday morning I was sent to 44 berth along with a lorry from Bill Hockin at Barnstaple. We got our loading and delivery tickets from the office and went in search of our friends. When we found them we were told to come through the back gate of the berth that they will open for us and they pointed to an empty shed. Park in there, one behind the other and we will see you in a minute.

We walked back to our lorries and to the amazement of other drivers we drove off. They were even more amazed when an hour later we were heading for the dock gates both fully loaded with paper pulp. They were never told where we loaded it. That night when our friends from Tilbury came into the King's Arms there were two pints sitting on the bar, waiting for them. It is who you know.

Car factories are were just as bad for loading and unloading. It was Friday afternoon and I was delivering to British Leyland, Cowley, Oxford. I drove around the factory until I came to a small yard next to the exit gate. I had one pallet for them so I undone the ropes and sheets ready for unloading. The forklift arrived, lifted his forks up, drove up to the trailer and then said, 'Sorry mate I have to go and wash my hands now, ready to leave work.' And he dropped his forks.

'What time do you leave work?'

'Four thirty but we get two hours to wash our hands.' He drove off. I phoned the office and asked what I should do.

'Go to Timbmet and load for Barnstaple. Bring that pallet for Cowley back with you.'

Monday found me back in Cowley. The exit gate to the factory was on a roundabout and I tried to go in through that gate but the gate man wouldn't let me in. 'You have to go all the way around the factory.'

'If I go all around the factory I will have to have an hour's break,' I told him.

'That's not my problem,' he said.

So I drove around the factory and then parked right in front of the exit gate. 'Is it alright to park here?' I asked'

'Yeah you've only got one pallet.'

So I put the tachograph on break. The pallet was unloaded in minutes and I sat down to eat my sandwiches. Loaded car transporters started to queue up behind me and the gate man asked me to move. I told him I had said that I would have to have an hour's break if I went around the factory and now I am on a break and I can't move until it's over. I told the same to the transporter drivers when they asked me to move and that the gate man said it was ok to park there. Twenty minutes later I left the factory. When I got back to the yard the next day Tony Smythe informed me that British Leyland had said I was barred from they're UK factories.

For Ford at Dagenham I had a parcel so small it was in the cab. I found the stores, went in and showed them the paper work and asked if it was for them. 'Yes,' said the lady behind the counter, 'If you can find someone to unload you I will sign the ticket.'

I went to the cab, got the parcel, put it on the counter and went into the office to get a signature. Just after I got a signature a bloke came in and told the woman that I had unloaded myself.

'Is that right?' she asked.

'Yes,' I said 'it was no bother. It's only a small box.'

'You can't unload yourself - the union blokes will complain.'

'Well next time I won't do it.' I told her.

Guess what, I am barred from Fords at Dagenham as well.

In 1985 Jerry, the shop steward, left the firm. There were those that said Tony Smythe, who didn't like unions, had given him a thousand pounds to leave.

Well I had this thought: if I could get myself elected as shop steward then perhaps he would pay me a load of money to leave. Needless to say we had an official election and I was the only one that put up for the job.

I was even allowed to have days off to go to union seminars.

One day I decided that we needed a pay rise. Smythe's pay scale had fallen behind other companies and was part of the reason for the regular turn-over of drivers. This was a valid reason for a pay rise. It meant that when we got good drivers they might stay.

There were several hours of discussion. The usual tactics were used: All lorries were to be left in the yard over the weekend. Then, on Monday morning drivers turned up and found the gate locked - no drivers were allowed in. A few drivers, the ones that did European deliveries had left on the Sunday along with a couple of others, one of whom had taken my unit.

It rained all day and we sat in cars waiting for something to happen. Television news companies filmed us and we were on the local news. It was claimed that we were on strike but we pointed out that we wanted to go to work but we were locked out. The next day we were allowed back to work and discussions continued.

When the continental drivers arrived back into Dover their lorries were searched. Some one (I know not whom) had told the customs that they were smuggling and one driver was fined a couple of hundred pounds when alcohol was found in his load. The same driver arriving back at the yard at two in the morning was promptly arrested. The police had been told that he was drug smuggling.

Tony Smythe stopped us using the drivers' room for union meetings so we arranged to have a meeting one evening at the Maidendown Stage transport café near Tiverton. Most of the drivers turned up but not the shunters as they were on a different pay scale. Decisions were made and when we finished I told them I don't condone breaking the law but I want every load delivered tomorrow on time. I don't care how you get there but I don't want Mr Smythe saying loads were delivered late.

I met with Tony Smythe a few days later and told him of the decisions made at a meeting.

He said, 'You can't have had a meeting as they are not allowed in the yard.'

I told him that we had independent witnesses who would confirm, in a court or an industrial tribunal, that we did have a meeting and all decisions were legal and above board. From then on we sat down and worked together to save money.

A note was put in everyone's pay packet: speed limits must be strictly observed. On the Monday morning we drove up the Ho Chi Minh trail at 40mpg - usually we would be doing 50, in places. It wasn't long before other companies were complaining to Smythe that his lorries were holding everyone up.

That Monday I rang Bob Lovelace and told him that I was empty at Copplestone.

'Thank God for that,' he said. 'I've got trailers here and no one is back to take them.'

I told him I would not be back either as my time was nearly up. I went to Lapford and parked-up. I stayed at my in-law's house, went down the pub with father-in-law and spent some of my night out money on beer for us both.

We were saving the firm money but there were still a lot of drivers speeding on the motorway. Police might have not worried about five miles over the speed limit but Tony Smythe and I did. We made it clear that any driver found exceeding the speed limit would receive a written warning. I agreed that stance with the company and told Smythe that Monday morning I would go up the motorway at sixty miles per hour and I would record the name of any driver that passed me and the registration number of the lorry.

As I proceeded along the M5 it wasn't long before I heard two drivers talking on the CB radio. As they passed me I waved my CB mike in a gesture that it was not working. Then I wrote down the time, the mile marker, their names and the registration numbers of the vehicles.

The next day I was waiting in the yard when they both returned. When they came into the drivers room I asked them to accompany me upstairs as witnesses to our pay negotiations and, of course, they followed me. We went into Mr Smythe's office.

'Written warnings for these two,' I said to Tony Smythe and read out what I had written down the day before. The drivers had both been with the firm for a long time and they were not very happy at my actions. Mr Smythe told them to leave the office. After they left we agreed a pay rise of seventy five percent, spread over twelve months, That would bring the pay in line with other local companies. I went downstairs to the drivers' room and the two drivers started on me. I held up my hand and they stopped speaking.

'Congratulations. You have assisted me in getting a seventy five percent pay rise. I knew someone would go over the speed limit and Smythe would give in (especially if it was one of his favourite drivers).'

'You devious bastard,' said one.

I took that as a compliment. 'Exactly,' I said'

Smythe's Transport used to deduct money from drivers' wages, most of the time it was because of parking charges at Services. At Heston Services, for example, it was five pounds for overnight parking, but drivers got a three pound meal voucher included in the payment. Tony Smythe argued that drivers got the meal voucher therefore the company would only reimburse them two pounds. There were other little things, for example if a bag of something fell off a trailer the driver had the cost of the item taken from his wages. It did not really affect me as I used to park most of the time at the stores I delivered to, or, if I was in London, outside of Bert Griffiths' or Edmonton.

At a union seminar one day I picked up a copy of a union magazine and on the back page was an article on the 1892 truck act and the 1963 payment of wages act both of which stated, quite clearly, that an employer cannot take money or stop payment from an employee's wages.

As Tony Smythe was not available I went back to Bob Lovelace and told him that what the company was doing was illegal and that any money stopped or deducted from an employee's wages must be returned. Bob said they didn't have trucks in 1892. I pointed out that it was something to do with woollen mills and not American lorries. A couple of weeks later all money that had been taken was paid back to employees. Only Ian Cuthbertson said thank you.

During the time that I worked for Smythe's the route out of North Devon had changed. A dual carriage way had been built from Junction 27 on the M5 to the outskirts of Tiverton.

Heavy traffic now turned right at the eastern end of Black Cat and went to Tiverton, through the village of Cove. A distance of around ten miles with some narrow parts in places.

After I left Smythe's Transport Adrian Richards took over TUO 800T as an owner-driver. Eventually it was sold into preservation and hopefully it is still out there somewhere. FDV 49Y an F12, driven by Jim 'Minder' Beveridge, was converted to a recovery vehicle and is now in Kent

When I started driving there were four transport cafés between Barnstaple and Taunton. Mount Sandford Road, Barnstaple; Red Deer (now a house of the same name); Petton Cross and Hillcommon.

I had worked for Smythe's Transport for five years and decided it was time for a change. Torridge Transport was looking for drivers so I thought I would give them a ring.

Above: Volvo F88 WFJ 701S. The first lorry the author drove for A.D.Smythe Transport.

Next page top: The dashboard of a Volvo F88. This lorry is under restoration hence the missing switches. Image by the Author.

Next page bottom: The centre consul of a Volvo F88. The black lever on the side is to split the gears. The small lever below it, with the black knob, is the handbrake. Image by the author.

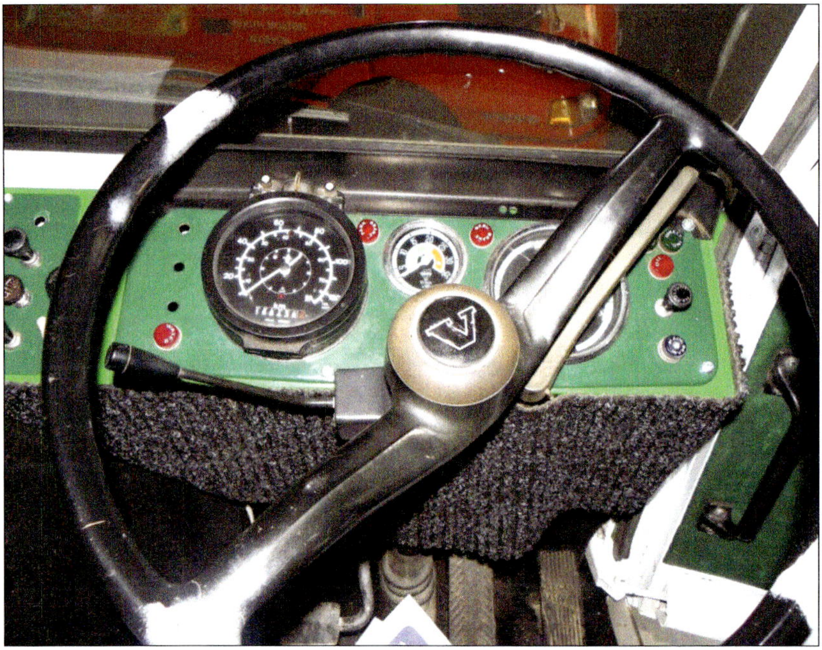

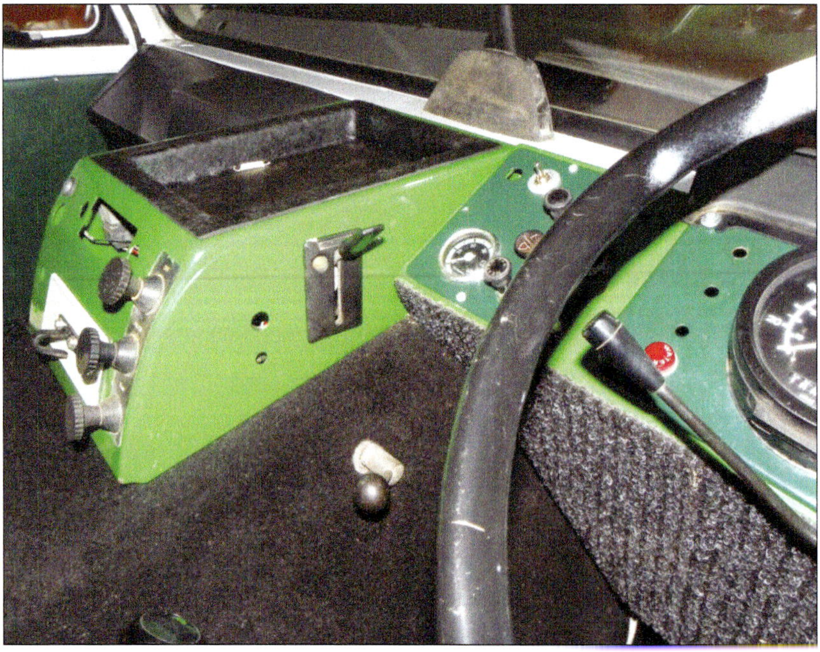

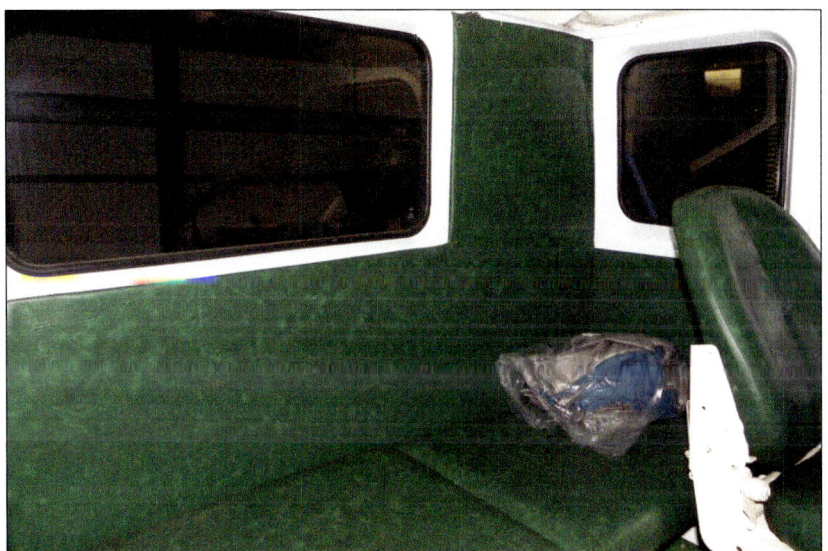

Above: The bunk bed of a Volvo F88 showing the rear and side window. The curtains are on the bunk. WFJ 701S had a padded cover for the rear window.

Image by the author

Below: Centre, the Fiat that I drove to London for William Hockin. There is an ERF A series on the left and on the right is a Volvo F88.

Image courtesy of Roxann E Cuthbertson

Above: the MAN radiator badge.   Image by the author.

Bottom: A selection of types of lorry that the author drove, in toy form.

Image from the author's collection.

Above: TUN 800T, in the old livery.   Image courtesy of Adrian Richards.

Below: Ian Cuthbertson's Volvo F12 in the new livery.

Image courtesy Roxann E Cuthbertson.

Above: Adrian Richards' Volvo F12. It is coupled to trailer 36 which is loaded with 8 x 6 sheets of chipboard. Adrian's daughter Louisa is stood at the front and another Smythe's trailer is in the background.

Image courtesy of Adrian Richards.

Right: Neil Russell chatting on his CB radio.

Image courtesy of Caroline Russell.

Above: Waiting to unload woodchips at the chipboard factory South Molton.
Image courtesy of Roxann E Cuthbertson.

Below: Jim Beveridge's Volvo F12 in the entrance to Smythe's Transport yard, Whiddon Valley, Barnstaple. The office building can be seen to the right.
Image courtesy of Andrew Jury.

Above: A small convoy heading home. The trailer on the left is loaded with slab wood and being pulled by an MAN, registration number WUO 132V.

Image courtesy of Roxann E Cuthbertson

Below: The author, Stephen Lock and wife Christine in front of Geoff Binding's Volvo F12, A902 KFJ at a Barnstaple carnival The low loader trailer is carrying school boy motorcycle scramblers.

11

Torridge Transport

Day one: The interview.

First I met two lovely ladies, Gilda and Marlyn, the secretaries, who pointed me in the direction of Mr Phil Jarrett, the transport manager.

I have to admit that I was a bit apprehensive about this meeting as he was supposed to be a bit of an ogre.

I really wanted this job, after five years with Smythe's Transport I was getting fed up and a change was on the cards. I had managed to get an interview with Torridge Transport. This is a company people did not leave: it was job-for-life for most drivers and I had a lot of friends working for them.

Mr Jerrett didn't seem as bad as most drivers made out, in fact he was quite a nice man. He asked me about my past experience, what type of vehicles and makes of lorry etc. I was in my late thirties and had been driving lorries (officially) since I was twenty-one. He was impressed.

The only make of lorry that I had not driven was Seddon Atkinson, of which Torridge Transport had many. He wanted to know if I was happy to drive anywhere including cities like London and Birmingham. 'Anywhere, anytime,' I replied.

Then he took me next door to meet Mr Brian Cobbledick, the big boss so to speak, although he is not that big. This is the man I needed to impress. He was actually quite pleasant and he also asked me what experience I had; after all he was going to give me a very expensive toy to play with and he did not want it damaged. He asked me why I wanted to leave Smythe's Transport and what I had done there.

I told him that I was married with two daughters and lived in South Molton and after five years I felt that it was time to change and perhaps look for new challenges. I told him that I was also the company shop steward. He seemed fairly happy with my answers.

He said that the company already had a union shop steward and I replied I was happy with that as I did not want to be one - I just wanted to be left alone to get on with the job.

After a few more general questions the interview was terminated and I was told there was another person that had also applied for the job and I would be told in the near future whether I was successful or no.

The following Saturday I was at my brother Philip's house when Mr Cobbledick rang and offered me the job - I immediately accepted. As I put the phone down I heard Mr Cobbledick say to someone else, 'He has accepted but the next available job will be yours.'

I found out later he was talking to Geoff Colwill whose father drove the Marathon for Greenaway's, Stratton.

The day I left Smythe's I was the driver of the oldest lorry on the fleet and proud to be so - and with a clean licence!

The following Monday week I arrived at Torridge Transport yard to discover my lovely Seddon Atkinson Four-Wheeled Artic unit was in the garage. The work wear was supplied by the company and I was given three work-coats but no trousers as there were none in the stores for my size.

I was then immediately promoted to 'General' and put on general duties. Even though it was in the garage I gave my new charge a good clean and polish which put me in the boss' good books. I was then informed the lorry would not be ready for a couple of days. Not the best news as Torridge Transport operated a bonus scheme (paid monthly) so I needed a couple of nights out that week to boost my wages.

Tuesday was the same as Monday: more time in the yard. With the wheel studs and nuts now painted white, the lorry looked great - pity it wasn't operable.

I was informed that Mr Jerrett wanted to see me. I hoped that I was not in trouble already but it turned out to be my first driving job for the company. A Fiat four- wheeler flat was to go to a local cheese farm to be unloaded (not a lot of bonus for this) but it did get me out of the yard. Five miles later and two shunts to get into the farm I was delighted to discover that I knew a couple of people that worked there: one of them was Tina, my brother Philip's daughter. With the Lorry unloaded it was back to the yard to discover I had to reload the lorry and return to the farm with another load of cheese. Well, at least I knew the way.

The couple of days in the yard gave me time to get to know the secretaries and the fitters, as the garage was located at the end of the yard. There was an old chap always wandering around the yard, quite an amiable sort of chap, and he always spoke to me. All I knew was that his name was Claude and I assumed he was an retired driver that used to come in and muck around for something to do. To be honest I wasn't really bothered who he was.

Thursday came with great news; I was off up the road but not with a 'Seddy Ak' as we called them but a Mercedes thirty-eight tonner. My destination was Northfleet in North Kent and the route plan was up the A361 to Taunton, then the A303 to the M25, head South to the A2, then five miles east to Northfleet, piece of cake. The return load was a load of slates from Rye, in Kent, to Teignmouth docks and then to take the Mercedes to a garage in Exeter. Claude would then pick me up and take me back to the yard.

A slight problem was that I had to finish Friday, at lunch time, because I had some people coming to tarmac the path at the entrance to our drive.

Thursday morning turned out to be not so good as I had over-slept. I grabbed my overnight bag, sandwiches which had been made the night before.

I had not driven a Mercedes for ten years, yet strangely enough this one seemed easier. Pushed for time I arrived at Northfleet in the afternoon. I had been to this company before and was unloaded pretty quickly. I needed to leave *tout suite* - as the French say - for Rye, and I hit the town soon after four o'clock - getting pretty stressed as the firm closed at four thirty.

Through the gate at four-fifteen, I was loaded by four thirty. I thanked the fork lift driver for hanging-on and loading me. The trucking gods were smiling on me.

After something to eat, I drove to Sevenoaks where I ran out of driving time so I parked up. I had the minimum break of eight hours, during which I grabbed some sleep, and got on my way again, heading for Teignmouth. It was two in the morning and I had never seen the M25 so quiet. I kept to the legal speed limit and started wondering how many lorries were going to be in front of me at Teignmouth docks. The weather was fine and traffic light - another moment of trucking heaven. I got to the docks at nine and unbelievably there was no one else there. Perhaps it does pay to get out of bed early.

Unloaded, I rang the office and told them I was empty. At first they did not believe me but eventually I was told to carry on to Exeter and Claude would meet me there.

By the time I got to Exeter I was feeling pretty pleased with myself and everything seemed fine, but this is the world of road haulage and the gods were about to take the rest of the day off.

The only space for a lorry was in front of the workshop door, the only door, but the manager said it was fine to leave it there.

I got into the minivan beside Claude after putting my sleeping bag, which I was using as a kit bag, into the back and we headed back to the yard at Torrington.

During the journey back to South Molton I began to ask Claude about himself, 'What do you actually do for Torridge Transport, Claude?'

'What do you mean Stephen?'

'Well this week I've seen you do all sorts of bits and pieces around the yard and now you are chauffeuring me around the countryside. I wondered if you were a retired driver and just helped out where necessary'.

He replied, 'My name is Claude Cobbledick and I own the firm. Don't you know who you are working for?'

Oops, this is not how to impress the boss.

'I don't really care as long as they leave me alone to get on with the job,' I replied.

Later, one of the girls in the office reported to me that Claude went back to office and told Brian that I was a proper chap and that all I wanted to do was get on and do the job and that I should be an asset to the firm.

Claude dropped me off at home just after one, in time for lunch. I then set off to find Chris Seatherton, a friend, who was supposed to be digging up the footpath at the end of the drive. The tarmac was coming at five o'clock and there was no sign of him. About thirty minutes later the phone rang - it was Claude. Did I have the keys to the Mercedes?

I told him no, they were in the lorry. I then checked my pockets and there they were. After a very large swear-word I apologised to Claude and said that I would take them to Exeter. He told me not to worry as he had obtained a spare key from the office and the drive to Exeter would give him something to do.

The good news was that my Seddy Ak was ready, I was to pick it up in the morning and bring the keys to the Mercedes with me.

Off to the New Inn to find Chris Seatherton. He said that the tarmac on the path was nine inches thick and impossible to dig up with a pick-axe and that he had hired a compressor but it wouldn't be available until three o'clock.

It arrived on time and we set-to. We had to dig up the path, remove the old kerbs and fit new dropped-kerbs to make a sloping entrance to the drive. We finished just as the tarmac lorry and the road gang arrived.

One and a half hours later, a new footpath at the end of the drive and, a bonus, a new tarmac garden path out the back, and we were all in the New Inn. All the guys were paid, I put some money behind the bar, and we all had a well-deserved drink.

Saturday Christine drove me to the yard, with the keys to the Mercedes, and after a bit of deserved mickey-taking from Claude and a few others, I got my hands on my lorry. One more aggravation the gear box was not a standard H pattern - it went around in a U, which means third and fourth were the opposite way around to most of the lorries I had driven. So for the first couple of days I had to think where the position of the next gear was before changing. As an end to an interesting first week I drove back up to Arronson's and strapped my load down ready for Monday.

Week two was the start of a weekly routine that was fine for me. My lorry was only plated for thirty-two tons gross weight while all the other artics on the fleet were thirty-eight tons.

There was one other slight shock when I discovered I was employed by North Devon Transport but under Torridge Transport colours. The wages and conditions were the same, so it made no difference to me.

Deliveries were to be mainly to superstores like B&Q and Homebase as well as other retail outlets and loads were often mixed sizes of chip-board, rarely more than my lorry could carry. Return loads were worked out to be a legal weight for the vehicle that I drove.

Another bonus was that my trailers were loaded by a shunter as the loads took a long time to load.

The thirty-eight tonners had to load their own as it was normally one type of board, usually destined for furniture makers. These did not take too long to actually load, but they may have had to wait a while depending on the lorry queue. Occasionally they did retail deliveries.

My deliveries were all over England and Wales, while Scotland was done by another firm.

A normal week would see me deliver a load that would mean three days away followed by a more local load which would take only two days. The following week it would be the opposite, two days out and then three. I could usually be finished by three o'clock Friday afternoons.

Because the deliveries to retail outlets paid a better rate than the factories there was little difference in bonus payments and as usual one or two of the other drivers started to complain about the new boy doing half the work and getting the same money.

I told them we can change: they could have this old lorry and I will have their nice new one. But don't forget that once a month you will have to load plaster board at Nottingham and deliver it, Saturday, to Plymouth. They declined.

Usually ten tons was delivered to UBM and the other ten tons to a building site and unloaded by hand. If all went well I could be home by two in the afternoon

With this particular run I would not start until lunchtime Monday, the following week.

The best paying load was to retail outlets across Lincolnshire, finishing at Great Yarmouth in Suffolk. The next best was the North West Coast finishing with two outlets in Carlisle.

One Monday I was sent on the Great Yarmouth run and on return, I was sent, first thing in the morning, to Portishead, empty to load chipboard for South Molton.

As I was leaving the docks Peter, another driver, commonly known as Hagar, arrived at the docks. 'Where have you been?' I asked.

'There's not much on, so why hurry?' he replied.

I went on my way to South Molton and when I had tipped I rang Phil Jerrett, 'Who else is there?' he asked.

'There is one of Billy Hockin's.'

'Is there any of ours?'

'Hagar is at Portishead'

'No, that'll be too late. There's a trailer loaded for Carlisle - you'll have to take it. I know you just done a long one but there's no one else.'

So off I went to Carlisle. It would have been Hagar if he had got out of bed a bit earlier. I got to Strensham services and there were three other lorries from Torridge Transport. Same old story.

'I hear you're off to Carlisle even though you just been to Great Yarmouth,' said one. How do they always know where everyone else is going?

'There's no one else in South Molton - so I had to do this run. If Hagar had got out of bed earlier you would be talking to him now. If you like I'll change trailers with you.'

'You're not the transport manger. You can't go arranging trailers like that.'

'If you want to change I'm quite happy to do so. I'll ring Jerrett and tell him.'

'It won't happen,' he said.

'If you're not going to do anything then I'm off,' I said and walked away from him.

He could have worked out that I couldn't swap trailers as he was thirty-eight tonnes gross and I was thirty-two.

Again other drivers started complaining that I was doing less than them, finishing early Fridays and getting the same money. To get over this I used to take an empty trailer to the Torrington Yard and bob-tail back with the wages for the South Molton drivers. The yard at Torrington was L shaped and not the easiest to manoeuvre in. I used to amuse the staff by first Jack-knifing the trailer and then reversing the trailer around to the direction that I wanted it to face. I found this much easier when in confined spaces, as one could turn around within the length of a trailer.

I was at the South Molton store early one Friday afternoon ready to give the drivers their wages when they arrived. I walked up to one and asked him how he was doing.

'What's it got to do with you?' he remarked. I thought there was no need to be so rude.

'To be honest I don't give a shit, but here's your wages and in future you can go and get them yourself.'

I never did bring his again.

I'd been on the firm for nearly a month and still not got any trousers. On the Friday I went to Torrington as usual. Out of sight of the office I took my jeans off, took off my coat and tied it around my middle. Then I went in to see Brian Cobbledick. 'Could I please have some trousers Mr Cobbledick?' I asked. 'Autumn is coming and it will be quite cold walking around like this.'

He stood and looked out of the window, with his back to me, his shoulders going up and down. He was obviously laughing. After a few moments he composed himself, turned around and said he would make it a matter of priority. I thanked him and left the office.

In the outer office the two girls were laughing their heads off having listened at the door, which I didn't completely close. True to his word, in a few days I received three pairs of company trousers.

Unlike Smythe's, Torridge Transport gave their drivers details of their return load before they left. All the driver had to do was ring in when empty to confirm that nothing had changed.

Soon after I had joined the firm I had a load up to the North East, the last drop being B&Q at Middlesbrough. The return load was fertiliser from ICI at Billingham to North Devon Farmers at Barnstaple. I set off from North Devon for Middlesborough on a Tuesday afternoon.

By thursday I was empty at ten in the morning, I phoned the office, and 'Radar' (Brian Cobbledick) answered the phone.

'Stephen Lock - empty at Middlesbrough,' I said.

'Why didn't you ring in last night?' he asked.

'You didn't expect me to get all those drops off yesterday, did you?'

'No, of course not.'

'Am I still loading back from ICI for Barnstaple.'

'Yes.'

'That's ok then, I will ring you when I get to North Devon Farmers.'

Before he could say anything else I put down the phone. I had a vision of him looking at the phone thinking, 'I didn't handle that very well.'

I did another trip up to the North East and I overslept in the morning. By the time I was unloaded I was too late to load. I rang Radar and he was not happy; the next load was for Kent and I had to be there first thing Thursday.

'Ring me in the morning when you are loaded,' he said.

The next morning I rang him just after eight and told him that I was loaded. 'You can't be, they don't open until eight.'

I told him that I would ring him when I got to Barnstaple. As I had eaten some cornflakes before loading I drove to Barnstaple with just one break and was empty in Barnstaple by three-thirty. When I rang Radar he told me that I had caught up a bit and told me to take the load for Kent. That made me happy: with up to fourteen drops it was worth two nights out and a lot of bonus.

Every four or five weeks I delivered to a company in Burnley, Lancashire on a Monday, the rest of the week I would be loaded at that company and deliver to outlets in the North of England. A typical example of those drops in a week was:

Tuesday 27th January 1987. Brighouse, Wakefield, Doncaster and Maltby.

Wednesday 28th January. York, Wetherby, Leeds, Barnsley, Dewsbury and Keighly.

Thursday 30th January. Two drops in Warrington, two drops in Widnes, Speke and Wallasey.

Friday 30th January, Morecambe, Southport, and drops in St Helens.

The return load was seventeen and a half tons from UKF Ince, for Crediton. UKF was a Dutch company that produced fertiliser. Four nights out and £2.40 for the Mersey Tunnel.

Other times I would load metal roofing sheets from St Helens.

I used to like doing the Burnley run as it was always four nights out. I didn't have to start until 8am Monday morning. I would park the lorry inside the factory at night to load and it would not be moved until the morning when I went off to deliver the load. The factory doors had to be opened before I started the lorry or the exhaust fumes would set off the fire alarm.

I would go to a newsagents, buy a paper and some 'Matchbox' toys. The shop had some old stock and by the time I finished going to Burnley I had bought them all. I still have them in my toy collection.

I would buy food on the way back to the factory every day. Meats would be brought from a delicatessen opposite Homebase at Stockport, general groceries form a shop at Rawtenstall. Cooking was done at the factory in the evening.

Most of the drivers doing the Burnley run used to start early and drive to the furthest point and then deliver on the way home.

I used to start at the nearest drop and finish at the furthest point then run back with an empty trailer to the factory this allowed me to go in a straighter line rather than have to stick to main roads and motorways. Once I even went to look at York Cathedral, not the easiest place to get to with an articulated lorry. Thruscross reservoir, near Harrogate, was easier to get to.

I tried to deliver to Huddersfield one afternoon. It was ten minutes to five and the forklift driver told me it was too late to unload and he would do it in the morning. I went to the cab of the lorry wrote on a bit of paper and then took the piece of paper to the forklift driver. 'What's this?' he asked.

'That is the address of the factory where your delivery will be stored until next week. If you want it earlier you can pop over to Burnley and get it. I am going back now to be loaded for tomorrow. If your comrades at the other stores had gotten off their asses and unloaded me when I arrived there, I would have been here an hour ago. Because of them you're not going to get your order until next week.'

I walked off toward my lorry and began to climb in. The forklift driver suddenly realised he did have time to unload me after all.

A lorry from Somerset had entered the yard while I was talking to the fork lift driver. While I was getting unloaded he came across to me.

'That was some story you just told him,' said the driver.

'It's the truth. This week I'm working out of Burnley and he knows I would have took it back. Not before I'd seen his manager, though.'

Another evening I was loaded by 8pm and went to strap down the load. It looked a bit bigger than normal and I queried the weight. The forklift driver went into the office and after a few seconds called me in.

'Mr Thornley wants a word with you,' he said.

I took the phone from him and said, 'Hello Keith how are you?' By the expression on the forklift driver's face he obviously had never heard anyone call Mr Thornley 'Keith'.

'Stephen, your load is worked out by computer and should not be above the correct legal weight. Go to a weigh bridge in the morning and weigh the lorry; if it is overweight then I will give you a written apology.'

I told him that I would weigh if I saw a weigh bridge but I am not going looking for one. I am happy to believe what he told me and that I would see him Friday.'

When I turned around the forklift driver was still stood there with his mouth open.

Next time I saw Mr Thornley I apologised for calling him 'Keith' but I am sure he understood why.

I set off on a Thursday night with four drops for London with a back load from either Sunbury on Thames or Tilbury Docks. I stopped overnight on the outskirts and at 8.30am in the morning I was outside a shop in Edgeware Road. There were double gates at the left side of the shop so I double-parked. I went into the shop and told them that I was ready to unload and I was blocking-in some illegally parked cars.

'I hope you're not blocking me in,' said a voice beside me.

'Is yours the white job with the blue light on top,' I asked.

'Yes,' the policeman answered.

'Yes. You are blocked-in and you are illegally parked.'

When I went outside a car in front of the police car had moved so he could get out.

The forklift driver took off the pallet on the nearside and I moved along the road a little so that he could unload the offside pallet. When he came out of the yard I stood in the road front of a small car with a lady driver. The pallet was unloaded and the car was on its way again within a couple of minutes. One drop done, three to go. The next one was at Potters Bar, a regular drop, and by using the M1 to Boreham Wood I made good time.

'I'll unload you in about half an hour,' said the forklift driver. As it was a sunny day I took off the straps and sheets. I folded the sheets and re-strapped the remaining load. With ten ton unloaded at Potters bar there was not a lot left; two lifts at B&Q and Homebase, both on the Mile End Road at Stepney.

From Potters Bar I drove through Enfield and then through Edmonton to Stepney. B&Q was tipped first and then it was couple of hundred yards to Homebase.

I was empty just after noon and I rang Radar, 'I'm empty so I'm off to Sunbury-on-Thames.'

'Nobody can get around London as fast as that. I told you earlier that if you have one drop left after lunch and you *can* get to Sunbury by four o'clock than go there, if not you will have to go to Tilbury docks and load in the morning.' I even got the forklift driver to confirm that I was empty and he still didn't believe me.

I went to Laconite Plastics, Sunbury-on-Thames and loaded plastic sheets for Aaronson, South Molton. I rang Radar and again told him that I was loaded and, again, he didn't believe me.

'I'll see you tomorrow morning,' I said.

I'd already had something to eat so I headed for Devon as fast as I legally could. At 7pm I was at Aaronson ready to unload but the chargehand told me that I would have to wait.

'Do you know where Torridge Transport's yard is?' I asked the chargehand.

'Of course,' he said.

'Well when you want your plastic you can pick it up from there. My time is nearly up and I have to park up for the night.'

The chargehand had worked for South Molton Concrete Works at the same time as I had. Now he was a chargehand he had turned into a right awkward sod so it gave me great delight to annoy him. He told me he was going to start unloading me straight away. Too late - I was off, and I went.

I used to deliver all across South Wales and when I first started I always joined the motorway, the M4, at junction 47, from Wales, West of Swansea. I was empty and heading for Bristol but automatically followed the sign for M4 West which meant that I had to go to junction 48 before I could head East the way I wanted to go.

From my diary: Monday 12th January 1987. Froze up. In freezing conditions diesel does not go solid but more like jelly. This only seemed to happen on English lorries. Often, in cold weather, there would be lorries on the hard shoulder with little fires burning under them as drivers tried to thaw out their diesel. I eventually tipped at Plymouth.

Tuesday 13th January 1987: Loaded for Leeds and had set off. Froze up at the bottom of the hill 400 yards from the chipboard factory. Got going, then froze up again. Got going, again froze up. Got going, stopped by the police half-way down the Black Cat Hill. Tony Yeoman on Smythe's Transport had suffered a 'head-on' with another lorry and the road was blocked. I felt sorry for the policewoman who's had to walk up the snowy hill and inform all the drivers of the situation. Diesel is warming up due to the shade from the trees. Black Cat Hill rarely froze.

Eventually we got going. Tony and the other driver were not hurt, just bent metal on the lorries. I was going along the M5 and my old

Smythe's lorry passed me. The driver had twiddled with something and now the lorry would do 70mph. As he passed, the young driver made a rude sign at me. This annoyed me so I changed down to a gear, accelerated and pulled out behind him. I drove into the fast lane and changed into top gear. I was doing 85mph when I passed him and gave him a rude sign back.

I had started to slow down a little when the other drivers in our convoy decided that they were going to park up in Taunton Dean Services. At the front I was rapidly approaching the Services and with no exhauster brake I was going to have to rely on ordinary brake shoes to stop me. Braking hard and changing down gears I slowed enough to take the off ramp but not to take the bend into the lorry park. I by-passed it and dropped enough speed to be able to use the petrol station as a roundabout. All the other lorries had parked together in one area of the lorry park, leaving no room for me. I parked a little way from them at the other side of the parking area. The night was spent in the services chatting away, like drivers do. The morning arrived and a little snow with it. I walked across to the others who were gathered near my old lorry. There among them was the driver of TUO 800T. He was dressed in his underpants and wearing his work boots. I sidled up and locked the driver's door. I still had a spare key for that lorry. When Smythe gave us blanks and told us all to get a spare key cut I had two made, just in case. In this instance the key was between two fingers of my right hand. A quick flip of the wrist and the door was locked.

Eventually our ex-forces driver was starting to feel the chill and decided to get back into his cab only to find the door would not open. 'Still playing up, this door then?' I asked the driver. He was level with the rear corner of the cab at the time.

I pointed to a spot on the corner of the cab and said, 'Watch this.' As I pointed to the cab with my left hand, my right hand unlocked the door. I hit the cab, flipped the door handle, and the door opened much to the amazement of all assembled. Small victories are still the best I thought as I walked back to my lorry. I hadn't got far when I heard all this banging. Every Volvo driver was hitting the corner of their cabs trying to unlock their door. What gullible people some drivers are.

One lunchtime I rang the office from Aaronson looking for my next load. 'There is nothing for you,' said Mr Jerrett. 'All I have is a tautliner (curtain side trailer) 1st drop at B&Q Bridgwater. The trailer is about two hundred weight over.'

I did not want to wait for another load as it could seriously alter my bonus pay.

'If I don't fill the diesel tank that would probably put me a very little over, and if I use the Ho Chi Minh trail to get to Bridgwater I should be ok as there is no weighbridge on that road,' I suggested.

Mr Jerrett agreed and so off I went. After delivering to Bridgwater it was off to B& Q at Weston-super-Mare and then to ABC Bristol (Portishead) and load some more chipboard for South Wales. I didn't want to be too late getting to South Wales so I had to get unloaded pretty quickly at Weston-super-Mare.

When I arrived at B&Q I explained to the forklift driver that I would like to unload early in the morning, if possible.

'I could come in after I take the girlfriend to work, about eight o'-clock,' he offered.

'That would be good but I would then catch a lot of traffic.'

'I only live down the road so I could come in at quarter past seven before I take her to work.'

'That would be great. I would really appreciate it if you could,' I said.

I tipped at Weston-super-Mare and I got to Portishead around eight o'clock.

'What are you doing here?' asked the storeman.

'You have some boards for South Wales for me.'

'They're not ready yet. We were told that you have to deliver to B&Q, Weston first.'

'I did that at seven thirty this morning.'

'They don't open until nine,' said one of them.

'They do for me,' I said.

I had to wait for an hour for my boards. Does life never go right?

Arriving around 6pm one evening at Homebase in Bury St Edmunds I found that the storage area of the shop was flooded. A lady manager came over to me and said, 'We can't unload you as we have a flood and the water will soak up through the pallets and damage the boards.'

I really wanted to get tipped so I could drive to the Norwich store and park overnight there. I would be at least two hours behind schedule the following day if I didn't make it to Norwich that night.

I pointed to the corner of the store, 'There are some plastic pallets over there. You could put the chipboard on those and it would stay dry. In fact you could put a lot of boxed stuff on them as well.'

'What a good idea,' she said. 'That's what we'll do.'

I got unloaded even though she did not have to. Unloading should be done between 9am and 5pm. Many DIY stores ignored this rule to avoid having a queue of lorries outside the store at opening time.

There was a good reason for letting lorries park overnight: added security. If I parked at a DIY store I very rarely went out anywhere. I Just sat in the lorry and watched telly. There was also the large skip. You wouldn't believe what stores throw away. I had two folding chairs from a skip in South Wales. The seats of both of them were broken, I repaired them and I am still using them today.

I was parked at a B&Q store in Birmingham and after having my dinner I went to put my rubbish in the skip. It was still daylight and when I looked in the skip there was this lovely white leather handbag. I thought Christine would like that and so I pulled it out. It was nice and I looked inside. I was surprised to find there was all sorts of stuff inside including a glasses case.

I put the hand bag back where I found it and called the police. When they turned up I told them that I had put the handbag back where I found it. While the policeman was looking inside the bag I was holding his torch so I shone it around the inside of the skip and revealed two more handbags.

A couple of months later I got a letter from the West Midlands Constabulary commending me for my action. All three handbags were claimed and one lady was especially happy to get back her very expensive glasses.

Driving along the M4 at Reading one afternoon I heard two shots ring out. My unit lurched to the left and I immediately drove onto the hard shoulder. I got out and found that both nearside tyres were flat. On further inspection I found that the inner wheel had broken up and a piece or pieces of the wheel had caused both tyres to puncture.

Help turned up and took the wheels off. The inner wheel had elongated holes and a chunk of metal missing. As I had checked the wheel nuts before setting off I was quite surprised. Tyres are easily replaced but not wheels. Temporary wheels were put on the unit and we managed to get it off the motorway. The next day I got to Edmonton, a lot later than expected, and Boxer was not happy. It was only the two new tyres on the rear that convinced him of my story.

I was parked up at Berwick-on-Tweed, a couple of miles from the Scottish border, one night when a Stowford's lorry from Willand pulled into the lorry park. I knew one or two of their drivers so I walked over to the lorry to say hello. Imagine my surprise - it was a very old friend from my biker days in South Molton. His name is Peter Ryan and he used to live in South Street, South Molton. When I had worked at North Devon Farmers, Peter's father was a storeman for the machinery department. The last time that I had seen Peter was back in the early 1970s when I worked for Shapcott and Son. Then Peter had been a slaughter man for Lloyd Maunders, Willand, and lived in Tiverton. He hadn't changed much since he was sixteen and still had long red hair. We had both been driving all day so we went for a long walk and caught up with what had been happening since we last met - the usual fish supper was consumed during our ramble. All too soon the night was over and sadly we had to part the next day as we were going in different directions. I have never seen him since, but you never know, maybe one day our paths may cross again. I do hope so.

Torridge Transport used to deliver John Deere tractors. They were loaded at Hull Docks and delivered all over the South West of England and South Wales. I arrived at the docks one evening and was told by the agent that it was too late to load.

'Go into Hull and have a couple of pints and come back in the morning,' he told me.

'I don't have much money left, so I won't bother,' I answered.

'Here, take this and have a drink on John Deere,' and he passed me a ten pound note.

I parked in Hull and cooked myself a meal. Then I went to sleep for a while. I woke up after eleven, too late for a drink. Still I had a good breakfast the next day courtesy of John Deere.

The procedure to load tractors was go to the office and get the delivery notes and then park at the loading ramp next to the car park for the ferry terminal. Then go and find the checker and give him the loading ticket. He would then find the key holder and get the correct key for that tractor.

On one occasion the key man could not be found so the loader and I went and found the first tractor. I tried all the keys in my possession and discovered the key to the yard diesel tank fitted the tractor ignition. We drove the tractor back to the ramp and while I loaded it, the loader took the key and went to find another tractor. He returned with a tractor and stopped at the bottom of the ramp and took the diesel key and went in search of the third tractor. Amazingly he returned with the third tractor. I loaded that tractor and then turned off the ignition to all of the three tractors. As I secured the tractors to the trailer the loader found the key holder and brought the keys to me. All this took place under the curious eyes of the ferry passengers. Discovering that the diesel key appeared to fit all John Deere tractors was a bonus. It would come in handy a few weeks later.

I was asked to pick up a tractor from an agricultural merchant in South Wales. It was at a farm and when I arrived I backed up to the loading ramp. I knocked on the door of the house and was told that the farmer was at a market and had took the tractor keys with him. I told the lady not to worry, I had seen the tractor parked in the yard. I checked, there were no keys in it, but the diesel key soon solved that problem.

As I loaded the tractor the lady was on the phone, probably to the farmer. I had pushed the collection ticket through the front door and now I had the tractor. This was obviously a repossession. In less than ten minutes I had gone. Who takes keys out of a tractor and then goes to market with them?

One Friday morning I arrived back at the South Molton yard when Radar called me into the office.

'I want you to take the low loader trailer to the West Midlands and pick up Micky Weeks' tractor unit, which has broken down, and bring it back to the yard. As it is extra to your normal work I will pay you hourly rate,' he said.

'That sounds ok to me as long as we keep it between ourselves.'

He gave me the address, I coupled up to the low loader, and was soon heading for Dudley. I found the lorry and unattached its trailer. As the engine of the unit started, I drove it onto the trailer and roped it down. With only a seven ton load the Ho Chi Minh was no problem. I dropped the trailer at the yard and was parked outside my house by 7pm - several pounds better off.

I finished my employment with Torridge Transport on Friday, 25th September 1987. I had twelve, mainly happy months working there.

I was invited to the Christmas dinner that year and some of the drivers were on about my late starts. We went to the bar and I asked Brian Cobbledick if he had any comments about my driving, apart from the day I overslept and didn't get loaded.

'Only one, Stephen. How could you leave the yard an hour after everyone else and do four or five drops in London and be empty the same day? The rest of them here, with the same load, never get empty the same day.'

I told him 'It's knowing the Job sir - knowing the job.'

One day someone parked his Atkinson tractor unit on the end of the sloping drive at the Torrington yard and the driver, who will remain nameless, went into the office. When he returned he found that the handbrake had failed and the lorry had rolled across the road and made a hole in the swimming pool wall. Since that day Torridge Transport was known as 'The Hole in the Wall gang.'

12

The Latter Years

My brother had started his own gas fitting company and offered me a job. In 1991 I took my exams and became a fully licenced gas fitter. Although I still did the odd driving job for my brother Maurice.

In 1996 I decided to start my own business so I went to my bank manager to get an overdraft on my business account.

'What is your business plan?' he asked.

'I am a qualified gas fitter and I hold a Heavy Goods Vehicle licence.' If I am not doing one I shall be doing the other. So basically the plan is work like shit.'

'It is not too comprehensive but is probably the most honest plan I have heard. I will allow the overdraft facility and would like to see you every month for the next three months.'

'I am happy with that. I do have three month's work and should be able to put some money in the bank very quickly.'

That's the job I did until I retired in 2019, a few months before my 70th birthday.

It wasn't long before my nephew, Alan Lock, phoned me. The chipboard factory was looking for an HGV driver for shunting . The factory insurance stated that all HGV drivers driving in the factory grounds must hold an HGV licence. It was summer and not a busy time for gas fitters. We agreed a rate and I started the following Monday. A minimum eight hours pay per day. Hours worked in excess of eight are to be paid at the same rate.

The job was no challenge and there was always two shunters working the same shift and employed by the factory. The first week I was driving a Ford D series tractor unit and the first day I drove it the seat nearly fell over. It was not secured to the rest of the lorry. The unit went into the workshop until it was fixed. There were some tautliners that I couldn't open the curtains, they went back to the trailer park empty. I was not straining myself because of someone else's lack of maintenance.

The summer holidays were covered by me and then came the winter. The Ford driver had a week's holiday and I was able to cover for him. I noticed that the brakes were not brilliant and reported the same to the workshop foreman. Only to be told that they were too busy to do anything that day.

Three hours later I went to drop a trailer at the trailer park and I couldn't get the Ford's handbrake to release. I tried rocking the unit but that didn't work so back to the workshop. I told them the Ford was stuck. Now they had to sort it out in a minus three degree wind in an open trailer park, on top of a hill. Needless to say the next time they listened to what I said.

The next time I did holiday relief the Ford had gone and an ex-petrol company Leyland had been purchased. The other shunter was a big Bedford, a little tall to keep getting in and out of but otherwise very sound.

I had an agreement with the factory manager that I could start at six in the morning and work until two in the afternoon, if I had a gas job to do. I also used to take paper work with me to do whilst I was being loaded. Indeed it was the best of both worlds.

I had done a couple of years relief and even done Sundays, usually ten hours starting at six and finishing about four in the afternoon. Eventually I may be doing a month's holiday relief at a time and I started to get a bit annoyed that other drivers were getting paid double time for Sundays and I was not getting any extra. After asking around it got even more bizarre. Caber Board were now the people that owned the chipboard factory and Caber Freight owned the transport side. One shunter, Trevor Colton was employed by Caber Board and got double time Sundays. Bill Taylor, ex Smythe's, worked for Caber Freight and got time and a half for Sundays. Ian Cuthbertson drove for Evans Transport and got an hourly rate.

I talked to the factory manager, Terry Robins, whom I had known since 1972, since the factory had opened. He told me that he would see what he could do. The answer from Caber Freight was as I was not Staff and they were not going to pay any extra. I missed a couple of Sundays which meant the others worked longer hours to get the trailers loaded.

The next Friday Terry came and personally asked if I would work the Sunday. I told him that I do not clock in as I am not staff therefore there is no record of the hours that I work. I suggested that instead of altering my hourly rate I just book a couple of extra hours. Terry came up with, for every two hours I worked, I was to book three.

It worked well especially as I was getting more and more relief work in the summer.

I arrived one Sunday to find Bill Taylor had come to work.

'I was told that you were on holiday,' I said to him.

'I was, we flew home last night and I slept all the way. I wasn't tired so I came to work.'

'That's fine by me, but as I have turned up, as agreed, I shall book eight hours any way.'

'There is no problem there. Evans' driver hasn't turned up so you can drive their shunter.'

It was a busy day and I worked ten hours, therefore I was paid for fifteen hours. The bill was sent to Evans. As their driver didn't get paid as much as me Caber Freight were asked not to use me again but to use one of their own drivers in the future.

To prove life is fun it started to snow heavily one Sunday as we worked, so before we went home Trevor and I drove the two Leylands (the Bedford had been replace by another Leyland) across to Torridge Transport's big yard and did some doughnuts with them.

In the trucking world news gets around fast. One evening I got a phone call from Paul Bennett, who had worked for Gregory and Son. He was now an owner driver for Readymix South West and also had a small-holding. He was looking for a driver for a couple of days as he had to market his pigs for Xmas.

I told him that I had a lot of paperwork to do but not so much gas fitting. He told me that there was only one load booked-in so I could do my paperwork in the office. That sounded good to me and I agreed. As it turned out there was more than one load but it worked out ok. Paul's lorry was an ancient Leyland and in the front was an hydraulic pump, the cover of which stuck out a few inches in front of the bumper. I can't remember the amount of times I hit that cover while manoeuvring on site.

The controls for the mixer were also very worn. One afternoon, while going up a long drive to a posh house, a bump in the road turned the mixer to discharge and I left a trail of concrete along the drive. The outcome was that Paul had to go out that night and clean it all up.

The dispatch plant for Readymix was situated at Venn Quarry, near Landkey, and had an extremely steep hill at the exit of the quarry. Like most quarries there was a one way system operating on the roads around it and woe betide anyone not knowing or ignoring the rules. Most days were run of the mill deliveries but one or two stand out.

A load of ready mix to Torrington sounds easy. Going along the North Devon Highway between Barnstaple and Bideford, I was following a tractor uphill with a Volvo estate behind me. Over the crest we went and I hung back and let the tractor get on a bit. As he approached the three lane road I started to accelerate. The road ahead was clear, I indicated, checked my mirror and started to pull out past the tractor. As I did, something in the mirror caught my eye. The woman driving the Volvo had decide to overtake and was crossing the double white lines. We were on a collision course, all I could do was go hard left hand down and brake as hard as I could. The liquid load did not like that and the lorry tilted at an alarming angle. I swear that I could see daylight under the offside rear wheels. To get it back down I had to steer right and accelerate. Which is what I did and sod the stupid Volvo driver who had now swerved right, across the road.

The lorry came back down on its wheels and I got control back. The Volvo driver took a long time before she attempted another overtake which she eventually managed to bring off.

Occasionally Landkey lorries were asked to go to another branch and help out and on this occasion it was Bude that needed help.

After lunch I was given a load to deliver about four hundred yards up the road from the plant. It was for new concrete bases for some chicken sheds with more loads to follow the next day. As the height of the sheds were low the concrete was moved using a dumper. When I was empty the farmer said that he wanted the rest of the loads that day. When I got back to the plant one of the Bude lorries was there. I told the plant batcher that the farmer wanted at least three more loads. The other driver complained that he wanted to go home. His fingers were twisted with arthritis and he must have been in agony all day. I told them I was happy to do all three loads. They were surprised by my enthusiasm as most of the time the drivers from Landkey went home at two o'clock. I told them that I was on an hourly rate and I would stay until the work was done. The Bude driver then decided he would stay. We delivered the three loads between us and I was on my way home by five o'clock.

Geoff Horrell was another owner who ran out of Venn Quarry. Geoff's lorry was a new Atkinson. While on holiday he hired a relief driver. The driver came back one day and the cab of the lorry had a long vertical dent on the rear corner of the cab. Geoff was not happy about that and so the next holiday he got me in to drive for a week. What a difference in power; the Atkinson would go up the hill, and out of the quarry, in third gear whereas the Leyland needed first gear. I remember going on hire to the Bude depot with the Atkinson and going down an overgrown lane. I was aware of the newness of the lorry and didn't want to scratch the paint. As luck would have it I got to the site before I got to the point that I could go no further. I think Geoff's lorry was one of the last that I drove.

Some of the makes of lorry that I have driven, many of them now just history are: AEC, Albion, Bedford, Commer, DAF, Dodge, ERF, Fiat, Foden, Ford, Guy, Leyland, MAN, Mercedes, Scammell, Seddon Atkinson, Volvo, and a Renault simulator at a Commercial Motor Show

When my Heavy Goods Vehicle Licence expired I decided that, as the gas business was booming, there was no need to supplement my income. So ended well over twenty years of living the dream. Something that I had wanted to do since I was ten years old came to an end.

I did miss the many friends that I had made on the road, God Bless Them all; the camaraderie and the cafés - a welcome site on a dark snowy night.

It was time for a new adventure - a new life - but that will be in another book.

Edward Gaskell
Publishers
DEVON

Drivers, Fitters and Shunters

Gregory and Son drivers

Paul Bennett
Geoffrey Binding
Clifford Cockram
Stephen Lock
Tony Morrison
Francis (Frank) Pidler
Steve Tapp
Jim White
John Williams
Maurice Williams

Smythe's Transport drivers:

Dave 'Butcher' Berry
Jeff 'Super Trooper' Binding
Jim 'Minder' Beveridge
Dougie 'Dougal' Braunton
Donald 'Corky' Courtney
Ian 'Whiteliner' Cuthbertson
Ray 'Glider' Davis
Mike 'Silver Bucket' Evans
Mike Fallon
Gordon Hartnoll
Richard 'Oyster Catcher' Holdsworth
Stephen 'Smurf' Lock, Author
Henry 'Redbeard' Miller
Derek Monk, Shop Steward
Colin 'Ginger' Paul, Yard man and shunter
Graham 'Whiskers' Reed
Adrian 'Side Winder' Richards
Jeff 'Rabbi' Roberts
Neil Russell

Bill 'Billy' Taylor, Yard man and shunter
Steve 'Waccy Baccy' Tucker
Mike 'Steamboat' Thorne
Colin Vanstone, Yard man and shunter
Peter Whitehead
Tony Yeoman
Bob Lovelace

Fitters:

Dave Helliman
Dave Underhill

Torridge Transport drivers:

Clive Boundy
Geoff Colwill
Peter 'Hagar' Ellis
Michael 'Ginger' Found
Bob 'Dr Hook' Grills
Terry Hookway
Arthur Jefferies
Alan Jones
Stephen 'Smurf' Lock, Author
Norman Richards
Chris 'Ben' Payne
Francis (Frank) Pidler
Steve Tapp, Storeman
Gerald Taylor
Ian Thomas
Richard 'Hank' Thornley
Michael 'Micky' Weeks
Tony Westacott

Fitters:

Brian Tetherbridge
Les Payne

Above : Geoff Horrell's mixer lorry.   Image courtesy of Geoff Horrell.

Below: Geoff Horrell and Paul Bennett's mixers after a hard day's work. Note the number plate fitted on the pump cover.

Image courtesy of Geoff Horrell.

Above: Black Cat bridge from the Bampton side.   Image by the author

Below: The narrow bridge at Waterrow on the old A361, now renumbered the B3227   Image by the author

Above: The narrow Black Cat bridge from the South Molton side.

Both images by the author

Below: The now defunct Black Cat garage and cafe.

Lazarus Press
DEVON